First Edition
First Printing, December 1996
5000 copies

Printed in U.S.A.
by PrintTech, division of York Graphic Services, Inc.
York, PA

concept & design:
Knezic/Pavone Advertising
Harrisburg, PA 17102

illustration:
Mike Fink

copy contribution:
Knezic/Pavone Advertising

editor:
Kyle D. Nagurny

for additional copies, please contact:
The Junior League of Harrisburg, Inc.
Cookbook Committee
3211 North Front Street • Suite 301
Harrisburg, PA 17110
(717) 238-1928 • Fax (717) 238-2945

a capital affair

The Junior League Of Harrisburg, Inc.

mission statement

The Junior League of Harrisburg, Inc. is an organization of women committed to promoting voluntarism, to developing the potential of women, and to improving the community through the effective action and leadership of trained volunteers. Its purpose is exclusively educational and charitable.

vision statement

We are an effective, progressive, multicultural volunteer organization of one heart in our commitment to enrich the lives of women and children in the greater Harrisburg community.

All proceeds from the sale of *a capital affair* will benefit the issues and concerns of domestic violence.

introduction

a *capital affair* is deliberately rich in meaning. First, it represents our region-the City of Harrisburg, capital of Pennsylvania, and its diverse surrounding areas: Carlisle, Boiling Springs, New Bloomfield, Gettysburg and Hershey, each with unique appeal. Harrisburg is a renaissance city. Having emerged from its own dark age, it is alive with attractions beyond its beautiful capitol building and the sparkling Susquehanna River in its front yard. The Harrisburg Senators baseball team, the Harrisburg Heat soccer team, the Harrisburg Symphony, Harrisburg Community Theater, Open Stage Theater of Harrisburg, Harrisburg Civic Opera, and many more entice us to the city. The question is still, "What to do?" but now it is a question with multiple options replacing the old one of frustration with no choices. Likewise, the surrounding areas provide diverse enticements: Carlisle, a beautiful historical city enhanced with intellectual climate of Dickinson College and The Dickinson School of Law; Boiling Springs, the trout fisher's mecca with its Yellow Breeches Creek; New Bloomfield, the county seat of rural Perry County, a wonderful place for a serendipitous drive; Gettysburg, replete with Civil War history and scenic battlefields; and Hershey, a fun stop for amusements, entertainment and chocolate indulgence.

We also chose a *capital affair* to connote the kinds of recipes selected for this cookbook -- exceptional ones we delight in preparing for special celebrations. You will find here the perfect tastes to prepare when you are the host of "a capital affair," those that make the cuisine a conversation piece of the party and inspire the guests to request recipes.

This is the first cookbook published by the Junior League of Harrisburg. We have been in existence for 68 years, and during that time have raised over 900,000 dollars through which we have benefited many organizations in the greater Harrisburg area. One Harrisburg attraction the Junior League seeded was the Museum of Scientific Discovery, a hands-on children's museum. Our current focus area is prevention of domestic violence, and we will channel our proceeds from this cookbook to education, advocacy and intervention projects to help reduce the incidence and painful effects of domestic violence.

Food brings people together. Almost from its inception, the production of this cookbook has been a joyful experience for our organization. Like people who break bread together, we bonded as we participated in each stage of the production. We hope that you have as much joy in preparing and presenting these recipes as we did in discovering, tasting and sharing them with you!

The Junior League Of Harrisburg, Inc.

a capital affair

The Junior League Of Harrisburg, Inc.

cookbook committee members

chairmen................... Linda Plesic
Patty Armbrust

committee members.......

Linda Askins	Mindy Holland	Mary Alice Rebman
Christina Barber	Carolyn Isom	Lynn Reutelheuber
Marla Bigeleisen	Toquaiah Jackson	Kirsten Rucker
Irene Bizzoso	Kim Johnson	Lorie Ruland
Jennifer Black	Kathy Joyce	Jill Crews Schiebel
Jennifer Scott Brubaker	Rita Latsha	Heather Schleicher
Carrie Curtis	Lisa Lutz	Mary Shotsberger
Diane Dalrymple	Jennifer Masters	Pam Smeltzer
Sharon DePamphilis	Sara McAskill	Julie Smith
Kim Dunkleberger	Julie McConahy	Robin Stuart
Delia Egan	Cheryl McCune	Pam Suan
Patrice Ridgeway Gallagher	Reesa Motley McMurtry	Edie Walsh
Karen Gunnison	Sheri Phillips	Kathy Wills
Amy Hammerschmidt	Carla Plouse	

corporate sponsors

Penn National Insurance
Bobby Rahal Dealerships

table of contents

9 - 48  appetizers

49 - 80 soup and salads

81 - 112 breads and brunches and lunches

113 - 160 entrees

161 - 192 vegetables and sides

193 - 218 desserts

219 index

appetizers

f or most auto-philes, their love affair with motorized vehicles is no passing fancy. And events held at Carlisle Fairgrounds continue to be a testimonial to that fact. From the first collective event organized in 1974 by Bill and Chip Miller, attendance has grown to nearly half a million devotees annually at the nine automotive and two antique events. French fries are the snack choice for the avid auto show goer at the fairgrounds - an area which would take over 19,000 fries placed end to end to surround.

caramelized onion quesadillas

1 tablespoon olive oil
1 red onion, halved and
 thinly sliced
4 green onions, sliced
3 cloves garlic, chopped
3/4 teaspoon ground
 cumin
1/4 teaspoon dried
 oregano
1 tablespoon fresh lime
 juice
Four 10-inch flour tortillas
1 cup shredded jalapeno-Jack
 cheese
1 cup shredded sharp
 Cheddar cheese
Sour cream and/or bottled
 salsa, optional

p reheat oven to 400 degrees. In large skillet heat olive oil over medium-low heat. Add red onion, green onion and garlic. Cover and cook 15 minutes or until softened, stirring occasionally. Add cumin and oregano. Cook, uncovered, 1 minute. Remove from heat. Stir in lime juice. On large baking sheet arrange 2 tortillas side-by-side. Top with onion mixture and spread evenly. Sprinkle with Jack and Cheddar cheeses. Top each with another tortilla. Bake 8 minutes or until heated through and golden around edges. Let stand 5 minutes. Cut into thin wedges. Serve with sour cream and/or salsa, if desired.

SERVES 6

mexicali roll-ups

Ten 6-inch flour tortillas
2 packages (8 ounces each)
 cream cheese
2 cups bottled salsa
2 cups shredded Cheddar
 cheese
5 to 6 green onions, chopped
1 can (8 ounces) pitted black
 olives, drained and
 chopped
1 avocado, peeled, pitted
 and thinly sliced

i n medium bowl beat cream cheese to soften. Stir in salsa. Spread on each tortilla. Sprinkle with Cheddar cheese. At one end of each tortilla sprinkle onions, olives and avocado. Carefully roll up tortillas, tightly enclosing ingredients. Place seam side down in flat dish. Cover and refrigerate several hours or overnight. Cut into 1-inch slices just before serving.

SERVES 10 - 12

crab quesadillas

3/4 cup butter, divided
Twelve 8-inch flour tortillas
1 pound crab meat, picked through and flaked
Salt and freshly-ground black pepper, to taste
4 cups shredded Monterey Jack cheese
Jalapeno peppers
Guacamole (recipe follows)
Bottled salsa

In large skillet melt 2 tablespoons of the butter over medium heat. Place 1 tortilla in pan. Sprinkle with 1/6 of the crab meat. Salt and pepper to taste. Sprinkle with 1/6 of the cheese. Top with another tortilla. Cook gently 5 minutes or until cheese begins to melt, turning once. Repeat with remaining tortillas, melting 2 tablespoons of the butter for cooking each time. Cut into thin wedges. Garnish with jalapeno peppers. Serve with guacamole and salsa.

guacamole:

In medium bowl coarsely mash 1 peeled and pitted ripe avocado with fork or potato masher. Add 1 peeled and diced tomato, 1 minced fresh jalapeno pepper, 2 tablespoons fresh lime juice and 1 tablespoon snipped fresh cilantro. Salt and pepper to taste. (May be made a day ahead. Place plastic wrap directly onto surface and refrigerate until ready to use.)

SERVES 8

smoked salmon tortillas

1 large cucumber, peeled, halved, seeded and thinly sliced
1/2 teaspoon salt
Six 10-inch flour tortillas
1 package (8 ounces) cream cheese, softened
1/4 cup snipped fresh dill
8 ounces smoked salmon, thinly sliced
12 leaves Boston lettuce, chopped with center ribs removed

In small bowl toss cucumber with salt. Let stand 20 minutes, stirring occasionally. Drain and dry with clean paper towels. Spread tortillas with softened cream cheese. Sprinkle with dill. Arrange salmon on tortillas. Top with cucumber and lettuce. Roll up tightly. Wrap each roll in plastic wrap and refrigerate 1 to 24 hours. Slice off ends and cut into 1-inch slices just before serving.

SERVES 8

southwest empanadas

1 package (8 ounces) cream
cheese, softened
1/2 cup butter, softened
1-1/2 cups all-purpose flour
1-1/2 packages (12 ounces)
cream cheese, softened
3 ounces goat cheese
3 tablespoons sun-dried
tomatoes, minced
3 tablespoons snipped fresh
cilantro
Salt and freshly-ground black
pepper, to taste
Cayenne (red pepper),
to taste
1 egg, slightly beaten
Salsa Fresca (recipe follows)
Vegetable oil

In food processor combine 8 ounces cream cheese and the butter, blending until smooth. Add flour and process until blended. Wrap dough in plastic wrap and refrigerate at least 1 hour.

In large bowl combine 12 ounces cream cheese, goat cheese, tomatoes and cilantro. Salt and pepper to taste. Add cayenne to taste. (Recipe may be made 1 day ahead to this point. Cover and refrigerate filling until ready to use.) On lightly floured surface roll out dough to 1/8-inch thickness. Using 3-inch plain or fluted cookie cutter cut out circles of dough. Spoon tablespoonful of filling onto center of each round of dough. Brush edges with egg. Fold dough over in half and crimp edges with fork to seal. In deep fryer or large, heavy skillet heat oil to 375 degrees. Fry filled dough, a few at a time, in oil 2 minutes or until lightly browned. Drain on paper towels. Serve with Salsa Fresca.

salsa fresca:

In medium bowl combine 4 seeded and chopped tomatoes, 1/2 minced medium onion, 1 clove minced garlic, 1/2 cup snipped fresh cilantro and 1 minced small jalapeno or other small hot pepper. Salt and pepper to taste. Puree half of mixture in food processor. Stir into remaining mixture. (May be made a few hours in advance. Cover and refrigerate until ready to serve.)

SERVES 10

cheese quesadillas with black bean salsa

Eight 8-inch flour tortillas
2 cups shredded Monterey
   Jack cheese
1 can (4 ounces) chopped
   green chiles, drained
4 teaspoons vegetable oil
Black Bean Salsa
   (recipe follows)

Sprinkle 4 of the tortillas with 1/2 cup of the cheese and 2 tablespoons of the chiles. Top each with another tortilla. Heat large skillet and brush with 1 teaspoon of the olive oil. Add one of the quesadillas. Saute 2 minutes or until lightly browned and cheese melts. Remove from pan. Keep warm. Saute remaining quesadillas, one at a time, using additional olive oil in skillet, as needed. Cut into thin wedges. Serve with Black Bean Salsa.

black bean salsa:

In medium bowl combine 1 can (16 ounces) drained and rinsed black beans, 3/4 cup frozen and thawed corn kernels, 1/4 cup vegetable oil, 1 can (4 ounces) chopped green chiles, 2 diced plum tomatoes, 4 thinly sliced green onions, 2 tablespoons chopped red onion, 2 tablespoons snipped fresh cilantro, 2 tablespoons fresh lime juice, 1/2 teaspoon ground cumin, 1/4 teaspoon salt and 1/8 teaspoon freshly-ground black pepper. (May also be served with tortilla chips.)

SERVES   10 - 12

almond-raspberry brie

12-ounce wedge Brie cheese
2 tablespoons seedless red
   raspberry jam
1 tablespoon Chambord or
   other raspberry-flavored
   liqueur
1-1/2 teaspoons packed
   brown sugar
3 tablespoons sliced almonds
1 tablespoon honey
Wafer cookies or gingersnaps

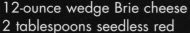

Slice Brie in half horizontally. Place bottom half on microwave-proof serving plate. In small bowl combine jam and liqueur. Spread on cheese, leaving 1-inch edge around side. Top with remaining half of cheese. Sprinkle with brown sugar and almonds. Drizzle with honey. Microwave on high (full power) 1 minute or just until soft. Serve immediately with wafer cookies or gingersnaps.

SERVES   6

glazed brie

3/4 cup packed light brown
   sugar
1/2 cup almonds
1/4 cup pecans
1/4 cup walnuts
1/2 teaspoon cinnamon
1/4 teaspoon ginger
Pinch nutmeg
Pinch allspice
1 to 3 tablespoons water
12-inch wheel Brie cheese
Dried apricots and figs
Assorted crackers and sliced
   fresh fruit

place brown sugar, almonds, pecans, walnuts, cinnamon, ginger, nutmeg and allspice in food processor. Process until nuts are finely ground. Add 1 tablespoon water. Process until mixture holds together, gradually adding more water, as needed. (Mixture should be moist, not runny, and hold together easily.) Spread mixture on Brie. Transfer to pan. Broil a few inches from heat just until topping is slightly browned, watching carefully. Remove from heat. Transfer to serving platter. Garnish with apricots and figs. Serve with assorted crackers and sliced fresh fruit.

SERVES   12

almond and prosciutto pizza

1 (10 inch) prepared pizza
   shell
1 clove garlic, minced
1 1/2 tablespoons olive oil,
   divided
3/4 cup ricotta cheese
1/2 cup mozzarella cheese,
   shredded
1/2 cup fontina cheese,
   grated
4 tablespoons Parmesan
   cheese, grated
2 tablespoons Prosciutto,
   finely chopped
1/4 teaspoon dried basil
1/4 teaspoon dried oregano
1/2 cup sliced almonds,
   toasted

preheat oven to 425 degrees. Mix garlic with 1/2 teaspoon oil. Brush dough with garlic oil. Spread ricotta on dough. Sprinkle with cheeses, basil and oregano. Lightly press almonds into toppings. Drizzle top with remaining oil. Bake for 20-25 minutes or until crust is golden. Serve immediately.

SERVES   8 - 10

spinach phyllo pizza

7 sheets phyllo dough

1-1/2 pounds fresh spinach, coarse stems removed

5 tablespoons sweet (unsalted) butter, melted and kept warm

6 tablespoons freshly grated Parmesan cheese

1 teaspoon dried mint leaves

Salt and freshly-ground black pepper, to taste

1/2 cup very thinly sliced red onion

2/3 cup finely crumbled feta cheese

1-1/2 tablespoons olive oil

S tack phyllo between two pieces of wax paper. Cover with damp towel. Set aside. Rinse spinach under cold water. Place in large kettle. Cover and cook over medium heat in water clinging to leaves 3 to 4 minutes or just until wilted. Rinse under cold water and set aside to drain in colander. Adjust rack to middle of oven. Preheat oven to 400 degrees. Lightly butter large baking sheet.

Place 1 sheet of phyllo on buttered baking sheet. Lightly brush with butter. Sprinkle with 1 tablespoon of the Parmesan cheese. Top with another phyllo sheet, gently pressing to adhere to bottom layer. Repeat layers of butter, Parmesan cheese and phyllo five more times, ending with phyllo. Lightly brush top with remaining butter. Bake 5 minutes on middle oven rack. Arrange spinach evenly over crust, leaving 1-inch border around edge. Crumble mint over top. Salt and pepper to taste. Scatter onion over top. Sprinkle with feta cheese. Drizzle with olive oil. Return to oven 15 minutes or until cheese is melted. Cut into squares. Serve immediately.

SERVES   6 - 8

california pizza

2 individual size (7-8 inch) baked pizza crusts

1/2 cup tapenade

5 ounces herb flavored goat cheese, crumbled

1 jar (7 ounce) roasted red peppers, drained and chopped

1 medium zucchini, thinly sliced

P reheat oven to 450 degrees. Place the pizza crusts on a baking sheet. Spread a thin layer of tapenade over both pizza crusts. Scatter the roasted red peppers and zucchini over pizza crusts. Bake 8 minutes or until crust is brown and toppings are heated through. Cut into wedges. Serve immediately.

SERVES   4

chicken pizza with barbecue sauce

1-1/2 cups shredded cooked
  chicken
3/4 cup spicy or hickory-
  flavored barbecue sauce
1 large (about 16 ounces)
  baked cheese pizza crust
  such as Boboli
1/2 medium onion, sliced
1/4 green bell pepper, sliced
1/4 red bell pepper, sliced
1/3 cup drained oil-packed
  sun-dried tomatoes, thinly
  sliced
1/4 cup pine nuts
2 teaspoons dried oregano
Salt and freshly-ground black
  pepper, to taste
1-1/2 cups shredded
  mozzarella cheese

preheat oven to 450 degrees. In medium bowl combine chicken and barbecue sauce. Let stand 15 minutes. (May be prepared 2 hours ahead to this point. Cover and refrigerate until ready to use.) Place pizza crust on large baking sheet or pizza screen. Spoon chicken mixture evenly over crust. Top with onion, bell pepper, tomatoes and pine nuts. Sprinkle with oregano. Salt and pepper to taste. Sprinkle with cheese. Bake 10 to 12 minutes or until crust is crisp and cheese is melted. Cut into wedges. Serve immediately.

SERVES 8

greek appetizer pizzas

4 pita rounds
3-4 tablespoons olive oil
1 clove garlic, minced
2 tomatoes, chopped
4 scallions, chopped
3/4 cup greek olives,
  chopped
1 1/2 teaspoons dried
  oregano
1 cup feta cheese, crumbled
1 cup provolone cheese,
  shredded

preheat oven to 350 degrees. Split pitas and brush with 2 tablespoons oil. Sprinkle pitas with garlic, tomatoes, scallions, olives, oregano, feta and provolone. Drizzle with remaining oil. Bake for 10 -12 minutes. Cut each round into fourths. Serve warm.

SERVES 6 - 8

french onion pizza

2 tablespoons olive oil
1-1/2 pounds onions,
  thinly sliced
2 cloves garlic, crushed
1 tablespoon snipped fresh
  thyme
1 teaspoon fennel seeds
1 can (2 ounces) anchovy
  fillets, drained*
Milk
Dough (recipe follows)
1 tablespoon olive paste
8 to 12 pitted black olives
Additional olive oil
1 egg yolk
1 tablespoon milk
Pinched salt
Creme fraiche, optional

Preheat oven to 475 degrees. In large skillet heat 2 tablespoons olive oil over medium-high heat. Add onions, garlic, thyme and fennel seeds. Saute 20 minutes or until onions are softened and lightly golden. Soak anchovy fillets in small amount of milk 10 minutes. Drain and pat dry. Set aside.

Spread dough with olive paste. Top with onion mixture, anchovies and olives. Drizzle with additional olive oil. Using sharp knife, cut small slits around edge of dough to make decorative edge. In small bowl whisk together egg yolk, 1 tablespoon milk and pinch salt. Brush on edge of dough. Bake 25 minutes or until golden. Cool slightly and cut into wedges. Serve with dollops of creme fraiche, if desired.

* 3 tablespoons drained sun-dried tomatoes in oil may be substituted

dough:

In large bowl combine 1-1/4 cups all-purpose flour, 1 teaspoon fast-acting dry yeast and 1/2 teaspoon salt. Make well in center. Work in 2 tablespoons olive oil and 1/2 to 2/3 cup tepid water to form pliable dough. Knead on lightly floured surface 5 minutes or until smooth and elastic. Place dough in lightly oiled bowl, turning to coat lightly with oil. Cover loosely with plastic wrap. Let rise in warm place until doubled. Punch down and roll out onto lightly floured surface to 10-inch round. Transfer to lightly greased baking sheet or pizza pan. Prick with fork.

SERVES 6 - 8

herbed cheese tarts

1/3 cup fine, dry bread
  crumbs
1 package (8 ounces) cream
  cheese
3/4 cup cottage cheese
1/2 cup shredded Swiss
  cheese
1 tablespoon all-purpose flour
1/4 teaspoon dried basil
1/8 teaspoon garlic powder
2 eggs
Vegetable oil cooking spray
Sour cream
Sliced olives
Snipped fresh chives
Cayenne (red pepper)

Preheat oven to 375 degrees. Coat mini-muffin pans with vegetable oil cooking spray. Sprinkle bread crumbs onto bottom and sides until coated. Shake pans to remove any excess crumbs. Set aside.

In large bowl beat cream cheese, cottage cheese, Swiss cheese, flour, basil and garlic powder just until fluffy. Add eggs. Beat on low speed just until blended. Spoon 1 tablespoon onto crust in muffin pans. Bake 15 minutes. Cool 10 minutes in pans. Remove from pans and cool completely on wire racks. Refrigerate until ready to serve. Garnish with sour cream, sliced olives, snipped fresh chives and cayenne.

SERVES   12

harris mansion cheese pate'

2 packages (8 ounces each)
  cream cheese
1-1/2 teaspoons dried Italian
  herb seasoning
Salt and freshly-ground black
  pepper, to taste
1/2 cup shredded Gruyere
  cheese
1/4 cup finely chopped
  pecans
3 ounces Roquefort cheese,
  crumbled
1/2 cup snipped fresh
  parsley
1/2 cup crumbled, crisply-
  cooked bacon
Fresh parsley sprigs
Assorted crackers

Lightly oil a 6- x 4-inch loaf pan. Line with plastic wrap, leaving a 2-inch overhang on each side. In medium bowl beat cream cheese to soften. Beat in herb seasoning. Salt and pepper to taste. Carefully spread 1/3 of the cream cheese mixture in pan. Top with the Gruyere cheese and pecans. Top with half of the remaining cream cheese mixture. Top with the Roquefort cheese, parsley and bacon. Top with remaining cream cheese mixture. Press down firmly. Cover with overhanging plastic wrap. Refrigerate overnight. Invert onto serving plate and remove plastic wrap. Bring to room temperature. Garnish with fresh parsley sprigs. Serve with assorted crackers.

SERVES   8 - 10

roasted garlic pate'

2 large bulbs of garlic
1 pound ripe Brie cheese, chilled
1/2 teaspoon cayenne (red pepper)
3 tablespoons olive oil
1 tablespoon hot water
Assorted crackers

Preheat oven to 300 degrees. Bundle whole, unpeeled bulbs of garlic in double thickness of foil. Twist ends of foil to seal shut. Roast 1 hour. Remove from oven. Set aside to cool to room temperature.

Meanwhile, trim and discard white rind from Brie. Cut Brie into 1-inch cubes. Place in top of double boiler over small amount of hot, not boiling, water. Heat 8 to 10 minutes or just until softened. Remove from heat. Peel garlic, clove by clove, dropping into blender or food processor. Add cayenne, olive oil and hot water. Blend or process 30 seconds or until pureed. Scrape down sides of blender or processor and blend additional 30 seconds. Add softened Brie, using 8 to 10 short, pulsing motions to blend in. Transfer to small serving bowl. If lumpy, whisk by hand until blended. Cover tightly and refrigerate until ready to serve. Bring to room temperature. Serve with assorted crackers.

SERVES   10 - 12

chicken pate'

1 1/2 - 2 pounds chicken breasts
4 teaspoons unflavored gelatin
1/4 cup chicken broth
1/2 small onion, quartered
1 tablespoon Dijon mustard
1/2 teaspoon nutmeg
2 tablespoons brandy
1/2 cup sweet (unsalted) butter
1/2 cup cream cheese
1/2 teaspoon salt
1/2 teaspoon freshly-ground black pepper
Assorted fresh vegetables and crackers

Lightly oil a 2 cup mold. In medium saucepan cover chicken breasts in water and cook until no longer pink. Remove meat from bones when cool. Add unflavored gelatin to chicken broth. In food processor place cooked chicken, onion, garlic, Dijon mustard, nutmeg and brandy. Process until smooth. Add butter, cream cheese, salt and pepper. Process for 10 seconds. Add reserved gelatin mixture. Process until smooth. Spoon into mold. Press down firmly. Refrigerate overnight. Run knife around edge of mold. Invert onto serving platter. Serve with fresh vegetables and crackers.

SERVES   12

smoked trout pate'

3/4 cup sweet (unsalted)
butter
6 ounces cream cheese
3 ounces soft, mild goat
cheese such as Montrachet
2 fillets (about 4 ounces)
smoked trout, skin and
bones removed
1 green onion, finely
chopped
2 tablespoons snipped fresh
parsley or chives
2 tablespoons fresh lemon
juice
1 tablespoon drained capers
1 teaspoon drained prepared
horseradish
1/2 teaspoon Tabasco sauce
Assorted sliced breads
Cucumbers

i n food processor combine butter, cream cheese and
goat cheese. Process until softened. Add trout and
process until blended with cheeses. Add green onion,
parsley or chives, lemon juice, capers, horseradish and
Tabasco sauce. Process 1 minute or until smooth. Transfer
to crock. Cover and refrigerate at least 2 hours or up to 2
days. Bring to room temperature. Serve with assorted
sliced bread and cucumbers.

SERVES   10 - 12

susquehanna shrimp dip

1 package (8 ounces) cream
cheese
1 cup sour cream
1 pound cooked medium
shrimp, shelled, deveined
and chopped
2 cups bottled salsa
2 cups shredded mozzarella
cheese
1 green bell pepper, chopped
1 tomato, chopped
3 green onions, chopped
Tortilla chips

i n medium bowl beat cream cheese to soften. Blend in
sour cream. In large round dish with edge layer cream
cheese mixture, shrimp, salsa, cheese, bell pepper, tomato
and green onions. Cover and refrigerate 3 to 4 hours.
Serve with tortilla chips.

SERVES   10 - 12

tri-color vegetable pate'

2 cans (15 ounces each) cannellini beans, rinsed and drained
1 tablespoon fresh lemon juice
4 tablespoons olive oil, divided
1 tablespoon fresh oregano, minced
4 cloves garlic, minced and divided
1 jar (7 ounces) roasted red peppers, drained and chopped
3/4 cup feta cheese, crumbled
1 cup fresh basil leaves
1 cup snipped fresh parsley
1/4 cup toasted pine nuts
1/2 cup ricotta cheese
Salt
Fresh herb sprigs
Freshly-ground black pepper
Sourdough bread slices

line a loaf pan with plastic wrap, overlapping sides.

for bean layer:

In large bowl, mash beans. Add lemon juice, 1 tablespoon olive oil, oregano and 2 cloves minced garlic. Blend until smooth. Season with salt and pepper, to taste. Spread evenly on bottom of prepared pan.

for red pepper layer:

In processor bowl combine red peppers and feta. Blend until smooth. Spread evenly over bean mixture in prepared pan.

for pesto layer:

In processor bowl, add 2 garlic cloves, basil, parsley and pine nuts. Mince. With machine running, gradually add 3 tablespoons olive oil. Process until smooth. Mix in ricotta. Spread evenly over red pepper layer. Cover with plastic wrap. Refrigerate overnight.

Invert pate' onto serving platter. Peel off plastic wrap. Garnish with herb sprigs. Serve with sourdough bread slices.

SERVES   12 - 14

cajun tuna dip

1 package (3 ounces) cream cheese, softened
3 tablespoons mayonnaise
1 teaspoon paprika
1/4 teaspoon freshly-ground black pepper
1/8 teaspoon garlic powder
1/8 teaspoon ground red pepper
1 can (6 1/2 ounces) tuna, drained and flaked
1/4 cup sweet red peppers, chopped
2 tablespoons green onion, chopped
2 tablespoons green olives, chopped
Sweet red, yellow and green pepper strips or assorted crackers

i n medium bowl beat cream cheese, mayonnaise, paprika, black pepper, garlic powder and red pepper. Stir in tuna, chopped red pepper, chopped onions and chopped olives. Refrigerate until ready to serve. Serve with pepper strips or assorted crackers.

SERVES   10

goat cheese log with cranberry-pecan crust

1/2 cup dried cranberries, finely chopped
1/4 cup pecans, finely chopped
1/4 teaspoon salt
1 (8 ounces) log soft goat cheese
Assorted crackers

O n a small platter combine cranberries, pecans and salt. Roll goat cheese log in mixture coating completely. Wrap in plastic wrap, refrigerating up to 3 days. Serve with crackers

SERVES   6 - 8

avocado dip with sesame seeds

1 red bell pepper, halved lengthwise, stemmed and seeded
1 tablespoon sesame seeds
3 ripe avocados, peeled, pitted and chopped
Juice of 1 lime
Grated peel of 1 lime
2 tablespoons sour cream
1 tablespoon snipped fresh cilantro
1 tablespoon minced shallots
1 teaspoon dark sesame oil
8 drops Tabasco sauce
Salt, to taste

a rrange bell pepper halves, skin sides up, on broiler rack over pan. Broil a few inches from heat 10 to 12 minutes or until skins are blackened. Cool and rinse under cold water. Pat dry. Finely dice and set aside. Arrange sesame seeds in single layer on baking sheet. Broil a few inches from heat 1 to 2 minutes or just until toasted, stirring occasionally. Set aside.

In large bowl combine avocados, lime juice, lime peel, sour cream, cilantro, shallots, sesame oil and Tabasco sauce. Salt to taste. Mound into serving dish. Garnish with toasted sesame seeds. Arrange bell pepper around dip.

SERVES   8 - 10

herb and olive dip

1-1/3 cups sour cream
1-1/3 cups mayonnaise
1 can (4 ounces) pitted black olives, drained and chopped
2 tablespoons parsley flakes
2 tablespoons minced dried onion
2 teaspoons seasoned salt
2 teaspoons snipped fresh dill
1 round loaf rye or pumpernickel bread, not sliced
Cherry tomatoes
Fresh dill sprigs

i n large bowl combine sour cream, mayonnaise, olives, parsley flakes, onion, salt and dill. Set aside. (Filling may be made 1 day ahead. Cover and refrigerate until ready to use.) Hollow out center of bread, leaving 1-1/2-inch bottom. Transfer to large serving platter. Fill center of bread with sour cream mixture. Cut remaining bread into bite-size pieces and arrange around bread for dipping. Garnish with cherry tomatoes and fresh dill sprigs.

SERVES   12 - 15

low-fat roasted pepper dip*

1 cup reduced-fat sour cream
1 cup reduced-fat mayonnaise
1 jar (7 ounces) roasted red
   peppers, drained and
   chopped
2 tablespoons grated
   Parmesan cheese
2 teaspoons dried basil
1/2 teaspoon salt
1/2 teaspoon freshly-ground
   black pepper
Assorted fresh vegetables,
   washed and sliced

In medium bowl combine sour cream, mayonnaise, red peppers, Parmesan cheese, basil, salt and pepper. Cover and refrigerate until ready to serve. Spoon into serving bowl. Serve with assorted fresh vegetables.

*64 calories and 4 grams fat per 2 tablespoons

SERVES   12 - 15

asparagus cheese fritters

24 fresh asparagus spears
Boiling water
1-1/2 cups all-purpose flour
1/2 teaspoon baking powder
Salt and freshly-ground black
   pepper, to taste
3/4 cup finely grated
   Gruyere cheese
1/2 teaspoon freshly grated
   lemon peel
1-1/4 cups milk
1 egg
Dash Worcestershire sauce
Vegetable oil
Lemon wedges
Fresh parsley sprigs

Wash, trim and cut asparagus about 1/2 inch below tips. (Reserve stems for other uses such as soups and stews.) Blanch tips in large amount of boiling water 1 minute. Drain immediately on clean paper towels.

In large bowl combine flour and baking powder. Salt and pepper to taste. Add cheese and lemon peel, blending well. In separate bowl combine milk, egg and Worcestershire sauce. Gradually add to flour mixture, blending to consistency of sour cream. Let stand 30 minutes at room temperature, or cover and refrigerate up to 2 hours. (If mixture becomes too thick, thin with small amount of milk.)

In large skillet or deep fryer heat 2 to 3 inches of vegetable oil to 375 degrees. Using long-handled fork, dip asparagus tips into batter. Deep-fry, a few at a time, several seconds per side or until puffed and golden. Remove with slotted spoon and drain on clean paper towels. Transfer to heated serving platter and keep warm until all tips are fried. Arrange lemon wedges on platter. Garnish with parsley sprigs. Serve immediately. (May be frozen. To reheat, arrange on baking sheet. Bake at 400 degrees for 10 to 12 minutes or until hot.)

SERVES   6 - 8

caponata

i n large saute pan or skillet heat olive oil over medium heat. Add eggplant, tomatoes with juice, onion, bell pepper and garlic. Cook 20 to 30 minutes or just until eggplant is tender, stirring occasionally. Add parsley, olives, vinegar, sugar, capers, tomato paste, basil, salt and pepper. Simmer 15 minutes, stirring occasionally. Set aside to cool to room temperature. Meanwhile, preheat oven to 350 degrees. Arrange pine nuts in single layer on baking sheet. Bake 8 minutes or until lightly toasted. Sprinkle over cooled caponata. Serve with pita triangles or baguette slices.

SERVES   12 - 15

1/2 cup olive oil

1-1/2 pounds eggplant, peeled and cubed

1 can (28 ounces) tomatoes with juice

3 cups sliced onion

2 cups chopped green bell pepper

3 cloves garlic, minced

1/2 cup snipped fresh parsley

1/2 cup drained pitted black olives, halved

1/3 cup red wine vinegar

2 tablespoons sugar

2 tablespoons drained capers

2 tablespoons tomato paste

2 tablespoons snipped fresh basil

1 teaspoon salt

1/2 teaspoon freshly-ground black pepper

3/4 cup pine nuts

Pita triangles or baguette slices

gingered cream cheese grapes

i n medium bowl beat cream cheese to soften. Blend in ginger. Shape 1 teaspoon mixture around each grape, rolling between palms to shape and cover completely. Transfer coated grapes to wax paper-lined tray. Cover and refrigerate 15 minutes. Roll in pecans. Cover and refrigerate until firm.

SERVES   6 - 8

2 small packages (3 ounces each) cream cheese

2 tablespoons finely chopped crystallized ginger

30 seedless green grapes, washed and thoroughly dried

1 cup toasted pecans, cooled and finely chopped

chutney cheese ball

2 packages (8 ounces each)
  cream cheese
1/2 cup sour cream
1/2 cup chopped salted
  peanuts
4 slices crisply cooked bacon,
  crumbled
1 tablespoon chopped green
  onion
2 teaspoons curry powder
1/4 cup flaked coconut
1/4 cup snipped fresh
  parsley
2 tablespoons chutney
Assorted crackers

i n large bowl beat cream cheese until softened. Add sour cream, blending until smooth. Add peanuts, bacon, green onion and curry powder, blending well. Shape into ball. In shallow ball combine coconut and parsley. Roll cheese ball in mixture until coated. Cover and refrigerate at least 4 hours. Top with chutney just before serving. Serve with assorted crackers.

SERVES   8 - 10

artichoke bottoms
with feta cheese and shrimp

2 cans (13-3/4 ounces each)
  artichoke bottoms,
  drained
2/3 cup medium shrimp,
  shelled, deveined and
  chopped
4 ounces feta cheese,
  crumbled
2 tablespoons pimientoes,
  diced
1 tablespoon snipped fresh

a rrange the artichoke bottoms on a serving platter. Toss the shrimp, feta cheese, pimientoes and parsley in a medium bowl. Spoon 1 tablespoon filling into the cavity of each artichoke bottom. Serve slightly chilled or at room temperature.

SERVES   6 - 8

chinese roasted chicken wings

1 cup packed brown sugar
1 cup soy sauce
3/4 cup water
3/4 cup melted butter
1 teaspoon dry mustard
1 teaspoon hot red pepper flakes
1/4 teaspoon Chinese 5-spice powder
30 chicken wings

I n large shallow baking pan combine brown sugar, soy sauce, water, melted butter, dry mustard, red pepper flakes and spice powder. Add chicken wings, turning to coat with mixture. Cover and refrigerate a few hours or overnight to marinate. Preheat oven to 350 degrees. Remove chicken from marinade and transfer to large pan. Roast 1-1/2 hours or until tender and cooked through. Baste and turn chicken occasionally during roasting.

SERVES   6

stuffed pea pods

1/2 pound large fresh sugar pea pods, washed and stemmed
1 pound smoked salmon
1/2 pound smoked rainbow trout
1/2 package (4 ounces) cream cheese
2 tablespoons prepared horseradish
1 tablespoon finely chopped pimientos
1 tablespoon fresh lemon juice
1 tablespoon chopped onion
1 tablespoon snipped fresh chives
Salt, to taste
Garlic powder, to taste
2 tablespoons Cognac, optional

S lit pea pods lengthwise along one side to form pockets. Set aside. In food processor puree salmon, trout and cream cheese until smooth. Add horseradish, pimientos, lemon juice, onion and chives. Pulse processor on and off until ingredients are combined. Add salt and garlic powder, to taste. Blend in Cognac, if desired. (Filling may be made 4 to 5 days ahead, or frozen up to 3 months.) Fill pea pods with mixture. Cover and refrigerate until ready to serve. Serve cold.

SERVES   8 - 10

caribbean curried chicken bites

2/3 cup raisins
2 tablespoons rum or
  pineapple juice
4 boneless, skinless chicken
  breast halves
1-1/3 cups soft cream cheese
3 tablespoons mango chutney
3 tablespoons mayonnaise
1 tablespoon teriyaki sauce
2 teaspoons curry powder
1/2 teaspoon ground ginger
1/2 teaspoon salt
1/4 teaspoon cayenne
  (red pepper)
1 cup sliced toasted almonds
1-1/2 cups flaked coconut
Fresh apricots, orange slices
  and kiwifruit slices

i n small bowl toss raisins with rum or pineapple juice. Set aside. Place chicken in large saucepan. Cover with water. Bring to boil. Reduce heat. Cover and simmer 25 minutes or until tender and cooked through. Remove chicken from water. Cool. Place half of chicken in food processor. Pulse 2 or 3 times or until coarsely chopped. Remove and set aside. Repeat chopping procedure with remaining half of chicken. Set aside.

In large bowl combine cream cheese, chutney, mayonnaise, teriyaki sauce, curry powder, ginger, salt and cayenne. Drain raisins. Add raisins, chicken and almonds to cream cheese mixture, blending well. Shape into 1-inch balls. Roll in coconut. Cover and refrigerate until ready to serve. (May be frozen in airtight container up to 1 week.) Arrange on serving platter. Garnish with fresh apricots, orange and kiwifruit slices.

SERVES   10

antipasto roll-ups

1 can (7 ounces) Italian-style
  tuna packed in olive oil,
  drained
1 hard-cooked egg
1/4 cup mayonnaise
2 teaspoons fresh lemon juice
4 ounces sliced deli
  mozzarella cheese
8 ounces sliced deli hard
  salami

i n medium bowl mash together tuna, egg, mayonnaise and lemon juice. Set aside. Cut each slice of cheese into 4 triangular pieces. Arrange each triangle on a slice of the salami. Spread 1 teaspoon tuna mixture along nearest edge of salami. Roll up and secure with toothpicks. Cover and refrigerate overnight.

SERVES   6 - 8

piroshki

i n large bowl beat butter to soften. Add cream cheese, beating until blended and smooth. Beat in cream. Add flour and salt, blending well. Shape into ball. Wrap in wax paper and refrigerate until cold. Preheat oven to 400 degrees. Lightly grease baking sheets. Cut dough in half, returning half to refrigerator until ready to use. On lightly floured surface, roll out remaining half of dough to 1/8-inch thickness. Using 2-1/2- to 3-inch biscuit or cookie cutter, cut into 30 rounds. Spoon teaspoonful Herbed Beef or Crab Filling onto center of each round. Brush edges with egg. Fold dough over in half and crimp edges with fork to seal. Transfer to prepared baking sheets. Cut small slit in top of each to allow steam to escape. Brush with egg. Bake 15 to 18 minutes or until golden brown. Repeat cutting, filling and baking procedures with remaining half of dough. Serve warm.

herbed beef filling:

In large skillet melt 2 tablespoons butter over medium-high heat. Add 2 large minced onions. Saute until golden. Add 3/4 pound lean, twice-ground beef. Cook until lightly browned and cooked through. Remove from heat and cool to room temperature. Stir in 2 chopped hard-cooked eggs, 1 teaspoon dried dill, 3/4 teaspoon salt and 1/8 teaspoon freshly-ground black pepper, blending well. Cover and refrigerate until ready to use.

crab filling:

In large bowl beat 1 package (8 ounces) cream cheese to soften. Stir in 1 can (7-1/2 ounces) drained minced clams, 3/4 cup flaked crab meat, 2 tablespoons snipped fresh chives, 2 teaspoons grated fresh onion, 1 teaspoon Worcestershire sauce, 1/2 teaspoon garlic powder and 1/2 teaspoon white pepper. Cover and refrigerate until ready to use.

SERVES   12 - 15

1-1/2 cups butter
1-1/2 packages (12 ounces) cream cheese
6 tablespoons heavy or whipping cream
3-3/4 cups all-purpose flour
1-1/2 teaspoons salt
Herbed Beef Filling (recipe follows)
Crab Filling (recipe follows)
2 to 3 eggs, slightly beaten

mushrooms stuffed with crab

24 (about 1-1/4 pounds) medium mushrooms
5 tablespoons butter, divided
2 tablespoons minced green onions
1/2 pound lump crab meat, picked through and flaked
3/4 cup shredded Monterey Jack cheese, divided
1/2 cup (about 1 slice) soft bread crumbs
1 egg, well-beaten
1 teaspoon fresh lemon juice
1/2 teaspoon snipped fresh dill
1/4 cup dry white wine

remove and chop stems from mushrooms. In large skillet melt 2 tablespoons of the butter over medium-high heat. Add mushroom stems and green onions. Saute until onion is soft. Remove from heat. Stir in crab meat, 1/4 cup of the Monterey Jack cheese, the bread crumbs, egg, lemon juice and dill, blending well. Set aside.

Melt remaining 3 tablespoons butter and pour into 13 x 9-inch oblong pan. Add mushroom caps, turning to coat with butter. Arrange upside down in pan. Fill each cap with crab meat filling, gently pressing into caps. (May be prepared 1 day in advance to this point.) Preheat oven to 400 degrees. Pour wine into pan with mushrooms. Sprinkle mushrooms with remaining 1/2 cup cheese. Bake, uncovered, 15 minutes. Serve immediately.

SERVES   10

italian sausage and sun-dried tomato tarts

2 sheets frozen puff pastry, thawed
1 pound ground Italian sausage
1-1/2 cups ricotta cheese
1/4 cup snipped fresh parsley
1/2 teaspoon fennel seed
3/4 cup grated Parmesan cheese
12 slices Muenster cheese
1/2 cup sun-dried tomatoes packed in oil, drained and sliced

preheat oven to 425 degrees. Using 2-1/2-inch biscuit or cookie cutter, cut pastry sheets into rounds. Place in mini-muffin tins, lining bottoms and sides of cups with pastry. In large skillet cook sausage. Drain and cool on paper towel-lined plate. In medium bowl combine ricotta cheese, parsley and fennel. Spoon into pastry-lined muffin cups. Top with sausage and Parmesan cheese. Cut Muenster cheese in small squares to fit top of each tart and place on each. Garnish with sun-dried tomato slices. Bake 8 minutes or until hot and cheese melts. Serve hot.

SERVES   10

sizzling mushrooms

1/4 pound oyster
  mushrooms
1/4 pound shitake
  mushrooms, stems
  removed and sliced
1/4 pound Portobello
  mushrooms, stems
  removed and chopped
1/4 pound chanterelle
  mushrooms
1/2 red onion, sliced
1 clove garlic, minced
2 tablespoons olive oil
1 teaspoon fresh rosemary,
  chopped
1 teaspoon fresh sage,
  chopped
1 teaspoon fresh thyme,
  chopped
1 teaspoon snipped fresh
  parsley
1 tablespoon balsamic
  vinegar
1/2 cup dry white wine
8 slices crusty bread,
  toasted

i n a medium bowl combine all ingredients except wine and bread. Place a cast-iron skillet on a hot grill. Heat until pan becomes very hot. Empty mushroom mixture onto hot pan. Close grill cover. Cook mushrooms 5 minutes. Remove from grill. Splash with wine to sizzle. Serve immediately with crusty bread.

Note: May be prepared in 500 degree oven.

SERVES   4

thai style seared scallops
with cucumber-pepper relish

1 stalk lemongrass, sliced
    thin crosswise
1/2 cup rice wine vinegar
1/4 cup sugar
1/2 teaspoon hot red
    pepper flakes
1/2 cup water
2 medium cucumbers,
    peeled, halved and thinly
    sliced
1 banana pepper, seeded
    and minced
1 small jalapeno pepper,
    seeded and minced
2 teaspoons snipped fresh
    cilantro
2 teaspoons snipped fresh
    basil
1/3 cup fresh lime juice
Salt and freshly-ground black
    pepper, to taste
1 pound sea scallops
Salt and white pepper
2 tablespoons olive oil

t o prepare relish place first five ingredients in nonreactive saucepan. Simmer until liquid is reduced to 1/2 cup, about 10 minutes. Strain. Cool slightly. Discard solids. Stir in next seven ingredients plus dash salt and pepper. Set aside.

Sprinkle scallops with 1/2 teaspoon salt and 1/4 teaspoon white pepper. Heat oil in medium skillet. Saute scallops, turning once, about 3 - 4 minutes. Spoon a portion of relish onto each plate. Arrange scallops over relish. Serve immediately.

SERVES 4

crab rangoon

1 package (8 ounces) cream cheese
1/2 pound lump crab meat, picked over and flaked
1 to 1-1/2 teaspoons minced fresh garlic
Dash Worcestershire sauce
1 to 2 drops Tabasco sauce
1 teaspoon salt
1/2 teaspoon white pepper
80 wonton wrappers
Vegetable oil

in large bowl beat cream cheese to soften. Add crab meat, garlic, Worcestershire sauce, Tabasco sauce, salt and pepper, blending until fluffy. Arrange wonton wrappers in rows. Place about 1/2 teaspoonful crab mixture on center of each. Fold over wrappers diagonally to form triangles. (Do not press edges together.) Place small dabs of crab filling on wrappers just to each side of center mound. Draw middle of each long edge over filling and pinch together. Fold bottom corners in to look like wings. Heat oil to 375 degrees. Deep-fry a few of the appetizers at a time until golden. Keep warm in 250-degree oven while frying remaining appetizers. Serve hot.

SERVES   15 - 20

clams napoli

3 tablespoons extra-virgin olive oil
2 cloves garlic, chopped
2 cups cherry tomato halves
1/2 cup dry white wine
1/4 cup snipped fresh herbs such as basil, oregano or marjoram
1/8 teaspoon fennel seeds or 1/2 cup chopped fresh fennel bulb
2 dozen fresh littleneck clams (or mussels), scrubbed and rinsed under cold water
Crusty Italian bread

in Dutch oven or stock pot heat olive oil over medium heat. Add garlic. Saute 3 to 5 minutes or just until browned. Reduce heat to medium-low. Add tomatoes, wine and herbs. Stir in fennel. Place clams (or mussels) in pot. Cover and cook over medium heat 10 to 15 minutes or until shellfish open, stirring occasionally. (Discard any unopened shellfish.) Arrange in shallow serving bowls with a small amount of stock from cooking pot. Serve immediately with crusty Italian bread for dipping. (Leftover stock is excellent over pasta.)

SERVES   4

jalapeno pesto-topped oysters on the half shell

1/3 cup freshly grated
  Romano cheese, divided
3 large jalapeno peppers,
  seeded
2 teaspoons hot red pepper
  flakes
4 cloves garlic
1/4 cup pine nuts
3 tablespoons freshly grated
  Parmesan cheese
3 tablespoons snipped fresh
  cilantro
Freshly grated nutmeg,
  to taste
1/2 cup melted sweet
  (unsalted) butter
2 to 3 cups rock salt
16 large fresh oysters on the
  half-shell
2 limes, each cut into 8
  wedges

Preheat oven to 400 degrees. Set aside 2 tablespoons of the Romano cheese. In food processor combine remaining Romano cheese, jalapeno peppers, red pepper flakes, garlic, pine nuts, Parmesan cheese, cilantro and nutmeg. Process until pureed. With processor running, add melted butter in thin stream, processing until blended well. Line 4 pie plates or rimmed oven-proof plates with rock salt. Arrange 4 oysters on top of salt in each plate. Top each oyster with a spoonful of Romano cheese mixture. Bake 6 to 8 minutes or until bubbly. Remove from oven. Sprinkle with reserved 2 tablespoons Romano cheese. Broil a few inches from heat just until cheese is melted. Garnish with lime wedges. Serve immediately.

SERVES   4

crab deviled eggs

- 6 eggs, hard-cooked and chilled
- 4 ounces lump crab meat, picked over and flaked
- 2 to 3 tablespoons mayonnaise
- 2 tablespoons finely chopped celery
- 2 tablespoons finely chopped onion
- 2 tablespoons fine, dry seasoned bread crumbs
- 1/2 teaspoon prepared yellow mustard
- 1 to 2 dashes Old Bay seasoning
- Paprika
- Fresh parsley

Peel and split eggs lengthwise. Remove yolks and set aside whites. Chop 2 of the yolks, reserving remaining yolks for another use. In large bowl gently combine the 2 chopped yolks, crab meat, mayonnaise, celery, onion, bread crumbs, mustard and seasoning. Fill egg whites with egg yolk mixture, mounding high. Sprinkle with paprika. Garnish with parsley. Cover and refrigerate until ready to serve.

SERVES   6 - 8

deviled shrimp

- 2 pounds cooked large shrimp, shelled and deveined
- 1 lemon, very thinly sliced
- 1 red onion, very thinly sliced
- 1/2 cup drained pitted black olives
- 1 bottle (8 ounces) Caesar salad dressing
- 1 to 2 teaspoons chopped garlic
- 1 teaspoon Dijon mustard

Arrange shrimp, lemon, onion and olives in clear shallow bowl. In separate bowl combine salad dressing, garlic and mustard. Pour over shrimp and other ingredients in bowl. Cover and refrigerate 1 to 2 hours. Serve with toothpicks.

SERVES   10

rosemary focaccia
with goat cheese and tomato stuffing

2 packages active dry yeast
1 cup lukewarm water
3-1/4 to 3-1/2 cups
    all-purpose flour
1-1/2 teaspoons salt
6 tablespoons olive oil,
    divided
1 tablespoon snipped fresh
    rosemary
Goat Cheese and Tomato
    Stuffing (recipe follows)

In small bowl sprinkle yeast. Stir in water. Set aside 10 minutes. In large bowl combine 3-1/4 cups flour, salt and 3 tablespoons of the olive oil. Stir in yeast mixture. Turn onto floured surface. Knead 15 minutes or until dough forms smooth ball, adding flour as needed or, place flour, salt and 3 tablespoons olive oil in food processor. Add yeast mixture and process 45 seconds or until smooth ball forms. Lightly coat large bowl with olive oil. Place dough in bowl, turning to coat with oil. Cover and set aside in warm place 1 hour or until doubled in volume.

Coat 13- x 9-inch oblong pan with 1 tablespoon olive oil. Gently press down dough to remove air. (Do not knead.) Stretch to fit bottom of pan. (If dough is too elastic, cover and set aside 15 minutes before stretching.)   Cover with dry cloth and set aside 30 minutes or until dough rises slightly. Adjust oven rack to lowest position. Preheat oven to 400 degrees. Using fingertips, make shallow indentations about 2 inches apart in dough. Drizzle remaining 2 tablespoons olive oil over dough. Sprinkle with rosemary. Bake 20 to 25 minutes or until golden brown. Cool completely. Remove from pan and split into 2 sheets. Spread one half with Goat Cheese and Tomato Stuffing. Top with other half, gently pressing down. Cut into small squares.

goat cheese and tomato stuffing:

In food processor place 3/4 cup sun-dried tomatoes and 5 fresh basil leaves. Pulse until coarsely chopped. Add 4 ounces goat cheese and 4 ounces mascarpone or cream cheese. Pulse just until blended. (Stuffing may be covered and refrigerated up to 4 hours before using.)

SERVES   10 - 12

mini beef wellingtons

7 ounces frozen all-butter puff pastry, thawed

1/3 cup Boursin cheese, room temperature

1/2 pound beef tenderloin, fat trimmed, cut into 1/2-inch cubes

Salt and freshly-ground black pepper, to taste

1 egg, slightly beaten

O n lightly floured sheet of parchment roll out pastry to 15- x 7-1/2-inch rectangle, about 1/8-inch thick. Cut into 1-1/2-inch squares. Spoon scant 1/4 teaspoon cheese in center of each square. Season the beef with salt and pepper to taste. Place beef cube on each pastry square. Fold pastry over beef, neatly tucking in corners. Arrange pastries, seam sides down, on large parchment paper-lined baking sheet. (May be prepared and frozen up to 1 week to this point.) Preheat oven to 400 degrees. Lightly brush each pastry with egg. Bake 10 to 12 minutes or until puffed and golden brown. Cool slightly. Transfer to large serving platter. Serve immediately.

SERVES   10 - 12

beef roulades
with watercress and blue cheese

4 ounces blue cheese, crumbled

1/4 cup sour cream

1 tablespoon fresh lemon juice

3/4 teaspoon freshly-ground black pepper, divided

1-1/2 pounds boneless sirloin steak, about 1-1/2 inches thick

1 teaspoon salt

48 sprigs fresh watercress, rinsed and dried

i n medium bowl combine blue cheese, sour cream, lemon juice and 1/4 teaspoon of the pepper. Set aside. (Mixture may be covered and refrigerated overnight. Bring to room temperature before using.) Sprinkle steak with salt and remaining 1/2 teaspoon pepper. Grill or broil a few inches from heat 8 minutes for medium-rare or to desired doneness, turning once. Transfer steak to cutting board. Let stand 7 minutes.

Holding sharp knife at angle, cut steak across grain into 24 1/4-inch thick slices. Spread 1/2 tablespoon cheese mixture on each slice. Place 2 sprigs watercress along one of the short edges of each steak slice. Starting at short edge, roll up each slice, enclosing watercress. Secure with toothpicks or small skewers. Transfer to large serving platter. Serve immediately or cover and refrigerate up to 1 hour.

SERVES   10

bruschetta with shrimp
and gruyere cheese

1 cup olive oil

2 teaspoons seasoned salt

2 baguettes, each cut into
about 24 1/4-inch-thick
slices

1 cup mayonnaise

1/2 cup freshly grated
Romano cheese

1/2 cup shredded Gruyere
cheese

1/4 cup chopped onion

1/4 teaspoon Worcestershire
sauce

Dash Tabasco sauce

1/2 pound cooked medium
shrimp, shelled, deveined
and finely chopped

preheat oven to 300 degrees. In small bowl combine olive oil and seasoned salt. Brush on baguette slices. Arrange on large baking sheet. Bake 15 minutes or until crisp. Set aside. In medium bowl combine mayonnaise, Romano cheese, Gruyere cheese, onion, Worcestershire sauce and Tabasco sauce. Add shrimp, mixing well. Spread on baguette slices. Broil a few inches from heat just until bubbly. Serve immediately.

SERVES   16 - 20

pesto toasts

1/4 cup olive oil

Snipped fresh basil, to taste

Snipped fresh parsley, to taste

2 cloves garlic, minced

10 plum tomatoes, thinly
sliced

2 baguettes, each cut into
about 24 1/4-inch thick
slices

Butter, softened

Homemade or bottled pesto

2 cups shredded mozzarella
cheese

in medium bowl combine olive oil, basil, parsley and garlic. Add tomato slices. Cover and refrigerate several hours or overnight to marinate. Lightly butter baguette slices. Toast until lightly browned. Cool. Spread pesto on one side of each toast slice. Top with marinated tomato slices. Sprinkle with cheese. Arrange on baking sheet. Broil a few inches from heat just until cheese melts. Serve immediately.

SERVES   16 - 20

italian lake bruschetta

1 cup snipped fresh basil
   leaves
1 medium tomato, seeded
   and coarsely chopped
15 Calamata olives, drained,
   pitted and coarsely
   chopped
3/4 cup (2-1/4 ounces)
   freshly grated asiago
   cheese
2 cloves garlic, minced
1/2 loaf French bread, cut
   into 1/4-inch thick slices

in medium bowl combine basil, tomato, olives, cheese and garlic. Arrange bread slices on baking sheet. Spread each with 1/2 tablespoon basil mixture. Broil a few inches from heat 3 minutes or until golden brown and cheese bubbles. Serve immediately.

SERVES 6

pepper-crusted beef crostini with arugula

1-1/2 teaspoons crushed
   black peppercorns
3/4 pound beef tenderloin,
   fat trimmed, tied
1/2 teaspoon salt
3 tablespoons olive oil
1 baguette, cut diagonally
   into 24 1/4-inch-thick slices
2 tablespoons tapenade
   (black olive paste)
12 medium fresh arugula
   leaves, halved

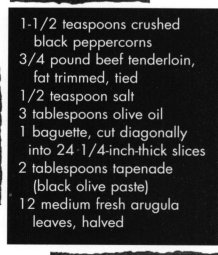

gently press crushed pepper into beef. Sprinkle with salt. In large saucepan heat 1 tablespoon of the olive oil over medium-high heat. Add meat. Cook 10 minutes or until well browned all over, turning frequently. Cool. Cover and refrigerate at least 2 hours or up to 2 days. Preheat oven to 350 degrees. Lightly brush both sides of bread slices with remaining 2 tablespoons olive oil. Arrange slices on large baking sheet. Bake 7 minutes or until lightly browned. Spread 1/4 teaspoon tapenade on each slice. Place arugula on top of each. Using sharp knife, cut chilled beef against grain into 24 very thin slices. Arrange 1 slice on each bread slice and serve.

SERVES 10

crostini with grilled vegetables and smoked mozzarella

3 tablespoons butter
2 tablespoons olive oil
1 medium onion, thinly sliced
2 medium carrots, julienned
1 medium green bell pepper, thinly sliced lengthwise
1 clove garlic, minced
2 small yellow squash, thinly sliced diagonally
4 medium plum tomatoes, peeled, seeded and diced
1/2 cup snipped fresh basil or parsley
1/2 teaspoon salt
1/4 teaspoon freshly-ground black pepper
1 cup shredded smoked mozzarella cheese
1 loaf French bread, cut into 16 1/2-inch-thick slices

place butter and olive oil in 13- x 9-inch baking pan. Place over hot, partially- vented grill. Add onion and carrots to pan. Cover grill and cook 5 minutes or until onions are soft. Add bell pepper and garlic. Cover grill and cook 3 minutes or until peppers begin to soften. Add squash and tomatoes. Cover grill and cook 4 minutes or until vegetables are tender. Stir in basil or parsley, salt and pepper. Sprinkle with cheese. Cover and cook 3 minutes or just until cheese melts. Remove pan from grill. Cover with foil and keep warm. Arrange bread slices around coolest edges of grill. Toast 1 minute or until golden, turning once. Transfer slices to large serving platter. Top with grilled vegetables. Serve immediately.

SERVES 8 - 10

beggars' purses with mushroom filling

2 tablespoons butter
1/2 pound fresh mushrooms,
    sliced
2 tablespoons white wine
1 tomato, chopped
2 teaspoons snipped fresh
    tarragon
Salt and freshly-ground black
    pepper, to taste
4 sheets phyllo dough
1/2 cup butter, melted

i n large skillet melt 2 tablespoons butter over medium-high heat. Add mushrooms. Saute 5 minutes or until soft. Add wine. Increase heat and cook 5 minutes or until most of the liquid is evaporated. Add tomato and tarragon. Salt and pepper to taste. Cook over low heat additional 5 minutes or until all of the liquid is evaporated. Set aside to cool. Butter a large baking sheet. Stack the phyllo sheets on top of each other. Cut into six 5-inch squares to make 24 individual squares. Brush 1 square with melted butter. Top with second square and brush with butter. Place squares, buttered side down, on buttered baking sheet. Top with cooled mushroom filling. Gather four corners together over filling. Twist to seal closed. Brush with butter. (Cover any remaining phyllo squares with plastic wrap and damp towel until ready to use.)

Repeat procedure until all of the phyllo squares and filling are used. (May be prepared a day in advance to this point. Cover and refrigerate until ready to use.) Preheat oven to 375 degrees. Bake 15 minutes or until golden brown. Serve immediately.

SERVES   6

marinated olives

1 pound brine-packed Gaeta,
    Nicoise or Picholine olives,
    drained
1 cup extra-virgin olive oil
2 to 3 cloves garlic, peeled
    and flattened
1 tablespoon hot red pepper
    flakes
1 tablespoon lightly toasted
    fennel seeds
Peel of 1 orange, julienned

p lace olives in colander. Rinse under cold water until water runs clear. Drain well, shaking to remove any excess water. In large, clean and dry jar combine olives with olive oil, garlic, pepper flakes, fennel seeds and orange peel. Cover tightly and shake well to combine. Marinate at room temperature 3 to 5 hours. Store in refrigerator up to 1 month until ready to serve.

SERVES   10 - 12

mini feta cheesecakes

1/2 cup fine, dry bread crumbs
1/2 cup ground pecans
1/4 cup butter
1 package (8 ounces) cream cheese
4 ounces feta cheese
1 egg
2 tablespoons milk
1/8 teaspoon Tabasco sauce
Herbed Tomato Sauce (recipe follows)
Sliced olives
Fresh parsley sprigs

Preheat oven to 350 degrees. In small bowl combine bread crumbs, pecans and butter, blending well. Line mini-muffin pans with paper liners. Spoon 1 teaspoonful of bread crumb mixture into each paper-lined muffin cup, pressing firmly onto bottom. Set aside.

In large bowl beat cream cheese until light and fluffy. Add feta cheese and egg, blending well. Mix in milk and Tabasco sauce. Spoon onto crust in muffin pans. Bake 10 to 12 minutes. Cool completely. Cover and refrigerate until well chilled. Top with Herbed Tomato Sauce. Return to refrigerator until ready to serve. Garnish with sliced olives and parsley sprigs.

herbed tomato sauce:

In small saucepan combine 1/2 cup tomato sauce, 2 tablespoons tomato paste, 1 tablespoon minced fresh onion, 1 clove minced garlic, 1/4 teaspoon dried basil, 1/4 teaspoon dried oregano and 1/8 teaspoon freshly-ground black pepper. Salt to taste. Cook and stir over medium heat 5 to 7 minutes or until heated through.

SERVES 10 - 12

new potatoes with bacon-horseradish filling

3 pounds (about 30) small, new red potatoes, scrubbed
1 cup mayonnaise
1 cup sour cream
1/4 cup crumbled, cooked bacon
1/4 cup prepared horseradish
Paprika

Prick potatoes with fork. Arrange on microwave-proof plate. Microwave on high (full power) 7 to 9 minutes or until tender, turning plate half-way after 3 to 4 minutes. Cool slightly. Slice open tops and scoop out potato. (May be made in advance to this point. Cover and refrigerate skins and potato until ready to use.)

In medium bowl combine mayonnaise, sour cream, bacon and horseradish. Add cooked potato, blending well. Reheat potato shells. Fill with potato mixture. Garnish with paprika just before serving.

SERVES 10 -12

stuffed camembert

8-ounce wheel Camembert cheese
1 cup shredded Cheddar cheese
1 small package (3 ounces) cream cheese
1-1/4 ounces blue cheese
2 tablespoons butter, softened
1 tablespoon snipped fresh parsley
1 clove garlic, minced
1 teaspoon dried Italian herb seasoning, or 1/4 teaspoon each dried basil, oregano, rosemary and thyme
1/4 cup thinly sliced green onion
Crackers or melba toast

refrigerate Camembert 2 to 3 hours or until very cold. Using sharp knife, cut around top, about 1/4 inch in from the edge and cutting down about 1/2 inch into the cheese. Using spoon, carefully scoop out cheese (including top rind), leaving 1/4-inch thick "shell" intact. Wrap and refrigerate shell until ready to use. Bring scooped Camembert, Cheddar cheese, cream cheese and blue cheese to room temperature. Beat with electric mixer until smooth and creamy. Beat in butter, parsley, garlic and herb seasoning. Stir in green onions. Mound in Camembert shell. Cover and refrigerate 1 to 4 days to blend flavors and temper. Let stand at room temperature about 1 hour before serving. Serve with crackers or melba toast.

SERVES   10 - 12

sesame shrimp

1/2 cup extra virgin olive oil
2 tablespoons sesame oil
2 cloves garlic, minced
1 tablespoon soy sauce
1/2 teaspoon red pepper flakes
1 pound medium shrimp, shelled and deveined

in shallow dish combine oils, garlic, soy sauce and red pepper flakes. Add shrimp tossing to coat with marinade. Seal tightly. Refrigerate 4 hours or up to 24 hours. Place shrimp in shallow baking dish. Preheat oven to 375 degrees. Bake, uncovered, for 10 minutes or until shrimp turns pink. Serve hot with toothpicks.

SERVES   10

city island crostini

1 French baguette, cut into 36 slices
1 package (8 ounces) cream cheese, softened
1/2 cup mayonnaise
1 package (1.7 ounces) dry Italian salad dressing mix
1/2 cup shredded Swiss cheese
Cucumber slices, quartered
Red bell pepper, chopped

Preheat oven to 400 degrees. Place baquette slices on baking sheet. Bake 5 minutes or until lightly browned. Remove from oven. Cool.

In small bowl mix cream cheese, mayonnaise, dressing mix and Swiss cheese. Spread on toasts. Bake 5 minutes. Remove from oven. Top with cucumber slice and chopped red peppers. Serve immediately.

SERVES 10 - 12

hummus with roasted garlic

2 cans (15 1/2 ounces) garbanzo beans, drained
1 head roasted garlic*, cloves removed
2/3 cup Tahini (sesame paste)
1/2 cup fresh lemon juice
2 tablespoons olive oil
Salt and freshly-ground black pepper
Snipped fresh parsley
Toasted pita triangles

In processor bowl place garbanzos, garlic, Tahini (sesame paste), lemon juice and olive oil. Process until smoothly pureed. Season to taste with salt and pepper. Transfer to shallow bowl. Garnish with parsley. Serve with pita triangles.

* Bundle whole, unpeeled bulb of garlic in double thickness of foil. Twist ends of foil to seal shut. Roast 1 hour. Remove from oven. Set aside to cool to room temperature.

SERVES 8

italian cheese terrine

1 package (8 ounces) cream
   cheese
2 tablespoons butter
1/2 cup grated Parmesan
   cheese
2 tablespoons prepared pesto
9 slices (about 1 ounce each)
   Muenster or mozzarella
   cheese
Basil-Tomato Sauce
   (recipe follows)
Fresh basil
Crackers or small wedges of
   baguette

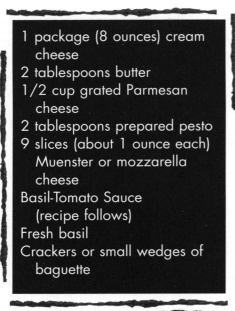

Line a 3-cup bowl or mold with plastic wrap, leaving 6-inch overhang around edge. Beat cream cheese to soften. Blend in butter, beating until smooth and creamy. Add Parmesan cheese and pesto, blending well. Set aside.

Cut 5 slices of the Muenster or mozzarella cheese in half diagonally to form triangles. Arrange in prepared bowl or mold. Spread 1/2 cup of the cream cheese mixture over cheese. Top with half of the Tomato-Basil Sauce. Cut remaining Muenster or mozzarella cheese slices in half crosswise. Arrange half over tomato sauce. Repeat layers with remaining cream cheese mixture, tomato sauce and Muenster or mozzarella cheese. Cover with overhanging plastic wrap and seal tightly. Place weight on top to lightly compress. Place on paper towel-lined plate to catch any drips. Refrigerate several hours or up to 3 days. Invert onto serving plate and remove plastic wrap. Garnish with fresh basil. Serve with crackers or small baguette wedges.

tomato-basil sauce:

Drain 1 can (14-1/2 ounces) whole tomatoes, reserving 1/4 cup juice. Chop and set aside tomatoes. In large skillet heat 1 tablespoon olive oil over medium heat. Add 3/4 cup chopped onion and 1 tablespoon minced garlic. Saute just until tender. Add chopped tomato, reserved 1/4 cup juice, 2 bay leaves, 1/2 teaspoon sugar and 1/4 teaspoon dried basil. Reduce heat and simmer 3 to 5 minutes or until thickened, stirring frequently. Remove from heat. Remove and discard bay leaves. Stir in 1 jar (7 ounces) drained and chopped sun-dried tomatoes. Cover and refrigerate at least 2 hours.

SERVES 10 - 12

baked chevre with tomatoes and french garlic toasts

3 tablespoons olive oil
1 cup chopped onions
4 cups peeled, seeded and chopped tomatoes, well drained
1-1/2 teaspoons finely chopped garlic
1/4 cup chicken stock or broth
1 teaspoon salt
Freshly-ground black pepper, to taste
8 ounces chevre cheese, room temperature
1 tablespoon snipped fresh parsley
French Garlic Toasts (recipe follows)
1/4 cup drained Nicoise olives

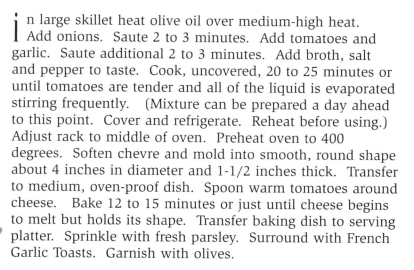

i n large skillet heat olive oil over medium-high heat. Add onions. Saute 2 to 3 minutes. Add tomatoes and garlic. Saute additional 2 to 3 minutes. Add broth, salt and pepper to taste. Cook, uncovered, 20 to 25 minutes or until tomatoes are tender and all of the liquid is evaporated stirring frequently. (Mixture can be prepared a day ahead to this point. Cover and refrigerate. Reheat before using.) Adjust rack to middle of oven. Preheat oven to 400 degrees. Soften chevre and mold into smooth, round shape about 4 inches in diameter and 1-1/2 inches thick. Transfer to medium, oven-proof dish. Spoon warm tomatoes around cheese. Bake 12 to 15 minutes or just until cheese begins to melt but holds its shape. Transfer baking dish to serving platter. Sprinkle with fresh parsley. Surround with French Garlic Toasts. Garnish with olives.

french garlic toasts:

Preheat oven to 300 degrees. Split 1 loaf crusty French bread in half lengthwise. Slice each half into 10 pieces and place on large baking sheet. Brush both sides with 1/2 cup olive oil. In small bowl beat 3/4 cup sweet (unsalted) butter until softened. Blend in 2 tablespoons snipped fresh parsley and 4 teaspoons minced fresh garlic. Spread butter mixture on top of each piece of bread. Bake 20 minutes or until golden. (May be made several hours in advance. Reheat in 300-degree oven.)

SERVES 8 - 10

soups and salads

ᖯoiling Springs Lake, from which the town derives its name, is the antithesis of the adage 'still waters run deep.' Far beneath its bubbly surface, the lake is fed by springs which are recognized as the seventh largest in Pennsylvania. Encased in subterranean caves, the springs propel the water upward with such enormous force that it causes the surface to assume the appearance of boiling - hence the lake's (and the town's) name.

chicken corn soup

2 stewing chickens, 3 to 4
   pounds each
3 quarts cold water
3 medium onions, minced
1 cup chopped celery
2-1/2 tablespoons salt
1-1/4 teaspoons nutmeg
1/4 teaspoon freshly-ground
   black pepper
10 ears fresh corn
1 egg
1 cup sifted all-purpose flour
1/2 cup milk
2 hard-cooked eggs,
   chopped
Snipped fresh parsley

In large stock pot simmer chicken in cold water with onions, celery, salt, nutmeg and pepper, covered, 2 to 2-1/2 hours or until chicken is tender. (Add water, as needed, during cooking.) Remove chicken from cooking broth, wrap and refrigerate. Cover and refrigerate broth until fat solidifies on surface. Skim and discard fat. (Broth should equal about 10 cups.) Using sharp knife, split corn kernels in half lengthwise and remove from cob. Add to chicken broth. Cover and bring to boil. Reduce heat and simmer until corn is tender.

Meanwhile, chop cooked chicken meat and set aside. In medium bowl beat egg until light in color. Add flour and milk. Beat until smooth. Add chopped chicken to broth. Using large serving spoon gradually add flour mixture in drops the size of cherry pits to broth, using knife to stop flow of batter as necessary. Cook, stirring constantly, 2 to 3 minutes or until batter forms noodles or "rivels" in broth. Add chopped hard-cooked eggs. Ladle into soup bowls and garnish with fresh parsley. Serve immediately.

SERVES 10 - 12

roasted garlic and onion cream soup

6 large sweet onions, cut
   into 1/2-inch slices
2 heads garlic, cloves
   separated and peeled
5 cups chicken broth
1-1/2 teaspoons dried thyme
1 teaspoon coarse (kosher)
   salt
1 teaspoon freshly-ground
   black pepper
1/4 cup butter, chopped
2 cups heavy or whipping
   cream
Snipped fresh parsley

Preheat oven to 350 degrees. Place onions and garlic in shallow roasting pan. Add 3 cups of the chicken broth. Sprinkle with thyme, salt and pepper. Dot with butter. Cover with foil. Roast 1-1/2 hours, stirring once or twice during baking. Remove from oven.

In food processor, puree small amounts of roasted onion-garlic mixture at a time, until smooth. Transfer to large saucepan. With processor running, gradually add remaining 2 cups chicken broth and the cream. Add to pureed mixture in saucepan, blending well. Heat through, stirring occasionally. (Do not boil.) Adjust seasonings, as desired. Ladle into soup bowls and garnish with fresh parsley. Serve immediately.

SERVES 6 - 8

sherried brie soup

2 cups cream sherry
2 tablespoons butter
6 cups sliced mushrooms
2/3 cup minced shallots
2 teaspoons fresh lemon
  juice
2 tablespoons all-purpose
  flour
4 cups beef stock or broth
4 ounces trimmed Brie
2 cups heavy or whipping
  cream
1 to 2 teaspoons salt
1/2 teaspoon freshly-ground
  black pepper
Additional Brie
Minced garlic
Snipped fresh chives

i n medium saucepan reduce sherry by half. In another medium saucepan melt butter. Stir in mushrooms, shallots and lemon juice. Saute 2 minutes. Remove from heat. Stir in flour until blended well. Return to heat. Add beef stock and reduced sherry. Cover and bring to boil. Reduce heat and simmer 25 minutes. Add trimmed Brie, stirring until melted. Add heavy cream, salt and pepper. Heat through, stirring occasionally. (Do not boil.) Ladle into soup bowls and garnish with additional Brie, minced garlic and snipped chives. Serve immediately.

SERVES   4

northern woods wild rice soup

1 quart half-and-half
6 cups cooked wild rice
2 cups cubed cooked
  chicken
1-1/4 cups chicken broth
1 cup cubed cooked ham
1/2 pound fresh spinach,
  thoroughly washed and
  coarsely chopped
1 cup shredded carrot
1 cup chopped celery
1 medium onion, chopped
1 tablespoon snipped
  fresh dill
1/2 teaspoon salt
1/4 teaspoon freshly-ground
  black pepper

i n large Dutch oven combine all ingredients. Bring to boil. Reduce heat and simmer, stirring occasionally, 15 to 20 minutes. Ladle into soup bowls and serve immediately.

SERVES   10

cajun crab soup

1/2 cup sweet (unsalted) butter
1 medium onion, chopped
2 cloves garlic, minced
1/4 cup all-purpose flour
2 bottles (8 ounces each) clam juice
2 cups chicken broth
1 package (10 ounces) frozen corn kernels
1 teaspoon salt
1/2 teaspoon white pepper
1/4 teaspoon dried thyme
1/4 teaspoon cayenne (red pepper)
2 cups heavy or whipping cream
1 pound lump crab meat
4 green onions, chopped

in large saucepan melt butter over medium heat. Add onion and garlic. Saute 5 minutes. Add flour, blending well. Cook, stirring constantly, 2 to 3 minutes. Stir in clam juice and chicken broth. Bring to boil, stirring occasionally. Add corn, salt, pepper, thyme and cayenne. Reduce heat. Cook, uncovered, 15 minutes, stirring occasionally. Add cream. Adjust seasonings, as desired. Stir in crab meat, being careful not to break up large lumps of meat. Add green onions. Heat through, stirring occasionally. (Do not boil.) Ladle into soup bowls and serve immediately.

SERVES   8 - 10

muffuleta's mushroom bisque

4-1/2 cups chicken broth
1/3 cup butter
1/3 cup finely chopped
  onion
1/4 cup finely chopped
  celery
6 tablespoons all-purpose
  flour
1/2 teaspoon dried thyme
1/2 teaspoon dried basil
1/2 cup dry sherry
3 bay leaves
1-1/4 pounds mushrooms,
  sliced
1 cup heavy or whipping
  cream
1 tablespoon fresh lemon
  juice
1-1/4 teaspoons salt
1/4 teaspoon Worcestershire
  sauce
1/4 teaspoon white pepper
1/8 teaspoon hot pepper

i n medium saucepan bring chicken broth to boil. Cover and set aside. In large saucepan melt butter over medium heat. Add onion and celery. Saute until translucent, about 5 minutes. Add flour, thyme and basil. Stir constantly 4 minutes. Whisk in hot broth and sherry. Add bay leaves. Bring to boil. Reduce heat. Simmer 3 minutes, stirring constantly. Add mushrooms. Cook 20 minutes, stirring occasionally. Add remaining ingredients, blending well. Simmer until slightly thickened, stirring occasionally, about 10 minutes. Remove and discard bay leaves. Ladle into soup bowls and serve immediately.

SERVES   4 - 6

garden vegetable chowder

2 tablespoons sweet (unsalted) butter
1 package (16 ounces) frozen corn kernels
2 small fresh yams, peeled and diced
3 stalks celery, diced
2 small zucchini, diced
1 large carrot, diced
1 small onion, diced
2 teaspoons dried thyme
4 bay leaves
6 cups canned low-sodium chicken broth
4 cups (about 5 ounces) packed fresh spinach, thoroughly washed
Salt
Freshly-ground black pepper

i n large Dutch oven melt butter over medium-high heat. Add corn, yams, celery, zucchini, carrot, onion, thyme and bay leaves. Saute 10 minutes or until vegetables are lightly browned. Add chicken broth. Cover and bring to boil. Reduce heat and simmer 45 minutes or until vegetables are tender. Remove and discard bay leaves. In blender puree 2-1/2 cups of the soup until smooth. Return puree to remaining soup. Add spinach and simmer 10 minutes or until wilted. Season with salt and pepper to taste. Ladle into soup bowls and serve immediately.

SERVES   6

kareen's tortellini and spinach soup

1 can (14 ounces) vegetable broth
1 can (14 ounces) chicken broth
1 can (14 ounces) "pasta-ready" tomatoes
1/2 of 10-ounce package frozen chopped spinach, thawed
1 cup uncooked small tortellini
1/4 cup grated Parmesan cheese

i n large pot combine vegetable broth, chicken broth, tomatoes and spinach. Cover and bring to boil. Add tortellini. Reduce heat and simmer about 15 minutes, stirring occasionally. Ladle into soup bowls and garnish with Parmesan cheese. Serve immediately.

SERVES   4 - 6

sensational shrimp bisque

1-1/2 pounds medium
  uncooked shrimp, peeled
  and deveined (reserve
  shells)
3 tablespoons olive oil
1/4 cup butter
1 large onion, diced
1 carrot, diced
1 stalk celery, diced
2-1/2 cups water
1 cup dry white wine
1/4 cup uncooked
  long-grain white rice
1 bay leaf
1 teaspoon salt
1/4 teaspoon cayenne (red
  pepper)
3 cubes chicken bouillon
1 can (16 ounces) whole
  tomatoes
2 cups heavy or whipping
  cream

i n large Dutch oven saute reserved shrimp shells in olive oil 3 minutes. Discard shells, reserving cooking liquid. Add shrimp. Saute additional 3 minutes and remove, setting aside. Add butter, onion, carrot and celery to Dutch oven. Cover and cook until tender. Stir in water, wine, rice, bay leaf, salt, cayenne and bouillon cubes. Cover and cook 15 minutes. Remove and discard bay leaf. Add tomatoes and shrimp. Puree mixture in food processor or blender until smooth. Return to Dutch oven. Stir in cream. Heat through, stirring occasionally. (Do not boil.) Ladle into soup bowls and serve immediately.

SERVES 4 - 6

cool cucumber and sweet yellow pepper soup

2 medium cucumbers,
  peeled, seeded and
  chopped
2 medium yellow bell
  peppers, chopped
2 cups peeled and cubed
  honeydew melon
1-1/2 tablespoons finely
  chopped shallots
1 fresh jalapeno pepper,
  seeded and chopped
1/2 cup plain yogurt
3 tablespoons fresh lemon
  juice
Salt
Freshly-ground black pepper
Marinated Crab Meat
  (recipe follows), optional
Diced yellow bell pepper,
  diced cucumber and
  snipped fresh chives,
  optional

i n food processor puree cucumbers, bell peppers, melon, shallots, jalapeno pepper, yogurt and lemon juice in small batches. Force through fine sieve into large bowl. Cover and refrigerate several hours or overnight. Season with salt and pepper to taste. Ladle into chilled soup bowls and garnish with Marinated Crab Meat, yellow bell pepper, cucumber and fresh chives, if desired. Serve immediately.

marinated crab meat:

In medium bowl combine 1/2 pound lump crab meat, 2 tablespoons extra-virgin olive oil, 2 tablespoons snipped fresh chives and 2 teaspoons white wine vinegar. Cover and refrigerate 1 to 2 hours or until ready to serve.

SERVES   4 - 6

vegetarian tortilla soup

6 cups chicken broth
1 red bell pepper, diced
1 red onion, chopped
2 cloves garlic, thinly sliced
2 teaspoons chili powder
2 teaspoons cumin
1 can (14 ounces) whole
    tomatoes, chopped
1 can (about 12 ounces)
    tomatoes with chiles
2 cans (16 ounces each)
    black beans, rinsed and
    drained
4 corn tortillas, cut into
    1/2-inch strips
Vegetable oil cooking spray
Peeled and chopped
    avocado, snipped fresh
    cilantro or shredded
    Monterey Jack cheese

i n large pot bring chicken broth to boil. Add bell pepper, onion, garlic, chili powder, cumin, tomatoes and tomatoes with chiles. Cover and return to boil. Reduce heat and simmer 15 minutes. Stir in beans.

Meanwhile, preheat oven to 400 degrees. Arrange tortilla strips in single layer on baking sheet. Spray with vegetable oil cooking spray. Bake 10 minutes or until crisp. Place a few of the tortilla strips in bottom of each soup bowl. Ladle soup over tortilla strips in bowls and garnish with avocado, cilantro or Monterey Jack cheese. Serve immediately.

SERVES   6

roasted red pepper soup

6 red bell peppers, cored, seeded and halved
1/4 cup sweet (unsalted) butter
1 cup chopped onion
1 cup chopped leeks
5 cups chicken broth
1/4 cup apple or orange juice
3 small boiling potatoes, peeled and sliced
2 tablespoons minced fresh garlic
2 tablespoons snipped fresh chives
2 tablespoons grated peeled fresh ginger
1/2 teaspoon freshly-ground black pepper
2 to 3 tablespoons Maggi seasoning
Hot pepper sauce, optional

Preheat broiler. Line large baking sheet with foil. Arrange 6 of the bell pepper halves, cut side down, on foil. Broil 2 inches from heat 5 to 10 minutes or until well charred. Transfer to plastic bag and seal. Set aside 10 minutes. Remove from bag. Slip off and discard charred skins. Coarsely chop peppers and set aside.

In large pot melt butter. Add onion and leeks. Saute over low heat 10 to 15 minutes or until soft and translucent. Coarsely chop remaining 6 bell pepper halves. Add with roasted peppers, chicken broth, apple or orange juice, potatoes, garlic, chives, ginger and pepper to sauteed onions and leeks. Bring to boil. Reduce heat and simmer, uncovered, until vegetables are tender. Add Maggi. Adjust seasonings, as desired. Ladle into soup bowls and serve immediately with hot pepper sauce, if desired.

SERVES 6

gazpacho with crab and pesto

2-1/2 pounds very ripe
  tomatoes, cored and
  quartered
1 green, red or yellow bell
  pepper, chopped
2 medium cucumbers,
  peeled, seeded and
  chopped
2 large celery stalks, cut into
  1-inch slices
3 tablespoons tomato paste
2 teaspoons salt
1/2 teaspoon freshly-ground
  black pepper
1/2 teaspoon cayenne (red
  pepper)
1/4 cup olive oil
1 tablespoon red wine
  vinegar
2 cups tomato juice
1 pound lump crab meat
1/2 cup pesto, optional

i n large bowl combine tomatoes, bell pepper, cucumbers,
  celery, tomato paste, salt, pepper and cayenne. Top with
olive oil and vinegar. Cover and refrigerate several hours
or overnight, stirring occasionally. In food processor,
process mixture in small batches just until coarse in
texture. Return to bowl. Add tomato juice. Adjust
seasonings, as desired. Cover and refrigerate until ready to
serve. Ladle into chilled soup bowls and garnish with crab
meat and if desired, pesto. Serve immediately.

SERVES   8

pineapple rice salad

1 package (3 ounces) lemon
   gelatin
1 cup boiling water
1 cup crushed pineapple,
   drained and juice reserved
1/2 teaspoon salt
2 cups cooked white rice,
   cooled
1 cup heavy or whipping
   cream
1/4 cup sugar

i n large bowl dissolve gelatin in boiling water. Add reserved pineapple juice. Stir in salt. Cover and refrigerate until slightly thickened. Beat until consistency of whipped cream. Stir in rice and pineapple. In separate bowl whip cream with sugar until soft peaks form. Fold into pineapple mixture. Cover and refrigerate several hours or overnight.

SERVES 8 - 10

impromptu salad with balsamic vinaigrette

1/2 cup olive oil
2 tablespoons balsamic
   vinegar
2 tablespoons snipped fresh
   flat-leaf parsley
1 small shallot, minced
1 clove garlic, minced
1/2 teaspoon whole-grain
   mustard
1/2 teaspoon salt
Freshly-ground black pepper,
   to taste
6 cups cleaned and torn
   salad greens such as
   arugula, radicchio and/or
   Bibb lettuce

i n food processor combine olive oil, vinegar, parsley, shallot, garlic, mustard, salt and pepper, to taste. Process until emulsified. Or, in medium bowl combine vinegar, shallot, garlic, mustard, salt and pepper, to taste. Gradually whisk in oil. Add parsley. Cover and refrigerate until ready to use. Whisk again just before serving. Lightly toss with greens. Serve immediately.

SERVES 6

green salad with pears and walnuts

1 tablespoon walnut oil
1/2 cup walnuts
1 large ripe Bartlett pear, peeled and cut into 1/4-inch thick slices
Olive Oil Vinaigrette (recipe follows)
10 cups cleaned and torn mixed salad greens such as watercress, red leaf and Boston lettuce
Freshly-ground black pepper, to taste

i n small skillet heat oil over medium-high heat. Add walnuts. Saute until lightly browned and fragrant. Set aside to cool. Place pears in shallow dish. Cover with Olive Oil Vinaigrette. Cover and refrigerate until ready to serve. (Salad may be prepared to this point several hours in advance.) Drain and reserve vinaigrette and pears. Toss reserved vinaigrette with salad greens. Add pepper, to taste. Arrange on chilled salad plates. Fan pear slices over top. Sprinkle with walnuts. Serve immediately.

olive oil vinaigrette:

In food processor mince 1 small shallot. Add 1/2 cup olive oil, 1-1/2 tablespoons red wine vinegar, 1 tablespoon Dijon mustard, 1/2 teaspoon sugar and 1/4 teaspoon salt. Process until well blended. Cover and refrigerate up to 4 days.

SERVES 4

watercress salad with lemon dressing

1/2 pound watercress, cleaned and stemmed
Lemon Dressing (recipe follows)
1/2 cup shredded Monterey Jack cheese
1/2 cup fresh blueberries or seedless green grapes
1/4 cup chopped toasted pecans

a rrange watercress on salad plates. Drizzle with Lemon Dressing. Top with cheese, blueberries or grapes and toasted pecans. Serve immediately.

lemon dressing:

In blender or food processor chop 1 clove garlic. Add 1/4 cup fresh lemon juice, 2 tablespoons sour cream and 1 tablespoon sugar. With blender or processor running, gradually add 1/2 cup safflower oil, blending well. Dressing may be prepared up to 1 day ahead. Cover and refrigerate until ready to use. Mix again just before serving.

SERVES 8

winter salad

8 cups cleaned and torn mixed salad greens such as spinach, red leaf lettuce, radicchio and Belgian endive
1 medium red onion, sliced
2 crisp apples, cored and thinly sliced
Crumbled blue cheese, to taste
Dried cranberries or pomegranate seeds, to taste
Olive Oil Vinaigrette (recipe follows)

a rrange salad greens on salad plates. Top with onion, apples, blue cheese and cranberries or pomegranate seeds. Serve with dressing on side.

olive oil vinaigrette:
In small bowl whisk together 3/4 cup olive oil, 3 tablespoons fresh lemon juice, 3 tablespoons balsamic vinegar and 1 tablespoon Dijon mustard. Whisk again just before serving.

SERVES   6 - 8

winter spinach salad

1 bunch spinach, cleaned and torn
3 green onions, thinly sliced
1 green apple, cored and thinly sliced
1/2 cup seedless red grapes, halved
1/3 cup dried sour cherries
1/4 cup coarsely chopped walnuts
2 tablespoons olive oil
2 teaspoons apple cider vinegar
Salt and freshly-ground black pepper, to taste
1/3 cup crumbled goat cheese

i n large bowl toss spinach, onions, apple, grapes, cherries and walnuts. In small bowl whisk together olive oil and vinegar. Salt and pepper, to taste. Toss with salad greens. Arrange on salad plates. Sprinkle with cheese. Serve immediately.

SERVES   4

cucumber and feta salad

8 ounces feta cheese
1/4 cup olive oil
2 to 3 tablespoons fresh
 lemon juice
1 tablespoon water
Salt and freshly-ground black
 pepper, to taste
1 large cucumber, peeled
 and diced
1 small red onion, chopped
1 tablespoon snipped fresh
 mint
1 tablespoon snipped fresh
 parsley
1 tablespoon snipped fresh
 dill
Fresh dill and mint
Lemon wedges
Warm pita bread

i n medium bowl crumble feta cheese. Add olive oil, lemon juice and water. Salt and pepper to taste. Add cucumber, onion, mint, parsley and dill. Lightly toss. Arrange on salad plates. Garnish with dill and mint sprigs. Serve with lemon wedges and warm pita bread. Salad may be prepared up to 1 day ahead.

SERVES 6

orzo and feta cheese salad with dill dressing

4 cups water
1 teaspoon salt
1 cup orzo, uncooked
3/4 cup crumbled feta
 cheese
1 tomato, diced
Dill Dressing (recipe follows)

i n medium saucepan combine water and salt. Bring to boil. Stir in orzo. Cook 30 seconds, stirring constantly. Reduce heat. Cover and simmer 15 minutes or until tender and water is absorbed, stirring frequently. Rinse in cold water. Drain. In large bowl combine cooked orzo, feta cheese and tomato. Lightly toss with Dill Dressing. Cover and refrigerate several hours or overnight. Lightly toss just before serving.

dill dressing:

In medium jar combine 1/3 cup olive oil, 1/4 cup fresh lemon juice, 3 tablespoons snipped fresh dill, 1 teaspoon salt and 1/4 teaspoon freshly-ground black pepper. Tightly seal jar and shake well. Shake again just before using.

SERVES 6

greek salad

1 small head lettuce such as romaine, Bibb or Boston, cleaned and torn
2 stalks celery with tops, thinly sliced
Cucumber slices, to taste
1 ripe tomato, quartered
2 green onions with tops, sliced
1 small jar or 1/2 large can artichoke hearts, drained and halved
1 small ripe avocado, peeled, sliced and dipped in fresh lemon juice
5 to 6 radishes, sliced or cut in rose-bud pattern
Anchovy fillets, to taste
5 to 6 cubes or crumbled feta cheese
Calamata olives, to taste
Greek Dressing (recipe follows)

i n large bowl lightly toss lettuce, celery, cucumbers, tomato, green onions, artichoke hearts, avocado slices and radishes, being careful not to bruise ingredients. Add dressing and lightly toss again. Arrange on chilled salad plates. Garnish with radishes, anchovies, feta cheese and olives. Serve immediately.

greek dressing:

In medium jar combine 2/3 cup olive oil, 1/3 cup wine vinegar, 1 teaspoon snipped fresh oregano or 1/2 teaspoon dried oregano, 1 teaspoon salt, 1/4 teaspoon freshly-ground black pepper and 1 clove crushed garlic. Tightly seal jar and shake well. Shake again just before using.

SERVES   4 - 6

orange-walnut salad

2 small heads Bibb lettuce, cleaned and torn
1 pound fresh spinach, cleaned and torn
2 oranges, peeled, seeded and sectioned
2 teaspoons butter
1/2 cup coarsely chopped walnuts
Sweet and Sour Dressing (recipe follows)

i n large bowl gently toss lettuce, spinach and oranges. In small skillet melt butter over medium-high heat. Add walnuts. Saute until lightly browned. Add to lettuce mixture. Toss with Sweet and Sour Dressing. Serve immediately.

sweet and sour dressing:

In medium bowl whisk together 1 cup vegetable oil, 1/2 cup vinegar, 1/2 cup sugar, 1 teaspoon each of salt, celery seeds, dry mustard, paprika and grated onion. Whisk again just before serving.

SERVES   6 - 8

greens with fried tortellini and prosciutto

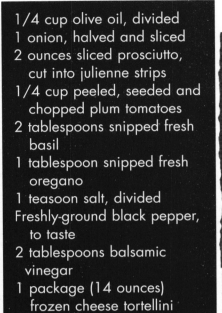

1/4 cup olive oil, divided
1 onion, halved and sliced
2 ounces sliced prosciutto,
    cut into julienne strips
1/4 cup peeled, seeded and
    chopped plum tomatoes
2 tablespoons snipped fresh
    basil
1 tablespoon snipped fresh
    oregano
1 teasoon salt, divided
Freshly-ground black pepper,
    to taste
2 tablespoons balsamic
    vinegar
1 package (14 ounces)
    frozen cheese tortellini
2 cups cleaned and torn
    mixed salad greens such
    as spinach and arugula
3 tablespoons freshly grated
    Parmesan cheese

i n large skillet heat 2 tablespoons of the olive oil over medium-high heat. Add onion, prosciutto, tomatoes, basil and oregano, 1/2 teaspoon of the salt. Add pepper, to taste. Saute 2 minutes. Stir in vinegar. Remove from heat. Transfer to large bowl and set aside.

In same skillet heat remaining 2 tablespoons olive oil over medium-high heat. Add tortellini, remaining 1/2 teaspoon salt. Add pepper, to taste. Saute 4 minutes or until golden brown, shaking skillet occasionally to toss pasta. Toss with prosciutto mixture in large bowl. Add greens and toss again. Arrange on salad plates. Sprinkle with Parmesan cheese. Serve immediately.

SERVES   6 - 8

spicy broccoli salad

3 pounds fresh broccoli,
    washed and trimmed
Salt and freshly-ground black
    pepper, to taste
Spicy Dressing
    (recipe follows)

C ut stems from broccoli and thinly slice on an angle. Cut broccoli head into small florets. Cook florets and stems in boiling water 4 minutes or just until tender. Drain. Salt and pepper to taste. Cool. Toss with Spicy Dressing. Serve immediately.

spicy dressing:

In small bowl combine 1/3 cup sherry wine vinegar, 2 tablespoons soy sauce and 1 tablespoon Dijon mustard. Whisk in 1/2 cup olive oil. Stir in 1 small seeded and minced hot green chile pepper, 3 tablespoons sugar and 1/4 teaspoon red pepper flakes.

SERVES   8 - 10

vermicelli and chicken primavera salad

1 package (12 ounces)
  vermicelli, uncooked
2 cups diced cooked chicken
1-1/2 cups julienned carrots,
  blanched
1-1/2 cups fresh broccoli
  florets, blanched
1-1/2 cups sliced mushrooms
1/3 cup pine nuts
1/4 cup snipped fresh basil
Vinegar-Oil Dressing
  (recipe follows)
Salt and freshly-ground black
  pepper, to taste

Cook vermicelli according to package directions. Drain and rinse under cold water. Drain again. In large bowl toss vermicelli with chicken, carrots, broccoli, mushrooms, pine nuts and basil. Add Vinegar-Oil Dressing. Lightly toss to coat. Salt and pepper to taste. Cover and refrigerate until ready to serve.

vinegar-oil dressing:

In small bowl whisk together 1/2 cup olive oil, 1/2 cup white wine vinegar, 1 teaspoon Dijon mustard and 1 clove crushed garlic.

SERVES   8

ravioli and broccoli salad

12 ounces cheese-filled
  ravioli, uncooked
3 tablespoons olive oil,
  divided
1 small bunch fresh broccoli,
  cleaned, trimmed and
  chopped
1 tablespoon finely chopped
  fresh chives
Salt and freshly-ground black
  pepper, to taste
Lemon Dijon Dressing
  (recipe follows)
7 tablespoons freshly grated
  Parmesan cheese
1/4 cup thinly sliced green
  onions
1/4 cup snipped fresh basil
Fresh basil leaves

Cook ravioli according to package directions. Drain. Place in large bowl and toss with olive oil. Set aside. Cook broccoli in boiling water 3 minutes or just until crisp-tender. Drain. Set aside to cool. Toss cooked broccoli and chives with ravioli. Salt and pepper to taste. Toss with Lemon Dijon Dressing, Parmesan cheese, green onions, snipped basil and pepper, to taste. Garnish with fresh basil leaves. Serve immediately.

lemon dijon dressing:

In small mixing bowl whisk together 6 tablespoons fresh lemon juice and 1 tablespoon Dijon mustard. Gradually whisk in 5 tablespoons olive oil. Whisk in 3 cloves minced garlic.

SERVES   6 - 8

portobello and prosciutto salad

1 small wedge Parmesan
   cheese
3 cups cleaned and torn
   salad greens such as
   romaine and/or arugula
1/4 cup balsamic vinegar
1/4 cup olive oil
1/4 cup minced shallots
1/4 cup snipped fresh
   parsley
1/2 teaspoon salt
1/4 teaspoon freshly-ground
   black pepper
4 large portobello
   mushrooms, stems removed
8 ounces thinly sliced
   prosciutto

Preheat broiler. Using vegetable peeler, shave 1/2 cup curls from Parmesan cheese. Set aside. Wrap and refrigerate remaining Parmesan for other uses. Arrange salad greens on large serving platter. Set aside.

In small bowl combine vinegar, olive oil, shallots, parsley, salt and pepper, mixing well. Brush mushroom caps with 1 tablespoon vinegar-oil mixture. Place on broiler rack over pan. Broil in closest position to heat source 4 minutes. Turn and brush with additional 2 tablespoons vinegar-oil mixture. Broil additional 5 minutes or until tender. Thickly slice mushrooms and arrange over greens on platter. Drizzle with remaining vinegar-oil mixture. Arrange prosciutto on same platter. Garnish with Parmesan cheese curls. Serve immediately.

SERVES   6

summer veggie slaw

1 bunch fresh watercress,
   cleaned and torn
6 cups shredded green
   cabbage
2 cups shredded red
   cabbage
1 cup shredded carrot
1/2 cup sliced green onions
6 tablespoons vegetable oil
3 tablespoons distilled white
   vinegar
2 tablespoons soy sauce
1/2 teaspoon freshly-ground
   black pepper
1/8 teaspoon Tabasco sauce

In large bowl combine watercress, green and red cabbage, carrot and onions. In small bowl whisk together oil, vinegar, soy sauce, pepper and Tabasco sauce. Drizzle over watercress mixture. Lightly toss. Serve immediately. (Vegetables and oil-vinegar mixtures may be prepared separately and refrigerated up to 8 hours.) Lightly toss just before serving.

SERVES   10 - 12

caesar margarita salad

Lime wedges, optional
Kosher or margarita salt, optional
1 large head romaine lettuce, cleaned and torn
1 cup shredded Monterey Jack cheese
1 red bell pepper, cut into thin strips
1/4 cup snipped fresh cilantro
Margarita Dressing (recipe follows)
Tortilla Wedges (recipe follows)

rub rims of 6 chilled salad plates with lime and dip in salt, if desired. Set aside. In large bowl lightly toss lettuce, cheese, bell pepper and cilantro. Add dressing and lightly toss again. Arrange on chilled salad plates. Serve immediately with Tortilla Wedges.

margarita dressing:

In medium bowl whisk together 1/3 cup canola or safflower oil, 1/4 cup fresh lime juice, 2 tablespoons egg substitute, 1-1/2 tablespoons tequila, 1-1/2 teaspoons orange-flavored liqueur, 1 clove minced garlic, 1 seeded and finely chopped serrano chile pepper, 1/4 teaspoon salt and 1/4 teaspoon ground cumin. Cover and refrigerate until ready to use. Whisk again just before using.

tortilla wedges:

Cut six 6-inch corn tortillas into small wedges. In small skillet heat 1/2 cup vegetable oil over medium-high heat. Add tortilla wedges. Fry until golden brown, stirring occasionally. Drain on paper towel-lined plate. Immediately sprinkle with kosher or margarita salt.

SERVES 6

first prize potato salad

4 pounds all-purpose potatoes (Do not peel)
2/3 cup red wine vinegar
2 tablespoons Dijon mustard
2 teaspoons salt
1 teaspoon freshly-ground black pepper
1/2 cup olive oil
3 cups chopped celery
1 cup minced red onion
1/2 cup snipped fresh parsley
1/4 cup snipped fresh tarragon

in large saucepan cover potatoes with cold water. Cover and bring to boil. Reduce heat and simmer 20 to 30 minutes or until tender. Drain and dice while warm. In large bowl whisk together vinegar, mustard, salt and pepper. Gradually whisk in olive oil. Add warm potatoes and lightly toss. (Mixture may be refrigerated at this point up to 24 hours.) Add celery, onion, parsley and tarragon. Lightly toss. Serve warm or chilled.

SERVES 10 - 12

smoked chicken salad
with pecans and sweet grilled pears

2 anjou pears, peeled and
  cored
Balsamic Dressing
  (recipe follows)
1 cup pecan halves
8 cups cleaned and torn
  baby lettuce
Meat sliced from small
  cooked, smoked chicken

C ut each pear into 8 wedges. Place in bowl. Top with
1/4 cup of the Balsamic Dressing. Marinate 10 minutes.
(Pears can be covered and refrigerated up to 8 hours at this
point.) Meanwhile, preheat oven to 325 degrees. Place
pecans in single layer on baking sheet. Bake 15 minutes.
Set aside.

Heat grill. Drain pears, reserving marinade. Place pears
on oiled grilling rack. Grill 2 minutes on each side or just
until heated through and slightly softened, brushing with
reserved marinade during grilling. Set aside. Place lettuce
in large serving bowl. Shake remaining Balsamic Dressing
and pour over lettuce. Lightly toss. Place lettuce mixture
on 4 to 6 dinner plates. Arrange pears, pecans and chicken
on top. Serve immediately.

balsamic dressing:

In medium jar combine 6 tablespoons walnut oil or extra
virgin olive oil, 1/4 cup balsamic vinegar, 1/4 cup fresh
orange juice, 1/4 cup snipped fresh cilantro, 2 tablespoons
honey, 1/2 teaspoon Asian or Caribbean chili sauce, 1/2
teaspoon salt and 1 clove minced garlic. Tightly seal jar
and shake well. Shake again just before using.

SERVES   4 - 6

chicken and tortellini salad with honey-mustard vinaigrette

1/4 cup olive oil, divided
2 cloves garlic, minced
3 skinless, boneless chicken breast halves, julienned
8 ounces tortellini, uncooked
1 green bell pepper, diced
3 stalks celery, diced
1 small red onion, thinly sliced
5 ounces smoked Gouda cheese, julienned
Honey-Mustard Vinaigrette (recipe follows)
3 ounces Canadian bacon, cooked and julienned

i n large skillet heat 2 tablespoons of the olive oil over medium-high heat. Add garlic. Saute just until browned. Remove from skillet and set aside. Add chicken to hot skillet. Stir-fry 3 to 4 minutes. Set aside to drain on paper towel-lined plate. Cook tortellini according to package directions. Drain and toss with remaining 2 tablespoons of the olive oil. Cool. In large bowl toss chicken, garlic, tortellini, bell pepper, celery, onion and Gouda cheese. Lightly toss with Honey-Mustard Vinaigrette. Top with Canadian bacon. Serve immediately.

honey-mustard vinaigrette:
In small bowl whisk together 3/4 cup olive oil, 3/4 cup vinegar, 1/4 cup honey, 2 tablespoons Dijon mustard and 1 teaspoon dry mustard.

SERVES   6 - 8

chicken salad with orange-ginger dressing

1 tablespoon oriental sesame oil
3 skinless, boneless chicken breast halves, cut into thin strips
1 red bell pepper, cut into thin strips
1 tablespoon soy sauce
1 small head red leaf lettuce, cleaned and torn
Orange-Ginger Dressing (recipe follows)
2 tablespoons toasted sesame seeds

i n large skillet heat oil over medium-high heat. Add chicken and bell pepper. Saute 5 minutes or until chicken is tender and cooked through. Transfer to medium bowl. Add soy sauce to skillet. Stir 30 seconds, scraping any brown bits from skillet into sauce. Pour over chicken. Lightly toss and set aside. In large bowl toss lettuce with just enough of the Orange-Ginger Dressing to coat. Divide among 6 salad plates. Top with chicken mixture. Sprinkle with sesame seeds. Serve with remaining Orange-Ginger Dressing.

orange-ginger dressing:
In blender combine 1/4 cup orange juice, 4 teaspoons peeled and chopped fresh ginger, 1 tablespoon minced shallot, 1 tablespoon rice vinegar, 1-1/2 teaspoons freshly grated orange peel and 1 teaspoon Dijon mustard. With blender running, gradually add 1/2 cup vegetable oil and 1 tablespoon oriental sesame oil. Salt and pepper to taste. Cover and refrigerate until ready to use. Let stand at room temperature 2 hours. Whisk again just before using.

SERVES   6

warm wild rice and roasted vegetable salad

4 firm plum tomatoes, quartered
2 small zucchini, sliced 1/4-inch thick
2 medium red or yellow bell peppers, cut into 1-inch squares
1 teaspoon snipped fresh rosemary
1 tablespoon olive oil
2 cups warm cooked wild rice
1/2 cup chopped prosciutto
Vegetable oil cooking spray
Vinaigrette Dressing (recipe follows)
Lettuce leaves
Fresh rosemary sprigs

Preheat oven to 450 degrees. Lightly coat a 15-1/2 x 10-1/2 x 1-inch jelly roll pan with cooking spray. In large bowl combine tomatoes, zucchini, bell peppers and rosemary. Drizzle with olive oil. Lightly toss to coat. Spread in single layer in prepared pan. Roast 15 to 20 minutes or until crisp-tender and lightly browned. Place in large bowl. Add cooked rice, prosciutto and Vinaigrette Dressing. Lightly toss. Arrange on large serving platter lined with lettuce leaves. Garnish with fresh rosemary sprigs. Serve immediately.

vinaigrette dressing:

In small bowl whisk together 2 tablespoons white wine vinegar, 1/4 cup orange juice, 1/4 cup olive oil, 1 tablespoon Dijon mustard, 2 teaspoons snipped fresh rosemary, 1-1/2 teaspoons salt, 1 teaspoon ground cumin and 1/4 teaspoon cayenne (red pepper).

SERVES   4 - 6

crab meat and pasta salad

12 ounces lump crab meat
1 pound pasta, uncooked
Herb Dressing (recipe follows)
1/2 pound fresh snow peas, washed, trimmed and blanched, or 1 package frozen, thawed
1 bunch fresh broccoli florets, washed, trimmed and blanched
2 cups cherry tomato halves
1/2 cup drained, thinly sliced water chestnuts
Fresh lettuce leaves
1/2 cup salted cashews

Pick through crab meat, removing shells and cartilage. Set aside. Cook pasta according to package directions. Drain and toss warm pasta with half of the Herb Dressing. Add snow peas, broccoli, tomatoes and water chestnuts. Stir in crab meat. Add enough additional Herb Dressing to coat mixture. Cover and refrigerate at least 30 minutes before serving. Spoon onto salad plates lined with fresh lettuce leaves. Sprinkle with cashews. Serve immediately.

herb dressing:

In medium bowl combine 1-1/2 cups mayonnaise, 1 tablespoon snipped fresh dill, 1 tablespoon snipped fresh basil and 1 tablespoon snipped fresh parsley, blending well.

SERVES   6

taco salad with shrimp and black beans

Avocado Dressing
(recipe follows)
2 medium tomatoes, chopped
1 green or yellow bell
  pepper, diced
1 can (16 ounces) black
  beans, rinsed and drained
1 pound cooked shrimp,
  shelled and deveined
4 cups sliced iceberg lettuce
4 cups tortilla chips
Sour cream, optional

i n large bowl combine Avocado Dressing, tomatoes, bell pepper, beans and shrimp. (Mixture may be prepared up to 3 hours in advance to this point. Cover and refrigerate until ready to use.) Arrange lettuce on large serving platter. Arrange 3 cups of the tortilla chips around edge. Crush remaining 1 cup chips. Stir into shrimp mixture. Spoon over lettuce. Garnish with sour cream, if desired.

avocado dressing:

In large bowl mash 1 peeled and diced ripe avocado. Stir in 1/2 cup sour cream, 1/3 cup mayonnaise, 3 tablespoons snipped fresh cilantro, 1 teaspoon fresh lemon juice, 1 teaspoon sugar, 1 clove minced garlic, 1/2 teaspoon chili powder, 1/2 teaspoon ground cumin and 1/4 teaspoon salt.

SERVES   6

fusilli and shrimp salad
with cucumber and orange

3 cups water
3/4 pound fresh medium
  shrimp, peeled and
  deveined
4 teaspoons salt, divided
12 ounces fusilli or other
  pasta, uncooked
2 tablespoons olive oil
1 small cucumber, peeled,
  halved lengthwise and
  thinly sliced
2 medium oranges, peeled
  and sectioned
6 green onions, thinly sliced
Spicy Dijon Dressing
(recipe follows)

i n medium saucepan bring water to boil. Add shrimp and 1 teaspoon of the salt. Cook 3 minutes or just until opaque. Drain and rinse under cold water. Drain again and set aside. Cook pasta according to package directions, using remaining 3 teaspoons salt in cooking water. Drain and rinse under cold water. Drain again. Place in large serving bowl. Toss with olive oil. Add shrimp, cucumber, oranges and green onions. Lightly toss. Add Spicy Dijon Dressing. Lightly toss to coat. Serve immediately.

spicy dijon dressing:

In small bowl combine 1/4 cup rice wine vinegar, 2 tablespoons brown sugar, 2 tablespoons soy sauce, 1 tablespoon Dijon mustard, 1 teaspoon salt, 1/2 teaspoon hot red pepper flakes and 1/2 teaspoon freshly-ground black pepper.

SERVES   8

grilled shrimp in chile marinade
with three melons

1/2 cup peanut oil

2 tablespoons fresh lime juice

1 tablespoon freshly grated
   lime peel

4 cloves garlic, minced

1 teaspoon Indonesian chile
   paste

1/4 teaspoon salt

24 (about 1 pound) fresh
   shrimp in shells

1/2 cup snipped fresh
   cilantro

1/2 medium honeydew
   melon, peeled, seeded and
   cut lengthwise into thin
   slices

1 small cantaloupe, peeled,
   seeded and cut lengthwise
   into thin slices

1/2 medium casaba melon,
   peeled, seeded and diced

i n medium bowl whisk together oil, lime juice, lime peel, garlic, chile paste and salt. If using wooden skewers, soak six 10-inch skewers 15 minutes in warm water. Thread shrimp on skewers. Brush with some of oil mixture. Cover and refrigerate remaining mixture until ready to use. Heat grill. Place skewers of shrimp on oiled grilling rack. Grill 2 minutes or just until opaque, turning once during grilling. Cool slightly. Peel and devein. Stir cilantro into remaining marinade. Add grilled shrimp and toss to coat. Marinate about 1 hour or cover and refrigerate overnight. Drain, reserving marinade. Alternate honeydew and cantaloupe slices in circular pattern on 4 dinner plates. Top with casaba melon and shrimp. Drizzle with reserved marinade and serve immediately.

SERVES   4

grilled seafood salad nicoise

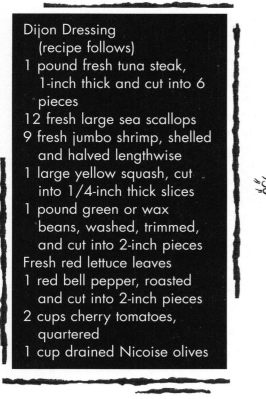

Dijon Dressing
(recipe follows)
1 pound fresh tuna steak,
1-inch thick and cut into 6
pieces
12 fresh large sea scallops
9 fresh jumbo shrimp, shelled
and halved lengthwise
1 large yellow squash, cut
into 1/4-inch thick slices
1 pound green or wax
beans, washed, trimmed,
and cut into 2-inch pieces
Fresh red lettuce leaves
1 red bell pepper, roasted
and cut into 2-inch pieces
2 cups cherry tomatoes,
quartered
1 cup drained Nicoise olives

brush 1 tablespoon Dijon Dressing on tuna. Repeat for scallops, shrimp and squash. Let stand 15 minutes. Meanwhile, in kettle of boiling water cook beans 5 minutes or just until crisp-tender. Drain and rinse under cold water. Drain again and transfer to bowl. Toss with 3 tablespoons of the Dijon Dressing. Grill the tuna 2-1/2 minutes on each side, the shrimp 4 minutes on each side, the scallops and squash 6 minutes on each side, 4 to 6 inches from heat source. Transfer to large tray as each is grilled. Line 6 salad plates with red lettuce leaves. Arrange 2 halved scallops, 3 shrimp halves and a piece of tuna on each plate. Spoon squash, beans, bell pepper, tomatoes and olives onto each plate. Drizzle with remaining Dijon Dressing or serve dressing separately. Serve immediately.

dijon dressing:

In small bowl whisk together 3 tablespoons red wine vinegar, 1 tablespoon Dijon mustard, 1 teaspoon anchovy paste, 1/2 teaspoon dried thyme, and 1/4 teaspoon sugar. Salt and pepper to taste. Add 1/3 cup olive oil in thin stream, whisking constantly. Continue to whisk until emulsified.

SERVES 6

radicchio and avocado salad
with warm monterey jack cheese

2 tablespoons fresh lemon
   juice
1 tablespoon Dijon mustard
1/2 teaspoon salt
1/4 teaspoon freshly-ground
   black pepper
3/4 cup olive oil
2 medium heads radicchio,
   cleaned and torn
4 small ripe avocados,
   peeled and diced
8 ounces Monterey Jack
   cheese, cut into 16 slices,
   2-1/2 x 1/2 x 1/4 inches
   each

In small bowl combine lemon juice, mustard, salt and pepper. Gradually whisk in olive oil. Set aside. Arrange radicchio on salad plates. Top with avocados. Drizzle with olive oil mixture. Arrange cheese in circular pattern on 12-inch microwave-safe plate. Microwave on medium power 3 minutes, rotating half turn after 1-1/2 minutes. Top each salad with 2 slices of the melted cheese. Serve immediately.

SERVES   6

ham and orzo salad

16 ounces orzo, uncooked
2 teaspoons salt
8 ounces cooked smoked
   ham, diced
2 plum tomatoes, diced
2 cups frozen corn kernels,
   thawed
8 green onions, thinly sliced
1 stalk celery, thinly sliced
1 medium red bell pepper,
   diced
Mustard-Thyme Vinaigrette
   (recipe follows)
Salt and pepper, to taste

Cook orzo according to package directions using 2 teaspoons salt in cooking water. Drain and rinse under cold water. Drain again. In large bowl toss orzo, ham, tomatoes, corn, onions, celery and bell pepper. Add Mustard-Thyme Vinaigrette. Lightly toss to coat. Salt and pepper to taste. Serve immediately.

mustard-thyme vinaigrette:

In medium bowl whisk together 3 tablespoons white wine vinegar, 1 tablespoon snipped fresh thyme or 1 teaspoon dried thyme, 2 teaspoons coarse-grain mustard, 1 clove minced garlic, 1/2 teaspoon salt and 1/4 teaspoon freshly-ground black pepper. Gradually whisk in 1/4 cup olive oil and 3 tablespoons vegetable oil. Whisk again just before using.

SERVES   8 - 10

beef salad with caper vinaigrette

Caper Vinaigrette
(recipe follows)
1-1/2 pounds rare roast
beef, sliced and cut into
strips
12 ounces fresh green beans,
washed, trimmed, cut into
pieces and blanched
1/2 red onion, thinly sliced
1/2 pound mushrooms, thinly
sliced
2 cups cherry tomato halves
2 jars (3 ounces each)
marinated artichoke hearts,
drained
1 bunch fresh watercress,
cleaned and torn
1 head leaf lettuce, cleaned
and torn

i n large bowl pour a third of the Caper Vinaigrette over roast beef. Cover and refrigerate at least 3 hours to marinate. Add green beans, onion, mushrooms, tomatoes, artichoke hearts and watercress. Toss with additional Caper Vinaigrette. Arrange on lettuce-lined salad plates. Serve immediately.

caper vinaigrette:

In medium bowl whisk together 1 cup vegetable oil, 1/2 cup red wine vinegar, 3 tablespoons fresh lemon juice, 2 tablespoons capers, 1 tablespoon Dijon mustard, 2 teaspoons sugar, 1 teaspoon salt and 1/2 teaspoon freshly-ground black pepper. Whisk again just before using.

SERVES   6 - 8

fruited spinach salad

8 cups cleaned and torn fresh
spinach
2 cups cantaloupe balls
1-1/2 cups fresh strawberry
halves
2 tablespoons seedless
raspberry jam
2 tablespoons raspberry
vinegar
1 tablespoon honey
2 teaspoons olive oil
1/4 cup chopped
macadamia nuts

i n large bowl lightly toss spinach, cantaloupe and strawberries, being careful not to bruise fruit. In small bowl whisk together raspberry jam, vinegar, honey and oil. Drizzle over spinach mixture. Lightly toss again. Sprinkle with macadamia nuts. Serve immediately.

SERVES   6 - 8

warm steak salad with papaya and red onion

2 tablespoons red wine
    vinegar
1 teaspoon salt, divided
1/2 teaspoon freshly-ground
    black pepper, divided
5 tablespoons olive oil
1 tablespoon snipped fresh
    rosemary or 3/4 teaspoon
    dried rosemary
1/4 teaspoon cayenne
    (red pepper)
1-1/2 pounds top sirloin
    steak, fat trimmed
1 small papaya, peeled and
    diced
1 small red onion, thinly
    sliced
1 small bunch curly endive or
    arugula, cleaned and torn

i n small bowl whisk together vinegar, 1/2 teaspoon of the salt and 1/4 teaspoon of the pepper. Gradually whisk in oil. Set aside.

In small bowl combine rosemary, cayenne, remaining 1/2 teaspoon salt and 1/4 teaspoon pepper. Rub into steak. Heat grill or broiler. Grill or broil steak 8 minutes or until medium-rare, turning once during cooking. Transfer to cutting board. Slice thin across grain, reserving juices. Toss steak and juices with papaya, onion and vinegar-oil mixture. Lightly toss to coat. Divide endive or arugula among 4 dinner plates. Top with steak mixture. Serve immediately.

SERVES   4

roast pork tenderloin salad
with creamy cilantro dressing

1-1/2 pounds pork
  tenderloin, fat trimmed
1 tablespoon vegetable oil
1/2 teaspoon salt
1/4 teaspoon freshly-ground
  black pepper
12 red lettuce leaves or 2
  quarts cleaned and torn
  mixed salad greens
1 cup thinly sliced mushrooms
1 small avocado, peeled,
  pitted and thinly sliced
2 small tomatoes, quartered
12 black olives such as
  Kalamata
Creamy Cilantro Dressing
  (recipe follows)

adjust oven rack to middle position. Preheat to 400 degrees. Place tenderloin in small roasting pan. Rub with oil. Sprinkle with salt and pepper. Roast 10 minutes to sear. Reduce oven temperature to 325 degrees. Insert meat thermometer in thickest part of meat. Roast 15 to 20 minutes or until thermometer registers 145 to 150 degrees. Cool to room temperature. (Meat may be wrapped and refrigerated overnight.) Thinly slice tenderloin across grain. Line 4 dinner plates with lettuce leaves or torn salad greens. Arrange tenderloin, mushrooms and avocado on top. Garnish with tomatoes and olives. Serve with Creamy Cilantro Dressing.

creamy cilantro dressing:

Halve, seed and mince 1 medium jalapeno chile pepper. In medium bowl toss jalapeno pepper with 2 cloves minced garlic, 3 tablespoons snipped fresh cilantro, 2 tablespoons snipped fresh parsley and 1 tablespoon fresh lime juice. Stir in 3/4 cup mayonnaise, 1/2 cup sour cream, 1/2 teaspoon salt and 1/4 teaspoon freshly-ground black pepper. Use immediately or cover and refrigerate up to 2 days.

SERVES   4

breads and brunches
and lunches

M any of nature's greatest treasures are found well off the beaten path. In 1920, a colony of the Box Huckleberry (Gaylussacia brachycera) - a rare shrub native to this region - was discovered along the northeast bank of the Juniata River between Newport and Duncannon. The plants of this particular colony are estimated to be 13,000 years old, making them the oldest living things in the world. The berries of this ancient form of vegetation are a delicacy for neighboring ruffed grouse.

apricot almond bread

3/4 cup sweet (unsalted) butter, room temperature
1-1/2 cups sugar
3 eggs
1-1/2 cups all-purpose flour
2 teaspoons baking powder
1-1/2 teaspoons baking soda
1-1/4 teaspoons salt
1/2 teaspoon cinnamon
1/2 cup sour cream
2 teaspoons almond extract
2 cups chopped dried apricots
1 cup toasted sliced almonds

Preheat oven to 325 degrees. Butter and flour two 9 x 5-inch loaf pans. In large bowl cream butter and sugar until smooth. Add eggs, one at a time, beating well after each addition. On low speed blend in flour, baking powder, baking soda, salt and cinnamon. Add sour cream and almond extract. Mix until smooth. Stir in apricots and almonds. Spoon into prepared pans. Bake about 1 hour and 10 minutes. Cool completely in pans before removing.

MAKES   2 LOAVES

chocolate lovers bread

1/2 cup butter, room temperature
1 cup sugar
2 eggs
1 cup buttermilk
1-3/4 cups all-purpose flour
1/2 cup unsweetened cocoa powder
1/2 teaspoon baking powder
1/2 teaspoon baking soda
1/2 cup chopped pecans
Honey Chocolate Butter (recipe follows)

Preheat oven to 350 degrees. Grease a 9 x 5-inch loaf pan. In large bowl cream butter and sugar until smooth. Add eggs, one at a time, beating well after each addition. Stir in buttermilk. On low speed blend in flour, cocoa powder, baking powder and baking soda. Stir in pecans. Spoon into prepared pan. Bake 1 hour or until toothpick inserted comes out clean. Cool 15 minutes in pan. Remove from pan and cool completely on wire rack. Serve with Honey Chocolate Butter.

honey chocolate butter:

In medium bowl beat 1/2 cup butter until softened. Add 2 tablespoons chocolate syrup and 1 tablespoon honey, beating until light and fluffy.

MAKES   1 LOAF

pecan bread

2 cups all-purpose flour
1 cup packed dark brown
   sugar
2 teaspoons baking powder
1 egg
1 cup milk
2 tablespoons melted butter
1 cup chopped pecans

preheat oven to 350 degrees. Butter a 9 x 5-inch loaf pan. In large bowl combine flour, brown sugar and baking powder. Add egg, milk and melted butter, stirring until blended well. Add nuts. Spoon into prepared pan. Bake 45 minutes. Cool 15 minutes in pan. Remove from pan and cool completely on wire rack.

MAKES   1 LOAF

low-fat banana bread*

2/3 cup sugar
2-1/2 tablespoons canola oil
   or softened margarine
2 egg whites
1 egg
1 cup (about 2 large) mashed
   ripe bananas
1/4 cup water
1-1/2 tablespoons
   unsweetened applesauce
1 teaspoon vanilla extract
1-2/3 cups all-purpose flour
1 teaspoon baking soda
1 teaspoon cinnamon
1/4 teaspoon baking powder
Vegetable oil cooking spray

preheat oven to 350 degrees. Lightly coat a 9 x 5-inch loaf pan with cooking spray. Lightly flour. In large bowl beat sugar and oil or margarine. Add egg whites, egg, mashed banana, water, applesauce and vanilla extract, beating well. In separate bowl combine flour, baking soda, cinnamon and baking powder. Stir into egg mixture just until moistened. Pour into prepared pan. Bake 45 to 50 minutes. Cool 10 minutes in pan. Remove from pan and cool completely on wire rack.

*160 calories and 4 grams fat per serving

MAKES   1 LOAF

carrot bread

1 cup sugar
3/4 cup vegetable oil
2 eggs
1-1/2 cups all-purpose flour
1-1/2 teaspoons cinnamon
1 teaspoon baking powder
1 teaspoon baking soda
1/4 teaspoon salt
1 cup packed grated carrots

preheat oven to 350 degrees. Grease a 9 x 5-inch loaf pan. In large bowl combine sugar and oil. Add eggs, one at a time, beating well after each addition. In separate bowl combine flour, cinnamon, baking powder, baking soda and salt. Blend into egg mixture. Stir in carrots. Spoon into prepared pan. Bake 55 to 60 minutes. Cool 15 minutes in pan. Remove from pan and cool completely on wire rack.

MAKES   1 LOAF

southwestern corn bread

1 cup crumbled fried bacon
   (reserve fat)
2 cups all-purpose flour
2 cups stone-ground
   cornmeal
1/4 cup sugar
2 tablespoons baking powder
1 teaspoon salt
4 eggs
1-1/2 cups milk
1/2 cup heavy or whipping
   cream
1/2 cup vegetable oil
1 cup diced onion
3 jalapeno peppers, diced

preheat oven to 425 degrees. Heat a 13 x 9-inch pan or large iron skillet in oven. Pour reserved bacon fat into hot pan or skillet. Return to oven. Meanwhile, in large bowl combine crumbled bacon, flour, cornmeal, sugar, baking powder and salt. Add eggs, milk, cream and oil, mixing well. Stir in onion and peppers. Spoon over bacon fat in hot pan. Bake 30 to 40 minutes. (Do not over-bake.) Serve warm.

SERVES   8

beer bread

3 cups self-rising flour
1/3 cup sugar
1 bottle (12 ounces) warm
(not hot) beer
Melted butter

preheat oven to 350 degrees. Grease a 9 x 5-inch loaf pan. In large bowl combine flour and sugar. Add beer, stirring just until dry ingredients are moistened. (Batter will be heavy.) Place in prepared pan. Bake 1 hour. Brush top with melted butter. Cover with foil until ready to serve. Serve warm.

MAKES 1 LOAF

pennsylvania herb potato bread

1 large (about 8 ounces) red
   or russet potato, peeled
   and chopped
1-1/2 cups water
1/4 teaspoon sugar
1 package active dry yeast
1/2 cup buttermilk
4 teaspoons snipped fresh
   thyme
1-1/2 teaspoons salt
4 cloves garlic, minced
3-1/4 to 4 cups all-purpose
   flour
1 egg yolk
2 tablespoons water

in medium sauce pan cook potato in 1-1/2 cups water, uncovered, 15 to 20 minutes or until tender. Drain, reserving 1/2 cup cooking liquid. Cool to lukewarm (110° to 115°). Stir in sugar and yeast. Let stand 10 minutes. In large bowl mash potato. Set aside.

In small saucepan heat buttermilk, thyme, salt and garlic just until warm (110° to 115°). Stir into mashed potato until smooth. Add yeast mixture and 2 cups of the flour. Stir until soft dough forms. Turn onto lightly floured surface. Gradually knead in enough of the remaining flour to make moderately stiff dough, 6 to 8 minutes. Place dough in lightly oiled bowl. Turn dough to coat with oil. Cover with damp cloth. Let rise in warm place 45 to 60 minutes or until doubled in volume. Punch down dough. Divide into six equal portions. Cover and let rest 10 minutes. Shape into 3-inch rounds or 5 x 2-inch ovals. Place on lightly greased baking sheet. Cover and let rise in warm place 30 minutes or until almost doubled. Preheat oven to 375 degrees.

In small bowl combine egg yolk and 2 tablespoons water. Brush on dough. Bake 20 to 25 minutes or until golden and hollow sounding when lightly tapped. Remove from baking sheet. Cool on wire rack.

MAKES 6 SMALL LOAVES

delicious dill bread

1/2 cup melted butter

1/3 cup grated Parmesan cheese

2 tablespoons snipped fresh dill

2 tablespoons snipped fresh parsley

1 teaspoon fresh lemon juice

1/2 teaspoon grated fresh lemon peel

2 packages (10 ounces each) refrigerated biscuits

Preheat oven to 400 degrees. Grease a large Bundt pan. In small bowl combine melted butter, Parmesan cheese, dill, parsley, lemon juice and lemon peel. Spoon into prepared Bundt pan. Arrange biscuits on edge over butter-Parmesan mixture in pan. Bake 20 to 25 minutes. Serve warm or at room temperature.

MAKES   1 LOAF

bacon braid

6 slices uncooked bacon, diced

1 package hot roll mix

1-1/2 teaspoons dried minced onion

1 egg, slightly beaten

1 package (3 ounces) cream cheese

1 teaspoon milk

1 egg, slightly beaten

Grease a 9 x 5-inch loaf pan. Fry bacon until cooked but not crisp. Drain and set aside. Prepare hot roll mix according to package directions, adding dried onion to mix. Cover with damp cloth and let rise in warm place 30 to 45 minutes or until doubled in volume. In small bowl beat cream cheese and milk until smooth. Set aside.

Transfer dough to lightly floured surface. Roll into 12-inch square. Spread with cream cheese. Sprinkle with bacon. Fold in half. Roll out again to 12-inch square. Cut into three 4-inch strips. Braid and pinch ends together to seal. Place in prepared pan. Cover with damp cloth and let rise in warm place until doubled in volume. Brush with beaten egg. Preheat oven to 350 degrees. Bake 35 minutes. Serve warm or at room temperature.

MAKES   1 LOAF

susie's orange muffins

1/2 cup sweet (unsalted)
   butter, room temperature
1 cup sugar
2 eggs
1 teaspoon baking soda
1 cup buttermilk
2 cups all-purpose flour
1/2 teaspoon salt
Peel of 1 orange, grated
Juice of 1 orange
1/2 cup sugar

Preheat oven to 400 degrees. Butter standard-size muffin tins. In large bowl cream butter and 1 cup sugar until smooth. Add eggs, beating until fluffy. Stir baking soda into buttermilk. In separate bowl combine flour and salt. Add alternately with buttermilk to egg mixture, stirring after each addition just until blended. Add orange peel. Spoon into prepared muffin tins, filling 2/3 full. Bake 20 to 25 minutes or until golden brown and firm to the touch. While warm, brush tops with orange juice and sprinkle with 1/2 cup sugar. Serve warm.

MAKES   1 DOZEN

peach muffins

1 egg
3/4 cup milk
2/3 cup packed light brown
   sugar
1/4 cup vegetable oil
1/2 teaspoon fresh lemon
   juice
1/2 teaspoon vanilla extract
1 cup whole-wheat flour
1 cup all-purpose flour
1-1/2 teaspoons baking
   powder
1 teaspoon cinnamon
1/2 teaspoon baking soda
1 cup diced peeled fresh
   peaches

Preheat oven to 375 degrees. Paper-line standard-size muffin tins. In large bowl beat egg lightly. Stir in milk, brown sugar, oil, lemon juice and vanilla extract, blending well. Add whole-wheat flour, all-purpose flour, baking powder, cinnamon and baking soda. Stir just until dry ingredients are moistened. Fold in peaches. Spoon into prepared muffin tins, filling 3/4 full. Bake 20 to 25 minutes or until toothpick inserted comes out clean. Serve warm.

MAKES   1 DOZEN

glorious morning muffins

5 eggs
2 cups vegetable oil
2 cups packed light brown
  sugar
4 teaspoons vanilla extract
4 cups whole-wheat flour
4 teaspoons baking soda
4 teaspoons cinnamon
4 cups grated carrots
2 apples, peeled and grated
2 cups chopped walnuts
1 cup raisins

Preheat oven to 350 degrees. Paper-line standard-size muffin tins. In large bowl combine eggs, oil, brown sugar and vanilla extract, beating well. In separate bowl combine flour, baking soda and cinnamon. Blend into egg mixture. Stir in carrots, apples, walnuts and raisins. Spoon into prepared muffin tins, filling 2/3 full. Bake 20 to 25 minutes. Serve warm.

MAKES   3 DOZEN

sweet potato muffins

1/2 cup butter, room
  temperature
1-1/4 cups sugar
1-1/4 cups mashed canned
  or baked sweet potatoes
2 eggs
1-1/2 cups all-purpose flour
2 teaspoons baking powder
1 teaspoon cinnamon
1/4 teaspoon nutmeg
1/4 teaspoon salt
1 cup milk
1/2 cup raisins
1/4 cup walnuts or pecans
Cinnamon-Sugar Topping
  (recipe follows)

Preheat oven to 400 degrees. Grease standard-size muffin tins. In large bowl cream butter, sugar and sweet potatoes until smooth. Add eggs, beating well. In separate bowl combine flour, baking powder, cinnamon, nutmeg and salt. Add alternately with milk to sweet potato mixture, stirring after each addition just until blended. Fold in raisins and nuts. Spoon into prepared muffin tins, filling 2/3 full. Sprinkle with Cinnamon-Sugar Topping. Bake 20 to 25 minutes. Serve warm.

cinnamon-sugar topping:

In small bowl combine 2 tablespoons sugar and 1 teaspoon cinnamon.

MAKES   2 DOZEN

stuffed french toast

3/4 cup apricot preserves, divided

3 tablespoons brandy or dark rum

1/2 teaspoon freshly grated orange peel

1-1/2 cups ricotta cheese

1/2 package (4 ounces) cream cheese, softened

1 cup grated Monterey Jack cheese

8 slices Italian or French bread, 2 inches thick

8 eggs

1-1/2 cups light cream

Dash nutmeg

1 tablespoon butter

1 tablespoon vegetable oil

Honey Orange Sauce or Apple Topping (recipes follow)

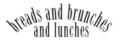

In small saucepan combine 1/2 cup of the apricot preserves, brandy or rum and orange peel. Heat to boiling, stirring occasionally. Set aside to cool to room temperature. In large bowl combine ricotta cheese, cream cheese and Monterey Jack cheese. Add cooled apricot mixture, mixing well. Set aside.

Starting at top of each slice, cut bread almost through to bottom to form pocket. Stuff with cheese mixture. Transfer to large baking sheet with sides. In large bowl combine eggs, cream and nutmeg. Pour over stuffed bread slices. Cover and refrigerate several hours or overnight.

In large skillet melt butter with oil. When bubbly, add 4 of the bread slices. Cook 5 minutes on each side or until golden brown. Transfer to clean baking sheet. Repeat cooking procedure with remaining bread slices and place on baking sheet. Preheat oven to 375 degrees. Brush bread slices with remaining 1/4 cup apricot preserves. Bake 15 minutes or until puffy and glazed. Top with warm Honey Orange Sauce or Apple Topping. Serve immediately.

honey orange sauce:

In medium saucepan heat 2 cups honey just until warm. Stir in 1/2 cup fresh orange juice, 4 teaspoons freshly grated orange peel, 4 teaspoons orange liqueur and 1/2 teaspoon freshly grated ginger. Heat through. Serve warm.

apple topping:

In large saucepan thoroughly combine 1 cup sugar, 2 tablespoons cornstarch, 1 teaspoon cinnamon and 1 teaspoon nutmeg. Stir in 2 cups water. Bring to boil over medium heat, stirring constantly. Cook, stirring constantly, until mixture thickens. Add butter. Stir until melted. Add 6 cups peeled and sliced apples. Heat through, stirring occasionally. Serve warm.

SERVES 8

homemade crescents

1/2 cup milk
1/4 cup vegetable oil
2 tablespoons sugar
1/2 teaspoon salt
1 egg, slightly beaten
1 package active dry yeast
2 cups all-purpose flour
2 tablespoons melted butter

In small saucepan scald milk. Set aside to cool to 105 to 115 degrees. In large bowl combine oil, sugar and salt, stirring until blended well. Stir in cooled milk and egg. Dissolve yeast in milk mixture. Add flour, mixing well. Cover with damp cloth and let rise in warm place 2 hours. Transfer to lightly floured surface. Roll into 15-inch round. Brush with melted butter. Cut into 16 wedges. Starting at wide end, roll each up to point. Transfer to large baking sheet. Cover with damp cloth and let rise in warm place additional 2 hours. Preheat oven to 400 degrees. Bake 6 to 8 minutes. Serve warm.

MAKES   16 CRESCENTS

dried cherry and cream scones

2 cups all-purpose flour
1/4 cup sugar
1 tablespoon baking powder
1/2 teaspoon salt
3/4 cup chopped dried
    cherries
1 tablespoon grated fresh
    lemon peel
1-1/4 cups heavy or
    whipping cream
3 tablespoons melted sweet
    (unsalted) butter
Lemon-Sugar Topping
    (recipe follows)

Preheat oven to 425 degrees. In large bowl combine flour, sugar, baking powder and salt. Stir in cherries and lemon peel. Add cream, stirring just until dough forms. Transfer to lightly floured surface. Knead gently just until dough holds together. Shape dough into 10-inch diameter, 1/2-inch round. Cut into 12 wedges. Transfer to large baking sheet. Brush with melted butter. Sprinkle with Lemon-Sugar Topping. Bake about 15 minutes or until lightly browned. Remove from pan and cool slightly on wire rack. Serve warm or at room temperature.

lemon-sugar topping:

In small bowl combine 2 tablespoons sugar and 1 teaspoon grated fresh lemon peel.

MAKES   1 DOZEN

oatmeal pancakes

2 cups milk, scalded
1-3/4 cups uncooked oats
3 tablespoons vegetable oil
3 eggs, slightly beaten
1 cup whole-wheat flour
2 tablespoons packed dark
    brown sugar
1 tablespoon baking powder
3/4 teaspoon salt
Butter
Warm maple syrup

i n large bowl combine scalded milk and oats. Let stand 5 minutes. Stir in oil and eggs, mixing well. In separate bowl combine flour, brown sugar, baking powder and salt. Add to oatmeal mixture, stirring just until moistened. Heat griddle until a few drops of cold water bounce off. Drop batter by generous spoonfuls onto hot griddle. Cook 2 to 3 minutes or until bubbles begin to appear on surface. Flip and cook 1 to 2 additional minutes or until done. Serve hot with butter and warm maple syrup.

SERVES 4

oat bran banana pancakes

1 cup oat bran
1 cup all-purpose flour
1 tablespoon sugar
2 teaspoons baking soda
1 very ripe, medium
    banana, mashed
2 teaspoons vanilla extract
1-1/2 cups plain low-fat
    yogurt
4 egg whites
2 tablespoons sweet
    (unsalted) butter or
    margarine, melted
Warm maple syrup
Fresh blueberries, optional

i n medium bowl combine oat bran, flour, sugar and baking soda. Stir in banana and vanilla extract. Add yogurt, mixing well. Beat egg whites until soft peaks form. Beat about a third of the egg whites into banana mixture. Fold in remaining egg whites. Fold in melted butter. Heat a large skillet over medium heat. Ladle 1/4 cupfuls of batter into hot skillet, spreading batter to form 3-1/2- to 4-inch circles.Cook until bubbles begin to appear on surface. Turn and cook 1 minute more or until bottoms are well browned. Serve with warm maple syrup and if desired, blueberries.

SERVES 4

apple almond coffee cake

1/2 cup butter or margarine
2 eggs
1-1/2 teaspoons vanilla extract
1/2 teaspoon almond extract
2 cups all-purpose flour
1 cup sugar
2-1/4 teaspoons baking powder
1/2 teaspoon salt
1/2 cup milk
2 medium apples, peeled and cut into wedges
1/3 cup apple jelly, slightly heated and stirred until smooth
1 tablespoon sliced almonds

Preheat oven to 400 degrees. Lightly grease and flour an 8-inch springform pan. In large bowl beat butter or margarine until softened. Blend in eggs, vanilla extract and almond extract.   In separate bowl combine flour, sugar, baking powder and salt. Add with milk to egg mixture, blending well. Spread batter in prepared pan. Arrange apple wedges on top. Brush with half of the heated apple jelly. Sprinkle with almonds. Bake 15 minutes. Reduce heat to 350 degrees. Bake 50 to 60 minutes or until toothpick inserted comes out clean. Cool 15 minutes on wire rack. Remove side of pan. Brush top of cake with remaining apple jelly. Cool completely. Serve at room temperature.

SERVES   6 - 8

coconut sour cream coffee cake

1 cup sweet (unsalted) butter
2 cups sugar
4 eggs
2 cups sour cream
2 teaspoons vanilla extract
3 cups all-purpose flour
2 teaspoons baking soda
1/4 teaspoon salt
Topping (recipe follows)

Preheat oven to 350 degrees. Butter a 13 x 9-inch oblong pan. In large bowl beat butter until softened. Add sugar. Cream until light and fluffy. Add eggs, one at a time, beating well after each addition. Blend in sour cream and vanilla extract. In separate bowl combine flour, baking soda and salt. Blend into egg mixture just until moistened. Spread in prepared pan. Sprinkle with topping. Swirl knife through topping and batter for marbled effect. Bake 45 to 50 minutes. Cool slightly on wire rack. Serve warm or at room temperature.

topping:

In small bowl thoroughly combine 1 cup sugar, 5 tablespoons chopped walnuts, 2 tablespoons shredded sweetened coconut and 2 tablespoons cinnamon.

SERVES   12

apricot nut roll

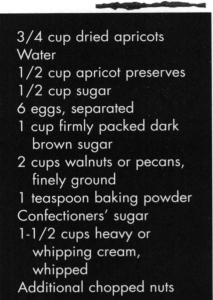

3/4 cup dried apricots
Water
1/2 cup apricot preserves
1/2 cup sugar
6 eggs, separated
1 cup firmly packed dark
   brown sugar
2 cups walnuts or pecans,
   finely ground
1 teaspoon baking powder
Confectioners' sugar
1-1/2 cups heavy or
   whipping cream,
   whipped
Additional chopped nuts

Preheat oven to 350 degrees. Butter a 15-1/2- x 10-1/2 inch jelly roll pan. Line with wax paper and butter again. In small saucepan cover apricots with water. Simmer until tender. Drain, reserving cooking liquid. Place apricots in blender container. Add preserves and sugar. Cover and blend 2 to 3 minutes, adding small amount of reserved cooking liquid if mixture is too thick. Set aside.

In large bowl beat egg yolks and brown sugar until doubled in volume. Blend in nuts and baking powder. In separate bowl using clean beaters beat egg whites until stiff but not dry. Fold about a third into egg yolk mixture. Fold in remaining egg whites. Pour evenly into prepared pan. Bake 20 minutes. Cover with clean damp towel and cool 15 minutes on wire rack. Invert onto wax paper which has been lightly dusted with sifted confectioners' sugar, leaving second layer of wax paper on top. Starting at long end, roll up cake. Cover roll with damp towel. Set aside to cool completely.

Carefully unroll and remove top layer of wax paper. Spread with apricot mixture and top with about 2/3 of the whipped cream, spreading to within 1 inch of cake edges. Removing bottom layer of wax paper, gently re-roll cake lengthwise. Transfer to serving dish, seam side down. Frost with remaining whipped cream. Sprinkle with additional chopped nuts. Refrigerate up to 4 hours or until ready to serve.

SERVES   12

apricot cream scones

2 cups all-purpose flour
1/4 cup plus 2 tablespoons
    sugar, divided
1 tablespoon baking
    powder
1/2 teaspoon salt
3/4 cup dried apricots
1 tablespoon plus 1
    teaspoon freshly grated
    lemon peel, divided
1-1/4 cups heavy or
    whipping cream
3 tablespoons sweet
    (unsalted) butter, melted

Preheat oven to 425 degrees. In large bowl combine flour, 1/4 cup of the sugar, baking powder and salt. Stir in apricots and 1 tablespoon of the lemon peel. Add cream, stirring just until dough forms. Turn onto lightly floured surface. Gently knead just until dough holds together. Shape into 10-inch diameter, 1/2-inch thick round. Cut into 12 wedges. Transfer to large ungreased baking sheet, spacing evenly.

In small bowl combine remaining 2 tablespoons sugar and 1 teaspoon lemon peel. Brush wedges with melted butter. Sprinkle with sugar mixture. Bake 15 minutes or until lightly browned. Transfer to wire rack and cool. (May be prepared a day ahead. Bake and cool completely. Wrap in foil. Store at room temperature.) Serve warm or at room temperature.

MAKES   1 DOZEN

mushroom crust quiche

5 tablespoons butter, divided
1/2 pound mushrooms,
    cleaned and coarsely
    chopped
1/2 cup finely crushed saltine
    crackers
3/4 cup finely chopped
    green onions
2 cups shredded Swiss
    cheese
1 cup cottage cheese
3 eggs
1/4 teaspoon cayenne
    (red pepper)
1/4 teaspoon paprika

Preheat oven to 350 degrees. In large skillet melt 3 tablespoons of the butter over medium-high heat. Add mushrooms. Saute until soft. Stir in crushed saltines. Press onto bottom and up side of 9-inch pie plate. In same skillet melt remaining 2 tablespoons butter over medium-high heat. Add green onions. Saute until transparent. Spread onions over crust. Sprinkle with Swiss cheese. In food processor puree cottage cheese, eggs and cayenne until smooth. Pour evenly over onions in crust. Sprinkle with paprika. Bake 20 to 25 minutes or until knife inserted just off center comes out clean. Let stand about 15 minutes before serving.

SERVES   4

vegetable quiche
with whole-wheat dill crust

2 cups whole-wheat flour
1 teaspoon salt
1 tablespoon snipped fresh
    dill or 1-1/2 teaspoons
    dried dill
1/2 cup cold sweet
    (unsalted) butter, chopped
1/2 to 3/4 cup ice water
1 tablespoon butter
2 tablespoons olive oil
1 cup finely chopped
    zucchini
1 cup finely chopped
    mushrooms
1/2 cup finely chopped
    green onions
5 eggs
1 egg, separated
1 cup milk
Pinch snipped fresh thyme or
    dried thyme
1-1/2 pounds grated French
    Gruyere cheese
Salt and freshly-ground black
    pepper, to taste

In large bowl combine flour and salt. Blend in dill with fork. Using pastry blender, fingers or food processor cut in cold butter until fine meal forms. Make well in center. Add 1/2 cup of the ice water. Blend with fork, adding additional water as needed to form dough into ball. Place on lightly floured surface. Knead two or three times to make smooth. Place in bowl. Lightly sprinkle with flour. Cover and refrigerate 2 to 3 hours. Preheat oven to 400 degrees. On lightly floured surface roll out dough to fit bottom and side of 9-inch quiche pan. Fit dough into pan, pressing firmly against bottom and side. Prick with fork. Bake 10 minutes. Set aside on wire rack. (Crust can be made up to 24 hours in advance. Cover and refrigerate unbaked crust until ready to bake.)

In skillet melt 1 tablespoon butter with olive oil over medium-high heat. Add zucchini, mushrooms and onions. Saute 6 to 7 minutes or until crisp-tender. (Do not brown.) Set aside to cool.

In large bowl combine eggs and egg yolk. Beat in milk until frothy. Add thyme. Stir in Gruyere cheese. Salt and pepper to taste. Alternate layers of sauteed vegetables and egg mixture in baked crust, ending with egg mixture. Beat egg white until frothy. Gently fold into top egg layer in crust. Bake 30 to 35 minutes or until golden brown. Cool about 15 minutes before serving.

SERVES   6

italian sausage quiche

3/4 pound Italian sausage, removed from casing

1 cup ricotta cheese

2/3 cup freshly grated Romano cheese

3 tablespoons snipped fresh parsley

3/4 teaspoon salt, divided

1/4 teaspoon freshly-ground black pepper

4 eggs

1-1/2 cups milk or light cream

2 tablespoons melted butter

1 tablespoon all-purpose flour

1/8 teaspoon nutmeg

10-inch pie shell, partially baked*

Preheat oven to 375 degrees. In large skillet break up sausage and saute until no pink remains. Drain. Stir in ricotta cheese, Romano cheese, parsley, 1/2 teaspoon of the salt and pepper. In separate bowl beat eggs slightly. Add milk or cream, melted butter, flour, nutmeg and remaining 1/4 teaspoon salt. Add to sausage mixture. Pour into partially baked pie shell. Bake 40 minutes or until puffy and golden brown. Let stand about 15 minutes before serving.

*to partially bake pie shell:

Preheat oven to 450 degrees or as your recipe specifies. Prick unbaked pie shell with fork. Bake 5 to 10 minutes. Set aside while preparing filling.

SERVES   6 - 8

brie quiche

6 ounces Brie cheese, crusts removed

1 package (8 ounces) cream cheese

2 tablespoons butter

3 tablespoons heavy or whipping cream

2 eggs

Salt and white pepper, to taste

Cayenne (red pepper), to taste

1/2 cup snipped fresh chives or sliced green onions

8-inch unbaked pastry shell

Preheat oven to 375 degrees. Using mixer, beat Brie, cream cheese and butter until softened. Blend in cream. Beat in eggs. Salt and pepper to taste. Add cayenne to taste. Stir in chives or green onions. Pour into pastry shell. Bake 30 minutes or until puffy and browned. Cool slightly before serving. (May be cooled completely and frozen until ready to serve. Thaw and reheat just before serving.)

SERVES   6

greek spinach quiche

3 tablespoons butter
1/2 Bermuda onion, sliced
2 cloves garlic, minced
3-1/2 cups sliced
  mushrooms
1 teaspoon fresh lemon juice
1 package (10 ounces)
  frozen spinach, thawed
1/4 teaspoon nutmeg
Salt and freshly-ground
  black pepper, to taste
4 to 6 ounces Feta cheese
1-1/2 cups half-and-half
3 eggs
9-inch unbaked pastry shell,
  fit into 9- or 10-inch
  quiche pan

Preheat oven to 350 degrees. In medium saute pan or skillet melt butter over medium-high heat. Add onion and garlic. Saute 5 minutes. Add mushrooms and lemon juice. Saute 8 minutes. Remove from heat. Squeeze all excess moisture from spinach. Add spinach and nutmeg to mushroom mixture. Salt and pepper to taste. Drain mixture and spoon evenly into pastry shell. Crumble Feta cheese over top. Whisk together half-and-half and eggs. Pour over mixture in pastry shell. Bake 35 to 45 minutes or until set. Cool slightly before serving. (Quiche may be made a day in advance. Reheat in 350-degree oven just until hot.)

SERVES   6 - 8

spinach and ricotta pie

Parmesan Pastry
(recipe follows)
1 tablespoon olive oil
2 leeks, thinly sliced
1 clove garlic, crushed
1 tablespoon snipped fresh
    thyme
4 cups cleaned and torn
    fresh spinach
1 cup ricotta cheese
2/3 cup light cream
3 eggs, slightly beaten
Pinch freshly grated
    nutmeg
Salt and freshly-ground
    black pepper, to taste
1/4 cup pine nuts

Prepare Parmesan Pastry and set aside to cool. Reduce oven to 375 degrees. In large skillet heat olive oil over medium-high heat. Add leeks, garlic and thyme. Saute 5 minutes. Add spinach. Stir 1 to 2 minutes. Set aside to cool slightly. Meanwhile, in large bowl beat ricotta cheese, cream and eggs until smooth. Stir in nutmeg. Salt and pepper to taste. Drain spinach mixture, squeezing out as much excess moisture as possible. Spoon and spread evenly onto prepared pastry. Top with ricotta cheese mixture. Sprinkle with pine nuts. Bake 30 to 35 minutes or until set and golden.

parmesan pastry:

In large bowl combine 1-1/4 cups all-purpose flour, 3 tablespoons freshly grated Parmesan cheese and pinch salt. Cut in 1/2 cup chopped butter. Stir in 1 egg yolk and 1 tablespoon cold water to form firm paste. Cover and refrigerate 30 minutes. On lightly floured surface roll out paste (dough) large enough to fit bottom and sides of 9-inch fluted pie pan. Fit pastry into pan and prick with fork in several places. Cover and refrigerate 15 minutes. Line pastry with foil and fill with dry beans. Bake at 400 degrees for 8 minutes. Remove beans and foil. Bake pastry additional 10 to 12 minutes or until crisp and golden.

SERVES   6 - 8

broccoli and cheese pie

8 phyllo pastry sheets
1 bunch (about 2 pounds)
  fresh broccoli, washed
  and trimmed*
1/2 cup boiling water
1/4 cup butter
1/2 cup finely chopped
  onion
3 eggs
1/2 pound feta cheese,
  crumbled
1/4 cup snipped fresh
  parsley
2 tablespoons snipped
  fresh dill
1/2 teaspoon salt
Dash freshly-ground black
  pepper
1/2 cup melted butter

Preheat oven to 350 degrees. Thaw phyllo sheets to room temperature according to package directions. Keep covered with damp paper towels until ready to use. Remove and discard stem ends from broccoli. Split large stalks. Coarsely chop stems and florets. Place in large skillet. Add boiling water. Cover and cook over medium heat 5 minutes. Drain well.

In separate skillet melt 1/4 cup butter over medium-high heat. Add onion. Saute 3 minutes or until golden. Add broccoli. Saute 1 minute. Remove from heat.

In large bowl beat eggs lightly. Add feta cheese, broccoli mixture, parsley, dill, salt and pepper. Line 9-inch springform pan with 6 of the phyllo sheets, allowing to overlap edge of pan. Brush with melted butter. Pour broccoli mixture into prepared pan. Fold overlapping ends of phyllo up and over top of filling. Using kitchen shears, cut four 9-inch circles from remaining phyllo sheets. (Tip: For guide, use 9-inch cake pan.) Brush each circle with melted butter. Layer on top of each other over filling in pan. Using shears, cut through phyllo layers to make eight wedges. Drizzle with any remaining melted butter. Place springform pan on baking sheet. Bake 40 to 45 minutes or until crust is puffy and golden brown. Cool 10 minutes on wire rack. Remove side of pan. Using sharp knife, cut into wedges using slices on top as guide. Serve immediately.

*3 packages (10 ounces each) frozen, thawed and drained chopped broccoli may be substituted

SERVES   6 - 8

watercress roulades with smoked salmon

8 ounces smoked salmon fillets
1-1/4 cups milk
4 cups cleaned and torn fresh watercress
1/4 cup butter
5 tablespoons all-purpose flour
1/2 cup grated gruyere cheese
3 eggs, separated
Salt and freshly-ground black pepper, to taste
Scant 1 cup cream cheese, softened
3 tablespoons ground almonds
3 tablespoons freshly grated Parmesan cheese
2 tablespoons snipped fresh herbs
1 tablespoon fresh lemon juice
1/2 teaspoon ground mace

Preheat oven to 400 degrees. Line a 13 x 9-inch oblong pan with parchment paper. Poach salmon fillets in milk 6 to 8 minutes or just until cooked through. Using slotted spoon, remove fish from stock and set aside, reserving stock. Dry watercress with clean paper towels. Remove and discard stalks. Finely chop watercress. Place in large bowl and set aside.

In medium saucepan melt butter over medium heat. Whisk in flour, blending well. Cook and whisk 1 minute. Add fish stock, whisking constantly. Cook and whisk until thickened. Remove from heat. Cool slightly. Whisk in gruyere cheese and egg yolks. Add to watercress and toss to combine. Salt and pepper to taste. Using clean whisk, beat egg whites until stiff but not dry. Fold into watercress mixture. Spoon into prepared pan. Smooth surface. Bake 20 to 25 minutes or until risen and set.

Remove from oven and cover with clean towel. Refrigerate until thoroughly chilled. Skin and flake salmon. Toss with cream cheese, almonds, Parmesan cheese, herbs, lemon juice and mace. When roulade is thoroughly chilled, invert onto clean towel and peel off parchment. Evenly spread salmon filling over top. Roll up tightly. Slice and serve immediately.

SERVES 6 - 8

ham and cheese torte

1 tablespoon butter
1-1/2 to 2 pounds fresh
    spinach, cleaned and torn
3 packages (8 ounces each)
    cream cheese
1/2 cup half-and-half
1 tablespoon prepared
    mustard
1/2 teaspoon salt
1/4 teaspoon dried oregano
4 eggs
2 cups shredded Swiss
    cheese
8 ounces chopped cooked
    ham
2 tablespoons snipped fresh
    parsley

Preheat oven to 350 degrees. Grease a 9-inch springform pan. In large saucepan melt butter over medium heat. Add spinach. Cook just until tender and wilted, stirring constantly. Using back of spoon press out and discard as much liquid as possible. Transfer spinach to cutting board and coarsely chop.

In large bowl beat cream cheese to soften. Add half-and-half, mustard, salt, oregano and eggs, beating well. Stir in Swiss cheese, ham, parsley and chopped spinach. Pour into prepared pan. Bake 1 hour and 15 minutes. Cool on wire rack. Cover and refrigerate overnight. Remove side of pan just before slicing.

SERVES   6 - 8

artichoke and sun-dried tomato frittata

10 sun-dried tomato halves
Boiling water
1 tablespoon butter
2 tablespoons olive oil
1 cup (about 5 ounces)
    frozen artichoke hearts,
    thawed and sliced
10 fresh basil leaves, snipped
8 eggs
Salt and freshly-ground black
    pepper, to taste
2 tablespoons grated
    Parmesan cheese
1/4 cup fresh goat cheese,
    room temperature

Place tomatoes in small bowl. Cover with boiling water. Let stand 10 minutes. Drain, cool and slice. In large skillet melt butter with olive oil over medium-high heat. Add artichoke hearts. Saute 5 minutes or until slightly browned. Add drained tomatoes and basil. Saute additional 1 minute. Remove from heat.

In separate bowl whisk eggs. Salt and pepper to taste. Add to tomato mixture in skillet. Return to medium heat. Cook and stir until eggs are softly scrambled. Reduce heat. Stir in Parmesan and goat cheeses. Smooth top of eggs. Continue cooking 5 minutes. Cover and cook additional 10 minutes over low heat or until firm and lightly browned on bottom. Run knife or metal spatula around edge to loosen. Invert onto large serving plate. Cut into wedges. Serve immediately.

SERVES   6 - 8

crab meat brunch casserole

2 eggs
2 cups milk
2 cups seasoned croutons
8 ounces shredded Cheddar cheese
1 tablespoon minced dried onion
1 tablespoon parsley flakes
1 pound lump crab meat
Salt and freshly-ground black pepper, to taste
Grated Parmesan cheese

Preheat oven to 325 degrees. In large bowl beat eggs. Add milk, croutons, Cheddar cheese, onion and parsley. Stir in crab meat. Salt and pepper to taste. Spoon into lightly greased shallow casserole dish. Sprinkle with Parmesan cheese. Bake 1 hour or until knife inserted in center comes out clean. Serve immediately.

SERVES   6 - 8

sensational sunday strata

16 slices bread, crusts removed
8 slices Old English cheese
1 cup mayonnaise
1/2 cup chopped onion
1/2 cup chopped green bell pepper
2 cups shredded mild cheddar cheese
5 eggs, slightly beaten
3 cups milk
1/2 teaspoon salt
1/4 teaspoon freshly-ground black pepper

Butter a lasagna-size baking pan. In prepared pan arrange 8 slices of the bread. Top each with slice of cheese. In small bowl combine mayonnaise, onion and bell pepper. Spread over cheese slices. Top with remaining bread slices. Combine cheddar cheese, eggs, milk, salt and pepper. Pour over bread slices. Cover and refrigerate overnight. Preheat oven to 350 degrees. Bake 45 to 50 minutes or until puffy and golden brown. Let stand about 15 minutes before cutting into squares.

SERVES   8

caramel strata

1 cup packed dark brown
    sugar
1/2 cup sweet (unsalted)
    butter
2 tablespoons light corn
    syrup
12 slices (about 10 ounces)
    white sandwich bread,
    crusts removed
1-1/2 cups whole milk
6 eggs
1 teaspoon vanilla extract
1/4 teaspoon salt
Assorted fresh fruit such as
    sliced kiwi, strawberries
    and pineapple

In small saucepan combine brown sugar, butter and corn syrup. Cook over medium-low heat until butter melts and sugar dissolves, stirring constantly. Bring to boil. Pour into 13- x 9-inch glass baking pan, tilting pan to coat bottom evenly with mixture. Cool. Arrange 6 slices of the bread over mixture in pan, trimming as needed to fit. Cover with remaining bread slices, trimming to fit. In medium bowl whisk together milk, eggs, vanilla extract and salt. Pour over bread. Cover and refrigerate overnight. Preheat oven to 350 degrees. Bake 40 minutes or until puffed and lightly browned. Let stand 5 minutes. Cut into 6 portions. Using spatula, invert onto serving plates, caramel side up. Garnish with fresh fruit. Serve immediately.

SERVES   6

blintz souffle

1/2 cup butter or margarine
1-1/2 cups sour cream
1 cup all-purpose flour
1/2 cup orange juice
1/3 cup sugar
2 teaspoons baking powder
6 eggs
1 package (8 ounces) cream
    cheese
2 cups small curd cottage
    cheese
2 egg yolks
1 tablespoon sugar
1 teaspoon vanilla extract
Additional sour cream
Blueberry syrup or assorted
    jams

Preheat oven to 350 degrees. Butter a 13 x 9-inch oblong pan. In blender or food processor blend butter or margarine until softened. Add sour cream, flour, orange juice, sugar, baking powder and eggs. Blend until smooth. Pour half of batter into prepared pan. Set aside.

In large bowl, blender or food processor blend cream cheese until softened. Add cottage cheese, egg yolks, sugar and vanilla extract. Blend until smooth. Drop by generous spoonfuls onto batter in pan. Spread evenly. Pour remaining batter over top. Bake 50 to 60 minutes or until puffy and golden brown. Serve with additional sour cream and blueberry syrup or assorted jams. (Unbaked souffle may be covered and refrigerated several hours or overnight. Before baking, bring to room temperature.)

SERVES   8 - 10

savory souffle roll

6 tablespoons butter, divided
4 green onions, finely
    chopped
4 medium mushrooms,
    chopped
1 cup chopped cooked
    spinach
1 cup chopped cooked ham
1 tablespoon Dijon mustard
1/4 teaspoon freshly grated
    nutmeg
2 packages (3 ounces each)
    cream cheese, softened
Salt and freshly-ground black
    pepper, to taste
1/2 cup all-purpose flour
1/2 teaspoon salt
1/8 teaspoon white pepper
2 cups milk
5 eggs, separated

i n large skillet melt 2 tablespoons of the butter over medium-high heat. Add green onions. Saute just until tender. Add mushrooms. Saute 3 minutes or until liquid is evaporated. Add spinach, ham, mustard and nutmeg. Heat through, stirring constantly. Reduce heat. Stir in cream cheese. Salt and pepper to taste. Keep warm over very low heat. Preheat oven to 400 degrees. Grease a 15-1/2 x 10-1/2 x 1-inch jelly roll pan. Line with wax paper. Grease wax paper. Lightly dust with flour.

In medium saucepan melt remaining 1/4 cup butter over medium heat. Blend in flour, salt and white pepper. Gradually add milk. Bring to boil, stirring constantly. Cook and stir 1 minute. Remove from heat.

In small bowl beat egg yolks slightly. Add small amount of hot milk mixture to yolks, stirring constantly. Return egg yolk mixture to milk mixture in saucepan, stirring constantly. Cook over medium heat additional 1 minute, stirring constantly. (Do not boil.) Cool to room temperature, stirring occasionally. Beat egg whites until stiff but not dry. Fold into cooled egg yolk mixture. Spread in prepared pan. Bake 15 to 20 minutes or until puffy and golden brown. Immediately invert onto clean towel. Top with warm mushroom mixture. Starting at a long end, roll up jelly roll style. Transfer, seam side down, to large serving platter. Slice and serve immediately.

SERVES   6 - 8

sweet noodle kugel

1 package (16 ounces)
  wide egg noodles,
  cooked al dente
6 tablespoons butter, melted
1/2 cup sugar
4 ounces cream cheese,
  room temperature
3 eggs
1 cup light cream
1 cup apricot nectar
1 cup apricot preserves
Topping (recipe follows)

toss noodles with butter until well coated. Cream sugar and cream cheese until smooth. Add eggs, one at a time, mixing well after each addition. Add cream and apricot nectar to the mixture. Pour over noodles. Mix well. Pour into greased 9 x 13 inch baking dish. Spread apricot preserves over noodles. Sprinkle topping over preserves. Bake at 350 degrees for 1 hour.

topping:
combine 1 cup crushed corn flake crumbs, 1/4 cup sugar, 12 tablespoons melted butter and 1 teaspoon cinnamon.

SERVES 12

broccoli reuben sandwich

3 scallions, chopped
2 cups fresh mushrooms,
  sliced
2 tablespoons softened
  butter or margarine
8 slices deli-style Rye bread
4 slices Swiss Cheese
1 large bunch broccoli,
  steamed and cut into
  bite-sized pieces
1 cup sauerkraut,
  well-drained
Thousand Island Dressing

in skillet saute scallions and mushrooms in 2 tablespoons butter. Drain. Butter one side of each slice of rye bread. Grill 4 slices of rye bread on heated griddle while layering each slice with Swiss Cheese, mushroom-scallion mixture, broccoli and sauerkraut. Spread Thousand Island Dressing on unbuttered sides of 4 remaining slices of bread. Place on each sandwich, buttered side up. Flip sandwich. Cover to grill and melt cheese. Serve immediately.

SERVES 4

barbecue turkey burgers

2 cloves garlic, minced
1/2 teaspoon salt
1/4 cup Worcestershire
  sauce
1/4 cup ketchup
2 tablespoons soy sauce
1 teaspoon chili powder
1/4 teaspoon ground cumin
1/4 teaspoon Tabasco sauce
Salt and freshly-ground black
  pepper, to taste
2 pounds ground turkey
1 small onion, minced
1/2 cup fresh bread crumbs
6 Kaiser rolls, split

In small bowl mash garlic with salt. Stir in Worcestershire sauce, ketchup, soy sauce, chili powder, cumin and Tabasco sauce. Salt and pepper to taste. In large bowl combine turkey, onion, bread crumbs and 1/4 cup of the sauce mixture. Form into six 3/4-inch thick patties. (Burgers may be prepared up to this point a day in advance. Cover and refrigerate burgers and remaining sauce until ready to cook.) Grill on a lightly oiled rack 5 to 6 inches from heat 6 minutes per side or until done. Brush frequently with sauce during grilling. Serve on Kaiser rolls, drizzled with remaining sauce.

SERVES   4 - 6

grilled gruyere, black forest ham and onion sandwiches

8 slices Italian bread, sliced
  1/2-inch thick
2 tablespoons butter, softened
8 thin slices (about 5 ounces)
  Gruyere or other Swiss
  cheese
8 slices (about 8 ounces)
  Black Forest or other
  smoked ham
1 cup sauteed chopped
  onions
Freshly-ground black pepper,
  to taste

Spread one side of each bread slice with butter. With buttered sides down, top four of the bread slices with 1 slice of cheese, 2 slices ham and 1/4 cup onions. Sprinkle with pepper. Top with remaining slices of cheese and bread, buttered sides up. Heat griddle over medium heat until a few drops of cold water bounce off. Arrange sandwiches on hot grill. Cook about 3 minutes per side or until cheese is melted and bread is golden brown. Serve immediately.

SERVES   4

indian beef patties in pitas

1-ounce (1-inch cube) fresh
  gingerroot
3 medium jalapeno chile
  peppers, seeded and
  coarsely chopped
2 cloves garlic
2 tablespoons snipped fresh
  mint leaves
1 medium onion, quartered
1 pound lean ground beef
2 teaspoons ground cumin
1 teaspoon salt
4 large pita breads, halved
Cucumber Sauce
  (recipe follows)

i n food processor mince gingerroot, jalapeno peppers, garlic and mint leaves. Add onions. Process until minced. Add ground beef, cumin and salt. Pulse just until combined. Form into 8 patties, each about 3 inches in diameter. Transfer to broiler rack over pan. Broil a few inches from heat 6 minutes or until browned on both sides and cooked to desired doneness, turning once. Slip into pita halves. Spoon Cucumber Sauce into each pocket. Serve immediately.

cucumber sauce:

Peel, seed and dice half of a small cucumber. Toss with 1-1/2 cups sour cream. Cover and refrigerate until ready to serve.

SERVES   4

calabrian smoked turkey sandwich

8 slices lean smoked bacon

8 slices round Peasant-style Italian bread, sliced 1/2-inch thick

6 ounces smoked turkey, thinly sliced

6 ounces Italian fontina cheese, thinly sliced

1 ripe avocado, peeled and pitted, cut into 1/4-inch thick wedges

1 large tomato, cut into 8 thin slices

Olive oil

in large skillet cook bacon 5 minutes or until crisp, turning once. Set aside to drain on paper towel-lined tray. Arrange 4 slices of the bread on clean surface. Top each slice with equal amounts of turkey, cheese, bacon, avocado and tomato. Top with remaining bread slices. Heat two large skillets or a large griddle over medium heat until a few drops of water bounce off. Lightly coat with oil. Arrange sandwiches in skillets or on griddle. Reduce heat to low. Weight sandwiches with heat-resistant plate or lid. Cook 5 minutes or until bread is golden brown on one side. Turn and cook 5 additional minutes or until cheese is melted and other side is golden brown. Cut in half. Serve immediately.

SERVES   4

sesame beef pitas

1 pound deli roast beef, julienned

Dressing (recipe follows)

4 large pita breads, cut in half

Seasame seeds

Alfalfa sprouts

Tomato slices

marinate beef in dressing for 4 hours or up to 8 hours. Drain. Fill 8 pitas halves with equal amount of beef. Sprinkle with sesame seeds. Garnish with alfalfa sprouts and tomato slices. Serve immediately.

dressing:

Combine 1 tablespoon honey, 1/4 cup rice wine vinegar, 1/4 cup tamari or light soy sauce, 1 tablespoon sesame oil, 1 tablespoon chili oil and 2 tablespoons vegetable oil.

SERVES   4

portobello mushroom burger
with basil mustard sauce

1 cup mayonnaise
1/3 cup snipped fresh basil
2 tablespoons Dijon mustard
1 teaspoon fresh lemon juice
Salt and freshly-ground black
  pepper, to taste
1/3 cup olive oil
1 clove garlic, minced
1-1/2 cups mesquite wood
  chips, soaked in cold water
  1 hour, optional
6 large portobello
  mushrooms, stems removed
6 large whole-grain
  hamburger rolls, split
6 leaves romaine lettuce
6 large tomato slices

i n small bowl combine mayonnaise, basil, mustard and lemon juice. Salt and pepper to taste. Cover and refrigerate until ready to use. In separate bowl whisk together olive oil and garlic. Set aside.

Heat barbecue to medium-high heat. When coals are white-hot, drain wood chips, if using, and scatter over coals. When wood chips begin to smoke, brush mushroom caps on both sides with oil-garlic mixture. Salt and pepper to taste. Grill 4 minutes per side or until tender and golden brown. Transfer to platter. Cover with foil and keep warm. Grill cut side of hamburger rolls 2 minutes or until lightly browned. Transfer bottom half of each roll to individual serving plates. Top each with mushroom cap, lettuce leaf and tomato slice. Top with mayonnaise mixture and top half of bun. Serve with remaining mayonnaise mixture.

SERVES   6

jim's big sandwich

1 package frozen bread
   dough, thawed, or 1
   recipe classic brioche
   dough
5 eggs
1/4 cup light cream
Snipped fresh or dried
   parsley and thyme, to taste
Salt and freshly-ground black
   pepper, to taste
2 pounds fresh spinach,
   cleaned and torn
1 tablespoon olive oil
1/2 cup chopped green
   onions
1 teaspoon nutmeg
1/8 teaspoon Tabasco sauce
2 large red bell peppers, cut
   into 1-inch strips
2 cups shredded Swiss
   cheese
12 ounces chipped baked
   ham
1 egg
1 tablespoon water

divide bread or brioche dough into two equal portions. Wrap and refrigerate until ready to use. Preheat oven to 400 degrees. Butter an 8- or 9-inch springform pan. In medium bowl lightly beat 5 eggs and cream. Add parsley, thyme, salt and pepper to taste. Pour into prepared pan. Bake 30 minutes or just until set. Cool completely on wire rack. Remove baked filling from side and bottom of pan. Set aside on wax paper. Reduce oven to 375 degrees.

In large saucepan cook spinach in small amount of boiling water just until wilted. Drain and squeeze out excess liquid. In large skillet heat olive oil over medium-high heat. Add spinach, green onions, nutmeg and Tabasco sauce. Saute until most of liquid has evaporated. Salt and pepper to taste. Set aside. Fill large skillet 1/4-inch deep with water. Add bell pepper strips. Place over medium-high heat. Steam, uncovered, until water evaporates. Continue cooking, stirring occasionally, until pepper skins begin to pop and brown slightly. Remove from heat and set aside.

On floured surface, roll out half of refrigerated dough to 1/8-inch thickness and large enough to line bottom and side of 8- or 9-inch springform pan with flat bottom. Press dough onto bottom and up side of pan. Top with 1 cup of the Swiss cheese, the baked egg filling, half of the spinach mixture, half of the chipped ham and all of the bell pepper strips. Layer with remaining ham, spinach and Swiss cheese. (Filling should mound slightly in center.) On floured surface roll out remaining dough to 1/8-inch thick round to fit over top of filling in pan. Lay over filling. Crimp seam to seal. Trim away excess dough. (If desired, excess dough may be rolled and cut into shapes to garnish top of crust before baking.) In small bowl beat egg and water. Brush onto crust. Using sharp knife gently slash crust a few times to allow steam to escape. Bake 30 minutes or until lightly browned. Cool in pan 15 to 20 minutes. Remove side of pan. Slice and serve hot, cold or at room temperature.

SERVES 8 - 10

entrees

t he Walnut Street Bridge stands as an iron clad
testimony to engineering innovations which stand the
test of time. From its opening to traffic in 1889, the
bridge has been a primary link between the Capital City
and all points westward. Throughout its life span, the
bridge has weathered many challenges to its existence,
including Hurricane Agnes which reduced its function to
walking only. In early 1996, nature's wrath once again
caused structural damage, destroying the western portion
and crippling the eastern span. It will take an estimated
$15 million to return the bridge as a pedestrian con-
veyance; the cost to build it in the late 19th century was
a mere $220,000.

seafood pastries with dill sauce

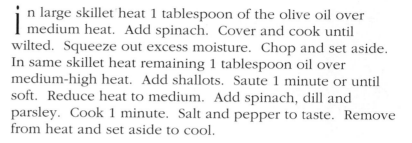

2 tablespoons olive oil, divided

10 ounces cleaned fresh spinach

3 shallots, minced

2 tablespoons snipped fresh dill or 2 teaspoons dried dill

2 tablespoons snipped fresh parsley

Salt and freshly-ground black pepper, to taste

8 sheets phyllo dough

1/2 cup melted butter

1/2 cup grated Parmesan cheese

4 fillets (6 ounces each) sole or flounder

Lemon Dill Sauce (recipe follows)

In large skillet heat 1 tablespoon of the olive oil over medium heat. Add spinach. Cover and cook until wilted. Squeeze out excess moisture. Chop and set aside. In same skillet heat remaining 1 tablespoon oil over medium-high heat. Add shallots. Saute 1 minute or until soft. Reduce heat to medium. Add spinach, dill and parsley. Cook 1 minute. Salt and pepper to taste. Remove from heat and set aside to cool.

Preheat oven to 450 degrees. Butter a baking sheet. Brush 1 phyllo sheet with melted butter. Sprinkle with 1 tablespoon of the Parmesan cheese. Place second phyllo sheet on top. Brush with butter. Arrange 1 fillet lengthwise in center of pastry, about 2 inches from bottom edge. Salt and pepper to taste. Spread about 1/4 cup of the spinach mixture lengthwise over half of fillet. Fold fillet in half over spinach mixture. Sprinkle with additional 1 tablespoon Parmesan cheese. Fold the bottom 2 inches of the phyllo over the fillet. Fold right and left sides of phyllo over fillet to enclose. Roll up phyllo with fillet. Transfer to prepared baking sheet, seam side down. Brush with melted butter. Repeat procedure 3 times with remaining ingredients. Bake, uncovered, 20 minutes or until golden. Spoon Lemon Dill Sauce onto serving plates. Place fish on top. Serve immediately.

lemon dill sauce:

About 5 minutes before fish is done baking, melt 1/2 cup butter in small saucepan over medium heat. Whisk in juice of 1 lemon and 1 tablespoon snipped fresh dill or 1 teaspoon dried dill. Salt and pepper to taste.

SERVES   4

spinach-stuffed trout

6 tablespoons sweet
(unsalted) butter, divided
2 shallots, minced
1/2 cup sliced mushrooms
1/2 bunch (about 6 ounces)
fresh spinach, cleaned
and chopped
1/4 cup snipped fresh
parsley, divided
1 teaspoon snipped fresh
tarragon
Salt and freshly-ground black
pepper, to taste
2 small trout (about 1/2
pound each), boned
2 tablespoons fresh orange
juice
1/2 teaspoon fresh lemon
juice
Orange slices

In medium skillet melt 2 tablespoons of the butter over medium-high heat. Add shallots and mushrooms. Saute briefly. Add spinach, 2 tablespoons of the parsley and tarragon. Reduce heat and cook, stirring constantly, until most of liquid has evaporated. Salt and pepper to taste. Stuff trout with spinach mixture.

In another skillet melt remaining 4 tablespoons butter over medium heat. Add trout. Saute about 5 minutes per side or until golden brown. Transfer to heated platter and keep warm. Add orange juice to skillet. Stir in lemon juice and remaining 2 tablespoons parsley. Cook over high heat, stirring constantly, until slightly thickened. Pour over trout. Garnish with orange slices and serve immediately.

SERVES   2

walnut-crusted sole

1/3 cup all-purpose flour
1/2 teaspoon salt
1/4 teaspoon freshly-ground
black pepper
1 cup finely chopped walnuts
1/4 cup cracker crumbs
4 fillets (4 ounces each) sole
or flounder
2 egg whites, slightly beaten
1/4 cup clarified butter
1 to 2 tablespoons vegetable
oil
Lemon wedges

In shallow bowl combine flour, salt and pepper. Set aside. In separate shallow bowl combine walnuts and cracker crumbs. Set aside. Dredge fillets through flour mixture. Dip into egg whites. Dredge through walnut mixture. In large skillet melt butter with oil over medium heat. Add breaded fillets. Fry 3 minutes on each side or until golden brown. Serve immediately with lemon wedges.

SERVES   4

sauteed sole fillets
with ginger and cilantro

- 2 tablespoons snipped fresh cilantro
- 2 teaspoons fresh lemon juice
- 1 teaspoon dried thyme
- 1 teaspoon minced fresh ginger
- 1 clove garlic, minced
- 4 fillets (5 ounces each) sole
- 1/2 teaspoon salt
- 1/4 teaspoon freshly-ground black pepper
- 1/4 cup all-purpose flour
- 2 tablespoons vegetable oil

In small bowl combine cilantro, lemon juice, thyme, ginger and garlic. Sprinkle fillets with salt and pepper. Rub with cilantro mixture. Dredge through flour. In large skillet heat oil over medium heat. Add fillets. Cook 2-1/2 minutes or until lightly browned, turning once. Serve immediately.

SERVES 4

mariner's walk tuna

- 2 pounds tuna or swordfish, cut into 4 steaks
- 1 cup all-purpose flour
- 6 tablespoons butter
- 2 cloves garlic, minced
- 1/2 cup white wine
- Juice of 1 lemon
- 2 tablespoons green peppercorns in brine, crushed
- 1 teaspoon salt
- Dash paprika
- Fresh snipped parsley, to taste

Preheat oven to 450 degrees. Lightly coat fish with flour. In large oven-proof skillet melt butter over medium heat. Add fish. Cook 2 minutes. Turn and add garlic. When garlic is lightly browned add wine, lemon juice, crushed peppercorns, salt, paprika and parsley, to taste. Transfer skillet to oven. Bake 10 minutes, basting fish occasionally with sauce from skillet. Serve immediately.

SERVES 4

grilled swordfish
with tomatillo-avocado salsa

1/2 pound tomatillos
3 cloves garlic
3 tablespoons olive oil
1-1/2 tablespoons balsamic
    vinegar
1 teaspoon salt, divided
4 (6-ounce) swordfish steaks
2 small jalapeno chiles,
    seeded and coarsely
    chopped
1/4 cup snipped fresh
    cilantro
1 large avocado, peeled,
    pitted and diced
1/2 small onion, minced
Fresh cilantro sprigs

heat grill or broiler. In small baking pan place tomatillos and garlic. Grill or broil 8 minutes or until lightly browned and soft, turning occasionally. Set tomatillos aside to cool. Mash garlic and blend with olive oil, vinegar and 1/2 teaspoon of the salt. Brush on swordfish. Grill or broil a few inches from heat 6 minutes or until opaque, turning once during cooking.

Meanwhile, in food processor puree cooled tomatillos, chiles and snipped cilantro. Add avocado. Using pulse feature, process a few seconds to combine. Transfer to medium bowl. Stir in onion and remaining 1/2 teaspoon salt. Transfer swordfish to serving plates. Spoon avocado salsa on side. Garnish with cilantro sprigs.

SERVES   4

less-fat caesar swordfish*

2 pounds swordfish steaks,
    1-inch thick
1/3 cup reduced-calorie
    Caesar salad dressing
Romaine lettuce leaves
1/4 cup freshly grated
    Parmesan cheese
2 tablespoons Caesar
    salad-style croutons
Vegetable oil cooking spray

arrange swordfish steaks in shallow dish. Pour salad dressing over top. Cover and refrigerate 1 hour to marinate, turning once. Remove fish from marinade, reserving marinade for basting. Place fish on grill which has been lightly coated with cooking spray. Grill 4 to 5 inches from heat 8 to 10 minutes per side or just until fish flakes with fork, basting occasionally with reserved marinade. Cut into 6 pieces. Arrange on romaine lettuce-lined serving plates. Sprinkle with Parmesan cheese and croutons. Serve immediately.

*252 calories and 11 grams fat per serving
SERVES   6

swordfish alla fiorentina

3 tablespoons olive oil, divided
3 cloves garlic, crushed
3 cups cleaned and torn fresh spinach
Salt, to taste
1 cup chopped onion
2 tablespoons drained Italian capers
1 cup Italian dry white wine
1/4 cup snipped fresh dill
3 tablespoons Dijon mustard
4 swordfish steaks
1/4 cup snipped fresh Italian flat-leaf parsley
Roasted red bell pepper strips or pimiento

i n large skillet heat 1-1/2 tablespoons of the oil over medium-high heat. Add garlic. Saute 1 minute. Add spinach. Saute additional few minutes. Remove from pan. Salt to taste. Add remaining 1-1/2 tablespoons oil to skillet. Add onions and capers. Saute 1 minute. Remove from heat.

In small bowl whisk together wine, dill and mustard. Add to onions and capers in skillet. Place swordfish in skillet and return to heat. Cook a few minutes on each side or until flesh is no longer translucent. Top with parsley. Keep warm. Reheat spinach-garlic mixture. Arrange in ring along edge of large serving platter. Place fish in center. Top with mustard mixture from skillet. Garnish with bell pepper strips or pimiento. Serve immediately.

SERVES 4

garlicky swordfish en papillote

1 tablespoon olive oil
1/2 teaspoon fennel seeds, crushed
4 cloves garlic, thinly sliced
1/4 cup fresh lemon juice
4 cups coarsely shredded carrot
4 (6-ounce) swordfish steaks
1/4 teaspoon salt
Four 15-inch squares parchment paper

i n small skillet heat olive oil over medium-high heat. Add fennel seeds and garlic. Saute 3 minutes. Cool slightly. Add lemon juice. Set aside. Fold each square of parchment paper in half. Open and place 1 cup carrot near each fold. Set aside.

In large skillet sear swordfish on both sides just until very lightly browned. Arrange over carrots on parchment. Spoon 1-1/2 tablespoons of the garlic mixture onto each steak. Sprinkle with salt. Fold parchment. Seal edges with narrow folds. (Fish can be prepared up to 1 day in advance to this point. Bring to room temperature before baking.) Preheat oven to 375 degrees. Transfer fish to large baking sheet. Bake 20 minutes or until puffed and lightly browned. Place on serving plates. Cut open and serve immediately.

SERVES 4

french-style grilled shrimp, scallops and swordfish

1 cup olive oil
1 teaspoon hot red pepper flakes
3 cloves garlic
12 small bay leaves
6 slices bacon
12 small, thin lemon wedges
12 raw shrimp, shelled and deveined
12 raw sea scallops
2 swordfish steaks, cut into 12 pieces
6 small, thin orange slices, halved
1/2 cup coarse fresh bread crumbs
Sage-Lemon Butter (recipe follows)
Freshly grated peel of 1/2 lemon
Fresh Italian parsley sprigs

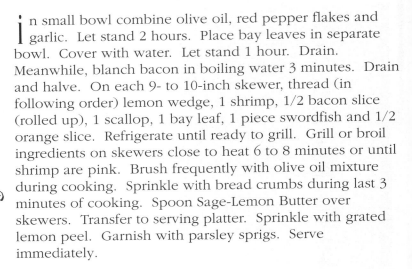

in small bowl combine olive oil, red pepper flakes and garlic. Let stand 2 hours. Place bay leaves in separate bowl. Cover with water. Let stand 1 hour. Drain. Meanwhile, blanch bacon in boiling water 3 minutes. Drain and halve. On each 9- to 10-inch skewer, thread (in following order) lemon wedge, 1 shrimp, 1/2 bacon slice (rolled up), 1 scallop, 1 bay leaf, 1 piece swordfish and 1/2 orange slice. Refrigerate until ready to grill. Grill or broil ingredients on skewers close to heat 6 to 8 minutes or until shrimp are pink. Brush frequently with olive oil mixture during cooking. Sprinkle with bread crumbs during last 3 minutes of cooking. Spoon Sage-Lemon Butter over skewers. Transfer to serving platter. Sprinkle with grated lemon peel. Garnish with parsley sprigs. Serve immediately.

sage-lemon butter:

In small saucepan melt 1/2 cup butter. Whisk in 1 tablespoon fresh lemon juice, 1 teaspoon dried and crumbled sage leaves and freshly grated peel of 1/4 lemon.

SERVES 6

mexican red snapper

- 3 large potatoes, peeled and quartered
- 3 to 4 tablespoons olive oil
- 1 large onion, thinly sliced
- 3 cloves garlic, minced
- 6 medium tomatoes, peeled and chopped
- 2 jalapeno peppers, seeded and chopped*
- 1 cup pimiento-stuffed green olives
- 2 tablespoons fresh lime juice
- 1/2 teaspoon salt
- 1/4 teaspoon sugar
- 1/4 teaspoon cinnamon
- 2-1/2 to 3-pound whole red snapper, cleaned, head and tail intact

i n medium saucepan cover potatoes with cold water. Bring to boil. Reduce heat. Cover and cook 15 to 20 minutes or almost tender. Remove from heat. Drain and set aside.

In large skillet heat oil over medium-high heat. Add onion and garlic. Saute 5 minutes. Stir in tomatoes, peppers, olives, lime juice, salt, sugar and cinnamon. Reduce heat and simmer 5 minutes. Remove from heat and set aside. Preheat oven to 375 degrees. Lightly grease a large baking dish. Arrange snapper and cooked potatoes in prepared dish. Top with tomato mixture. Bake on middle oven rack 12 to 15 minutes or until fish is slightly firm and translucent when separated with fork at thickest part. Serve hot from baking dish.

*Never touch your eyes when working with jalapenos. Wear rubber gloves or wash your hands when finished.

SERVES   5 - 6

red snapper with leeks and chives

- 1 liter red Burgundy wine
- 6 shallots, finely chopped
- 1 tablespoon red wine vinegar
- 6 tablespoons sweet (unsalted) butter
- Salt and freshly-ground black pepper, to taste
- 2 fillets (8 ounces each) red snapper
- 3 leeks (white part only), julienned
- 2 tablespoons snipped fresh chives
- 2 chive blossoms, optional

i n large saucepan combine wine, shallots and vinegar. Bring to boil. Boil until reduced to 1/4 cup. Remove from heat. Add butter, small amount at a time, swirling pan to melt and blend. (Do not stir.) Salt and pepper to taste. Keep warm. Salt and pepper fillets to taste. Place in steamer with leeks. Cook 8 to 10 minutes or just until fish turns opaque. Transfer fish to serving plates, mounding leeks on top. Spoon butter mixture around fish. Sprinkle with chives. Garnish with chive blossoms, if desired. Serve immediately.

SERVES   2

salmon with avocado butter

1/4 cup butter or margarine
1/3 cup mashed ripe avocado
1 tablespoon fresh lemon juice
1 tablespoon mayonnaise
1/2 teaspoon Worcestershire sauce
1/8 teaspoon salt
1 clove garlic, minced
3 drops Tabasco sauce
2 tablespoons snipped fresh parsley
4 (6- to 8-ounce) salmon steaks, 1-inch thick
1 lime, quartered

in small bowl beat butter or margarine until softened. Add avocado, lemon juice, mayonnaise, Worcestershire sauce, salt, garlic and Tabasco sauce. Beat until smooth. Stir in parsley. Cover and refrigerate 1 hour. Let stand at room temperature 10 minutes before serving. Place salmon steaks on lightly greased broiler rack over pan. Broil 4 to 5 inches from heat 5 to 7 minutes per side or until fish flakes easily with fork. Serve with lime wedges and avocado butter.

SERVES   4

baked salmon with lemon grass

1 stalk fresh lemon grass, outer leaves removed, bulb minced, or grated peel of 1 lemon
1-1/2 ounces chopped fresh ginger
3 cloves garlic
1 small hot red chile, seeded
4 tablespoons Asian sesame oil, divided
1-1/2 tablespoons rice wine vinegar
1 teaspoon salt
1/4 teaspoon freshly-ground black pepper
6 fillets (about 5 ounces each) salmon

in food processor combine lemon grass or lemon peel, ginger, garlic, chile, 3 tablespoons of the oil, vinegar, salt and pepper. Process until smooth paste forms. Brush salmon with remaining 1 tablespoon oil. Arrange in baking dish, skin side down. Spread 2 tablespoons of the lemon paste on each fillet. Cover and refrigerate 2 hours. Preheat oven to 400 degrees. Bake salmon 12 minutes or until opaque. Serve immediately.

SERVES   6

lacquered salmon

1 cup low-salt soy sauce
2 tablespoons cornstarch
2 tablespoons oriental
    sesame oil
2 tablespoons minced fresh
    ginger
2 tablespoons rice wine or
    dry Sherry
1 tablespoon honey
1 teaspoon Tabasco sauce
1 teaspoon freshly-ground
    black pepper
2 cloves garlic, chopped
1/2 teaspoon ground
    turmeric
8 fillets (8 ounces each)
    salmon, about 1-inch thick
2 bunches green onions,
    ends trimmed
2/3 cup water, optional
Chopped green onions

i n blender or food processor puree soy sauce, cornstarch, sesame oil, ginger, wine or Sherry, honey, Tabasco sauce, pepper, garlic and turmeric. (Can be prepared 1 day ahead to this point.) Cover and refrigerate until ready to use.

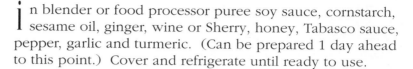

Preheat oven to 400 degrees. Lightly oil 2 medium baking dishes. Divide fish between dishes. Add 1 bunch of the whole green onions to each dish. Top with half of soy sauce mixture. Bake 20 minutes or until cooked through, basting with remaining soy sauce mixture during baking. Add 1/3 cup water to each dish as needed during baking to prevent burning. Transfer fish and green onions to serving plates. Garnish with chopped green onions. Serve immediately.

SERVES   8

scallop and bacon jambalaya

2 slices (2 ounces) bacon or
    ham, cut into 1/2-inch
    pieces
1 medium onion, chopped
1 clove garlic, minced
1 small green bell pepper,
    diced
1 stalk celery, diced
3/4 cup long-grain white
    rice, uncooked
1-1/2 cups chicken stock or
    water
1 teaspoon salt
1/2 teaspoon freshly-ground
    black pepper
1/8 teaspoon cayenne
    (red pepper)
1 pound raw bay scallops
2 green onions, sliced

In large saucepan saute bacon over medium-high heat 4 minutes or until crisp and fat is rendered. Add onion. Saute 3 minutes or until soft. Add garlic. Saute 30 seconds. Add bell pepper, celery and rice. Saute 3 minutes or until rice is golden and vegetables soften slightly. Stir in chicken stock or water, salt, pepper and cayenne. Bring to boil. Reduce heat. Cover and simmer 18 minutes or until liquid is absorbed. Add scallops. Cover and simmer 4 minutes or just until opaque. Stir in green onions. Serve immediately.

SERVES   4

orzo with spinach, shrimp and scallops

2 packages (10 ounces each)
    frozen spinach, thawed
2 quarts water
8 ounces raw medium
    shrimp, peeled and
    deveined
8 ounces raw bay scallops
1-1/2 cups orzo
1 teaspoon salt
3 tablespoons olive oil
3 tablespoons pine nuts
6 cloves garlic, minced
3/4 cup freshly grated
    Parmesan cheese
Salt and freshly-ground black
    pepper, to taste

Drain spinach and press with back of spoon to squeeze out excess moisture. (About 1-1/2 cups spinach should remain.) Set aside. In large pan bring 2 quarts water to boil. Remove from heat. Add shrimp and scallops. Cover and let stand 8 minutes or until seafood is opaque. Using slotted spoon, transfer seafood from cooking water to large bowl. Cover and keep warm. Return cooking water to boil. Add orzo and salt. Boil 8 to 10 minutes or just until tender. Drain. Cover orzo and set aside.

In large saucepan heat olive oil over medium heat. Add pine nuts. Cook 6 minutes or until golden, stirring frequently. Remove from pan and set aside. In same pan heat olive oil over medium-high heat. Add garlic. Saute 1 minute or just until tender. Add spinach and orzo. Stir until heated through. Stir in seafood, pine nuts and cheese. Salt and pepper to taste. Serve immediately.

SERVES   6

grilled scallops provencal

1/4 cup olive oil
3 medium tomatoes,
  blanched, skinned and
  diced
1 small green zucchini, diced
1 small yellow zucchini,
  diced
1 small green bell pepper,
  diced
1 small red bell pepper,
  diced
1 small yellow bell pepper,
  diced
1 small eggplant, peeled and
  diced
12 pitted Nicoise olives
1 clove garlic, crushed
Salt and freshly-ground black
  pepper, to taste
4 snipped fresh basil leaves
12 raw large scallops
Additional olive oil
Fresh watercress

in large skillet heat olive oil over medium-high heat. Add tomatoes, zucchini, bell pepper, eggplant, olives and garlic. Saute just until vegetables are crisp-tender. Salt and pepper to taste. Add basil, cooking a few minutes to blend flavors. Brush scallops with additional olive oil. Grill a few inches from heat 20 seconds per side or just until marked and golden. Place vegetable mixture on dinner plates. Top with scallops. Garnish with watercress. Serve immediately.

SERVES   2

shrimp and sea scallop stir-fry
with julienned vegetables and soba noodles

1 pound soba (buckwheat) noodles or angel hair pasta, uncooked

6 tablespoons vegetable oil

8 ounces raw shrimp, peeled and deveined

8 ounces raw sea scallops

4 stalks celery, cut on angle into 1-inch pieces

3 carrots, julienned

2 green bell peppers, julienned

2 red bell peppers, julienned

2 yellow bell peppers, julienned

12 mushrooms, sliced

3 tablespoons minced fresh garlic

1 bunch fresh cilantro, cleaned and snipped

1 bunch green onions, cut on angle into 1-inch pieces

1/4 cup dry sherry

Juice of 2 limes

1 teaspoon hot red pepper flakes

1/3 cup soy sauce

Cook noodles or pasta according to package directions. Drain and keep warm. In wok or saute pan heat oil over medium-high heat. Add shrimp and scallops. Stir-fry 3 minutes. Add celery, carrots, bell peppers, mushrooms and garlic. Stir-fry 2 minutes. Add cilantro and green onions. Lightly toss. Add sherry, lime juice and red pepper flakes. Cook and stir until liquid is reduced by about half. Stir in soy sauce. Lightly toss with cooked noodles. Serve immediately.

SERVES   4

angel hair pasta with shrimp and herb sauce

1/4 cup sweet (unsalted)
  butter
1-1/2 cups heavy or
  whipping cream
1/2 teaspoon salt
1/8 teaspoon grated fresh
  nutmeg
Generous pinch cayenne
  (red pepper)
3/4 cup finely chopped fresh
  watercress
1/2 cup freshly grated
  Parmesan cheese
1/4 cup snipped fresh herbs
  such as oregano or basil
9 ounces fresh angel hair
  pasta, uncooked
1/2 pound cooked, shelled
  and deveined shrimp
Salt and freshly-ground black
  pepper, to taste

in large skillet melt butter over medium heat. Whisk in cream, salt, nutmeg and cayenne. Simmer 15 to 20 minutes or until thickened, stirring occasionally. Stir in watercress, cheese and herbs. Meanwhile, cook pasta according to package directions. Drain and keep warm. Just before serving, add shrimp to cream mixture in skillet. Cook 1 minute or just until shrimp is heated through. Lightly toss with pasta. Salt and pepper to taste. Serve immediately.

SERVES   4

penne in tomato sauce with crab meat

1/4 cup olive oil
1 medium onion, minced
3 tablespoons snipped fresh Italian parsley
1 can (28 ounces) plum tomatoes, coarsely chopped, juices reserved
1/4 cup dry white wine
1/2 pound lump crab meat, picked over and flaked
1/2 teaspoon salt
1/4 teaspoon freshly-ground black pepper
12 ounces penne, medium shells or rotini, uncooked

In medium skillet heat oil over medium-high heat. Add onion and parsley. Saute 3 minutes or until onions are soft. Reduce heat. Add reserved juices from tomatoes. Simmer 10 minutes or until slightly thickened, stirring occasionally. Add tomatoes and wine. Simmer 5 minutes to blend flavors. Add crab meat. Simmer 3 minutes or just until heated through. Stir in salt and pepper. Meanwhile, cook pasta according to package directions. Drain and return to cooking pot. Add tomato mixture. Lightly toss. Serve immediately.

SERVES 4

baked flounder
with mustard and herbs

8 fillets (about 4 ounces each) flounder
2 tablespoons Dijon mustard
3/4 cup fine dry bread crumbs
1/2 teaspoon seasoned salt
1/4 teaspoon dried thyme
1/8 teaspoon freshly-ground black pepper
3 to 4 tablespoons Italian salad dressing or vinaigrette
1/2 cup butter, divided
8 lemon wedges
Snipped fresh parsley

Preheat oven to 450 degrees. Arrange fillets in single layer in shallow baking pan. Spread evenly with mustard. In small bowl combine bread crumbs, salt, thyme and pepper. Sprinkle over fillets. Drizzle with salad dressing or vinaigrette. Bake 5 to 7 minutes or until fish flakes easily with fork. Dot each fillet with 1 tablespoon butter. Top with lemon wedges. Garnish with parsley. Serve immediately.

SERVES 4 - 6

cajun pasta

1-1/2 cups water
1/2 pound raw medium shrimp
1 tablespoon olive oil
2 skinned and boned chicken breast halves, cut into 1/4-inch strips
1/2 pound andouille, Cajun-smoked or other smoked sausage, sliced
1/2 cup chopped onion
1 clove garlic, minced
1/2 cup Chablis or other dry white wine
1/2 cup chicken broth
1 teaspoon all-purpose flour
1 cup heavy or whipping cream
1 tablespoon Cajun or Creole seasoning
2 tablespoons tomato paste
1 teaspoon freshly-ground black pepper, optional
1 green bell pepper, cut into thin strips
1 red bell pepper, cut into strips
16 ounces fettuccine, uncooked

In medium saucepan bring water to boil. Add shrimp. Cook 3 to 5 minutes or just until shrimp turns pink. Drain. Rinse under cold water. Peel and devein. Set aside. In large skillet heat olive oil over medium-high heat. Add chicken, sausage, onion and garlic. Saute until meat is lightly browned. Remove mixture from skillet and set aside.

Add wine to skillet. Bring to boil. Reduce heat. Simmer 3 to 5 minutes or until wine is reduced to 1/4 cup. In separate bowl combine chicken broth and flour, stirring until smooth. To wine in skillet add chicken broth mixture, cream, Cajun or Creole seasoning, tomato paste and pepper, if desired. Bring to boil. Reduce heat. Simmer 20 minutes. Stir in chicken mixture and bell pepper. Cook and stir just until heated through. Reduce heat and keep warm. Cook fettuccine according to package directions. Drain and lightly toss with chicken mixture and cooked shrimp. Serve immediately.

SERVES 8

tuna steaks with wasabi butter

3 to 3-1/2 pounds tuna, cut into 6 steaks, about 1-1/2 inches thick
1/2 cup vegetable oil
1/4 cup oriental sesame oil
1/4 cup soy sauce
1/4 cup rice wine vinegar
2 tablespoons sweet vermouth
1 tablespoon packed brown sugar
2 tablespoons chopped fresh ginger
3 cloves garlic, minced
1/2 cup sweet (unsalted) butter
1-1/2 to 2 teaspoons green wasabi paste
3 tablespoons snipped fresh cilantro

arrange tuna steaks in shallow dish. In small bowl whisk together vegetable oil, sesame oil, soy sauce, vinegar, vermouth and brown sugar. Stir in ginger and garlic. Pour over tuna. Cover and refrigerate at least 4 hours to marinate, turning tuna occasionally. In small bowl beat butter until softened. Add wasabi paste. Beat until creamy. Add cilantro, blending well. Cover and refrigerate until ready to use. Bring to room temperature before grilling. Remove tuna from marinade, reserving marinade for basting. Grill a few inches from heat 5 to 6 minutes on each side or just until fish flakes with fork, basting occasionally with reserved marinade. Top with heaping spoonfuls of wasabi butter. Serve immediately.

SERVES   6

orange roughy with basil sauce

2 tablespoons butter or margarine
2 tablespoons all-purpose flour
1/2 cup chicken broth
1/2 cup dry sherry
2 tablespoons snipped fresh chives
1/2 teaspoon dried basil
1/2 teaspoon dried thyme
8 fillets (4 ounces each) orange roughy
1/2 teaspoon salt
1/4 teaspoon freshly-ground black pepper
3 medium tomatoes, peeled and sliced

preheat oven to 300 degrees. In medium saucepan melt butter over low heat. Stir in flour until smooth. Cook 1 minute, stirring constantly. Gradually add chicken broth and sherry. Cook over medium heat, stirring constantly, until thickened and bubbly. Stir in chives, basil and thyme. Remove from heat and set aside. Arrange fillets in lightly greased 13 x 9-inch oblong pan. Sprinkle with salt and pepper. Arrange tomato slices over fillets. Spoon butter mixture over top. Bake, uncovered, 30 to 40 minutes or until fish flakes easily with fork. Serve immediately.

SERVES   6 - 8

chicken marabella

6 to 8 boneless, skinless
   whole chicken breasts,
   halved
Salt and freshly-ground black
   pepper, to taste
1 cup pitted prunes, chopped
1 cup Spanish olives
3/4 cup capers with juice
1/2 cup red wine
1/4 cup olive oil
2 teaspoons dried oregano
8 bay leaves
1 clove garlic, minced
1 cup packed brown sugar
1 cup dry white wine
Hot cooked rice
Snipped fresh parsley

rub chicken with salt and pepper to taste. Arrange in shallow baking pan. In medium bowl combine prunes, olives, capers with juice, red wine, olive oil, oregano, bay leaves and garlic. Spoon mixture over chicken in pan. Cover and refrigerate overnight to marinate. Preheat oven to 350 degrees. Top chicken with brown sugar and white wine. Bake 50 to 60 minutes or until tender and cooked through, basting occasionally with pan juices. Spoon over hot rice. Garnish with parsley. Serve immediately. (Leftover marinade may be covered and refrigerated until ready to use for another purpose.)

SERVES   10

chicken with pasta and sun-dried tomatoes

12 ounces fettuccine,
   uncooked
1/4 cup olive oil
3 large boneless, skinless
   chicken breast halves, cut
   into 1-inch cubes
1 onion, chopped
1 clove garlic, chopped
1/2 teaspoon fennel seeds
1 carrot, julienned
1/2 cup oil-packed sun-dried
   tomatoes, drained and
   finely chopped
1 cup freshly grated
   Parmesan cheese

Cook fettuccine according to package directions. Drain and keep warm. In large skillet heat olive oil over medium-high heat. Add chicken. Saute 6 minutes or until browned and cooked through. Using slotted spoon, transfer chicken to large bowl. Keep warm. To same skillet add onion, garlic and fennel seeds. Saute 6 minutes or just until onion is tender. Stir in carrot and tomatoes. Cook 2 minutes or just until carrot is crisp-tender, stirring occasionally. Lightly toss tomato mixture, cooked fettuccine and Parmesan cheese. Serve immediately.

SERVES   4

roast pesto chicken

6- to 7-pound roasting
    chicken
3/4 cup pesto sauce, divided
3 tablespoons dry white wine
3/4 cup plus 2 tablespoons
    low-salt chicken broth,
    divided
2 tablespoons all-purpose
    flour
3 tablespoons heavy or
    whipping cream
Salt and freshly-ground black
    pepper, to taste
Fresh basil leaves

P at chicken dry with clean paper towels. Slide hands between chicken skin and meat over breast and legs to form pockets. Set aside 1 tablespoon pesto. Spread remaining pesto in chicken breast and leg pockets. Tie legs together. Tuck wings under body. Place in large roasting pan. (Chicken may be prepared up to 4 hours ahead to this point. Cover and refrigerate until ready to bake.)

Preheat oven to 450 degrees. Roast chicken 15 minutes. Reduce temperature to 375 degrees. Continue roasting 1-1/2 hours or until tender and juices run clear. Baste occasionally with pan juices. Transfer to large serving platter. Keep warm. Pour pan juices through cheesecloth into glass measuring cup to remove fat. Set aside.

Whisk wine into pan juices. Bring to boil, scraping up any browned bits. Add to pan juices in measuring cup. Add enough of the chicken broth to make 1 cup. Place in small saucepan. In small bowl whisk together 2 tablespoons of the remaining chicken broth and flour. Add to chicken broth in saucepan. Bring to boil, whisking constantly. Boil 5 minutes or until reduced to sauce consistency, whisking frequently. Whisk in cream and reserved 1 tablespoon pesto. Salt and pepper to taste. Slice chicken and garnish with fresh basil. Serve immediately with pesto gravy.

SERVES   4

chicken and leeks over linguine

1 pound linguine, uncooked
2 tablespoons olive oil
1 pound boneless, skinless
   chicken breast halves
Salt and freshly-ground black
   pepper, to taste
1/4 cup butter
3 large leeks (white and pale
   green portions only), thinly
   sliced
4 cloves garlic, minced
2 cans (14-1/2 ounces each)
   chopped tomatoes
2 tablespoons dry vermouth
1 cup freshly grated
   Parmesan cheese
1/4 cup snipped fresh basil

Cook linguine according to package directions. Drain and keep warm. In large skillet heat olive oil over medium-high heat. Add chicken. Salt and pepper to taste. Saute chicken 3 minutes per side or just until cooked through. Cool slightly. Thinly slice crosswise. Set aside.

In same skillet melt butter over medium heat. Add leeks and garlic. Saute 10 minutes or until leeks are very tender. Stir in tomatoes, vermouth and cooked chicken. Cook 2 minutes or just until heated through. Salt and pepper to taste. Lightly toss chicken mixture, cooked linguine and 1/2 cup of the Parmesan cheese. Sprinkle with fresh basil. Serve immediately with remaining Parmesan.

SERVES   4

grilled chilied chicken breasts
with sauteed corn and red pepper salsa

2 tablespoons fresh lime juice
2 tablespoons olive oil
1 teaspoon chili powder
1 tablespoon snipped fresh
   cilantro
4 (about 1-1/2 pounds)
   boneless, skinless chicken
   breast halves
Sauteed Corn and Red
   Pepper Salsa
   (recipe follows)

In large shallow bowl combine lime juice, olive oil, chili powder and cilantro. Add chicken, turning to coat with mixture. Let stand 15 minutes to marinate. Grill or broil a few inches from heat 3 minutes per side or until tender and cooked through. Transfer to serving plates. Spoon Corn and Red Pepper Salsa along side. Serve immediately.

sauteed corn and red pepper salsa:

In medium skillet heat 1 tablespoon olive oil over medium-high heat. Add 4 thinly sliced green onions, 1/2 minced jalapeno pepper and 1 diced red bell pepper. Saute 2 minutes or until vegetables are tender. Add 2 cups fresh or frozen, thawed corn kernels. Saute 2 minutes or until tender. Stir in 1/4 cup snipped fresh basil, 1/2 teaspoon salt and 1/4 teaspoon freshly-ground black pepper. Reduce heat and keep warm until ready to serve.

SERVES   4

mayor reed's cranberry glazed chicken

1/2 cup all-purpose flour
1 teaspoon salt
1/8 teaspoon freshly-ground black pepper
3 to 3-1/2 pounds boneless, skinless chicken breast halves, cut into pieces
2 to 3 tablespoons butter
1-1/2 cups fresh cranberries
1 cup packed brown sugar
3/4 cup water
1 tablespoon wine vinegar
1 tablespoon all-purpose flour
1/2 teaspoon cinnamon
1/4 teaspoon cloves
1/4 teaspoon allspice

In large shallow bowl combine 1/2 cup flour, salt and pepper. Dredge chicken through mixture. In large skillet heat butter over medium heat. Add chicken. Cook until browned and cooked through. Remove chicken from skillet. Set aside.

To drippings in skillet, add cranberries, sugar and water. Cook and stir 5 minutes or until cranberry skins pop. In small bowl whisk together vinegar, 1 tablespoon flour, cinnamon, cloves and allspice. Add to cranberry mixture. Cook and stir until mixture thickens. Return chicken to cranberry mixture. Simmer 30 minutes, turning chicken frequently. Serve immediately.

SERVES 4 - 6

moroccan chicken stew

8 boneless, skinless chicken breast halves
Salt and freshly-ground black pepper, to taste
3 tablespoons olive oil
2 onions, chopped
1-1/2 tablespoons paprika
2 teaspoons ginger
1/2 teaspoon turmeric
1/4 teaspoon cayenne (red pepper)
2 cups low-fat chicken broth
3 lemons, each cut lengthwise into 3 pieces
1 cup pitted Calamata olives
1 cup pitted green olives
Hot cooked rice

Season chicken with salt and pepper to taste. In large skillet heat oil over medium-high heat. Add chicken. Saute 5 minutes per side or until lightly browned. Remove from skillet and set aside. Remove all but small amount of drippings from skillet. To same skillet add onions. Saute 5 minutes. Stir in paprika, ginger, turmeric and cayenne. Return chicken to skillet. Add chicken broth and lemons. Cover and simmer 30 minutes. Add olives. Serve immediately over hot rice.

SERVES 8

chicken cerubi

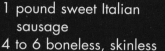

1 pound sweet Italian
sausage

4 to 6 boneless, skinless
chicken breast halves, cut
into pieces

1/4 cup all-purpose flour

Salt and freshly-ground black
pepper, to taste

2 tablespoons butter

2 tablespoons vegetable oil

1 cup sliced mushrooms

4 shallots or green onions,
sliced

1 clove garlic, minced

1/2 cup chicken stock or
broth

1/4 cup Madeira wine

2 cups fresh or frozen,
thawed snow peas

2 to 3 pimientos, thinly
sliced, optional

t horoughly cook sausage. Slice and set aside. Dredge
chicken through flour. Salt and pepper to taste. In large
skillet heat butter and oil over medium-high heat. Add
chicken. Saute until golden brown. Add mushrooms,
shallots or green onions and garlic. Saute 6 minutes. Add
cooked sausage, chicken stock or broth and wine. Salt and
pepper to taste. Stir in snow peas and if desired, pimientos.
Cook just until crisp-tender, stirring occasionally. Serve
immediately.

SERVES   6

island drumsticks with grilled pineapple

1/4 cup dark rum

1 tablespoon chili powder

1 tablespoon fresh lime juice

1 tablespoon packed brown
sugar

1/2 teaspoon hot red pepper
flakes

1 clove garlic, crushed

8 large chicken drumsticks

1 pineapple peeled and cut
into 1/2-inch slices

i n small bowl whisk together rum, chili powder, lime
juice, brown sugar, red pepper flakes and garlic. Arrange
chicken in large shallow dish. Pour rum mixture over top.
Cover and refrigerate at least 1 hour to marinate. Grill 5 to
6 inches from heat until tender and cooked through,
turning occasionally. Baste chicken and pineapple with
marinade during grilling. Serve immediately.

SERVES   6

chicken and shrimp stir-fry

2 tablespoons vegetable oil
1 whole (about 3/4 pound) boneless, skinless chicken breast, cut into 1- x 1/2-inch strips
1 small carrot, diced
1 small celery stalk, diced
1 small onion, diced
1 clove garlic, minced
4 ounces shiitake mushrooms, stemmed and quartered
1 can (6-1/2 ounces) minced clams with juice
1-1/2 cups light cream
1 teaspoon dried thyme
4 raw jumbo shrimp, peeled and deveined
1 tablespoon oriental oyster sauce
1 tablespoon fresh lemon juice
1/2 teaspoon salt
1/8 teaspoon white pepper
1 tablespoon cornstarch
2 tablespoons cold water
1 medium avocado, peeled, pitted and diced
1 tablespoon toasted pine nuts

In wok or large skillet heat oil over medium-high heat. Add chicken, carrot, celery, onion, garlic and mushrooms. Stir-fry 3 minutes or until lightly browned. Add clams with juice. Cook over high heat 1 minute or until juice is reduced slightly. Stir in cream and thyme. Bring to boil. Cover and cook 3 minutes or until slightly thickened. Add shrimp. Cook over high heat 2 minutes or just until shrimp turns pink, stirring occasionally. Stir in oyster sauce, lemon juice, salt and pepper. Thoroughly dissolve cornstarch in cold water. Whisk into hot mixture. Cook and stir over high heat 45 seconds or just until thickened. Stir in avocado. Transfer to large serving platter. Sprinkle with pine nuts. Serve immediately.

SERVES 4

hawaiian chicken with tropical fruit salsa

2-1/2 cups vegetable oil
1-1/2 cups pineapple juice
1 cup crushed pineapple
1-1/4 cups soy sauce
1 cup red wine
1 tablespoon ground ginger
8 boneless, skinless chicken breast halves
Tropical Fruit Salsa (recipe follows)

in large shallow bowl combine oil, pineapple juice, pineapple, soy sauce, wine and ginger. Add chicken, turning to coat with mixture. Cover and refrigerate up to 12 hours to marinate. Grill 5 to 6 inches from heat until tender and cooked through, turning occasionally. Baste with marinade during grilling. Serve immediately with Tropical Fruit Salsa.

tropical fruit salsa:

In large bowl lightly toss 2 cups each chopped fresh strawberries, pineapple, papaya and mango. Add 3/4 cup finely diced jalapeno pepper, 3/4 cup finely diced red onion, 3/4 cup fresh lime juice and 1/3 cup snipped fresh cilantro. Add salt and white pepper, to taste. Lightly toss. Cover and refrigerate until ready to serve.

SERVES   8

garlic lime chicken

1/2 cup reduced-sodium soy sauce
1/4 cup fresh lime juice
1 tablespoon Worcestershire sauce
2 cloves garlic, minced
1/2 teaspoon dry mustard
1/2 teaspoon freshly-ground black pepper
4 boneless, skinless chicken breast halves
Vegetable oil cooking spray, optional

in large shallow bowl combine soy sauce, lime juice, Worcestershire sauce, garlic, mustard and pepper. Add chicken, turning to coat with mixture. Cover and refrigerate at least 30 minutes to marinate. Grill 5 to 6 inches from heat until tender and cooked through, turning once. Baste with marinade during grilling. Or, spray a large non-stick skillet with cooking spray. Heat over medium heat. Add marinated chicken. Cook 6 minutes per side or until tender and cooked through, basting occasionally with marinade. Serve immediately.

SERVES   4

french country chicken

- 4 boneless, skinless chicken breast halves
- 1/2 teaspoon salt
- 1/8 teaspoon freshly-ground black pepper
- 2 tablespoons sweet (unsalted) butter
- 1 tablespoon vegetable oil
- 2 tablespoons chopped shallots or green onions
- 1 cup thickly sliced mushrooms
- 1/3 cup dry white wine
- 1/2 cup heavy or whipping cream
- 1 tablespoon Pommery mustard
- 2 teaspoons Dijon mustard
- 2 tablespoons snipped fresh parsley

Pat chicken dry with clean paper towels. Sprinkle with salt and pepper. In large skillet heat butter and oil over medium-high heat. Add chicken. Saute 6 minutes or until golden brown. Turn chicken. Reduce heat. Saute additional 4 minutes or until tender with no pink remaining. Cover and cook 2 minutes more.

Remove chicken to large serving platter. Keep warm. Remove all but 2 tablespoons fat from skillet. Add shallots or green onions. Saute 30 seconds. Add mushrooms. Saute additional 1 minute or until lightly browned. Add wine. Bring to boil, scraping up any browned bits from skillet, 3 minutes or until consistency of syrup. Whisk in cream and any juices from chicken. Cook and stir 3 minutes more or until slightly thickened. Add mustards. Adjust seasonings to taste. Stir in parsley. Pour over chicken. Serve immediately.

SERVES   4

chicken scallopini
with hazelnut-parsley pesto

4 (about 1-1/4 pounds) boneless, skinless chicken breast halves
1/4 teaspoon freshly-ground black pepper
1 tablespoon plus 1 teaspoon hot pepper-flavored oil, divided
1/2 cup low-salt chicken broth
1 tablespoon sweet (unsalted) butter
1 tablespoon drained capers
6 Calamata olives, pitted and slivered
1 teaspoon anchovy paste
Hazelnut-Parsley Pesto (recipe follows)
Julienned lemon zest

Pound chicken to 1/2-inch thickness. Sprinkle with pepper. In large skillet heat 1 tablespoon of the oil over medium-high heat. Add chicken. Cook 3 minutes per side or until browned and cooked through. Remove chicken to large serving platter. Keep warm. To same skillet add chicken broth, butter, capers, olives and anchovy paste. Bring to boil, scraping up any browned bits. Blend 2 tablespoons of broth mixture into Hazelnut-Parsley Pesto. Spoon 1/4 cup of the pesto mixture onto each of 4 heated dinner plates. Top with chicken and caper mixture. Drizzle with remaining 1 teaspoon oil. Garnish with lemon zest. Serve immediately.

hazelnut-parsley pesto:

In food processor chop 1 clove garlic. Add 1/3 cup toasted hazelnuts and 1/2 cup each packed fresh basil and Italian parsley. Process until finely chopped. Add 3 tablespoons low-salt chicken broth, 3 tablespoons olive oil, 2 tablespoons grated Parmesan cheese and 2 tablespoons fresh lemon juice. Process until smooth.

SERVES   6

golden chicken chili

2 cups dry Great Northern
   beans
3 cups water
2 tablespoons vegetable oil
2 onions, chopped
1 pound summer squash
1 can (15 ounces) hominy,
   drained, or 1 package (16
   ounces) frozen corn,
   thawed
3 pickled jalapeno peppers,
   seeded, deribbed and
   chopped
2 cloves garlic, minced
1 tablespoon cumin
1 teaspoon chili powder
1-1/2 pounds boneless,
   skinless chicken breasts, cut
   into 1-inch pieces
1/2 cup low-fat sour cream
1/4 cup snipped fresh
   cilantro
1 tablespoon fresh lime juice
2-1/4 teaspoons salt
Additional sour cream
Fresh cilantro leaves
2 plum tomatoes, chopped

i n large bowl combine beans and water. Cover and refrigerate overnight to soak. Rinse and drain. Cook according to package directions, reserving 1 cup cooking liquid. Drain beans and set aside.

In Dutch oven heat oil over medium heat. Add onions. Cover and cook 10 minutes. Stir in squash, hominy or corn, jalapeno peppers, garlic, cumin and chili powder. Add reserved 1 cup bean cooking liquid. Cover and simmer 12 minutes. Add chicken. Cook 10 minutes or until chicken is tender and cooked through. Remove from heat. Stir in sour cream, cilantro, lime juice and salt. Ladle into deep serving bowls. Top with additional sour cream, cilantro leaves and chopped tomatoes. Serve immediately.

SERVES   8

roast turkey breast with herb stuffing

8 slices stale cracked wheat bread
1/2 cup butter
1 onion, chopped
2 cloves garlic, minced
2 tablespoons snipped fresh parsley
1 tablespoon snipped fresh savory or 1 teaspoon dried savory
1 tablespoon snipped fresh thyme or 1 teaspoon dried thyme
1 tablespoon snipped fresh sage or 1 teaspoon dried sage
1 egg, slightly beaten
1 teaspoon salt
1 teaspoon freshly-ground black pepper
1 large (about 5 pounds) turkey breast
2 tablespoons softened butter

trim crust from bread. Place in food processor. Process until fine crumbs form. Set aside. In large skillet melt 1/2 cup butter over medium-high heat. Add onion and garlic. Saute 5 minutes or until soft.

In large bowl combine bread crumbs, sauteed onion and garlic, parsley, savory, thyme, sage and egg. Add salt and pepper. Loosen skin on turkey breast, leaving attached along edges. Stuff bird with Herb Stuffing between skin and breast meat, securing any loose edges with toothpicks. Rub turkey with 2 tablespoons softened butter. Transfer to large, shallow roasting pan. (Turkey can be prepared 2 hours in advance to this point. Cover and refrigerate until ready to roast.)

Preheat oven to 350 degrees. Sprinkle turkey with salt and pepper to taste. Add wine to roasting pan. Roast 1-1/2 hours or until turkey reaches internal temperature of 165 degrees, basting every 15 minutes with melted butter. Remove from pan. Keep warm and let stand about 30 minutes before slicing. Slice thin to reveal stuffing along edge. Serve immediately.

SERVES   4

turkey chili

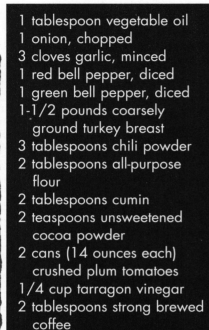

1 tablespoon vegetable oil
1 onion, chopped
3 cloves garlic, minced
1 red bell pepper, diced
1 green bell pepper, diced
1-1/2 pounds coarsely
  ground turkey breast
3 tablespoons chili powder
2 tablespoons all-purpose
  flour
2 tablespoons cumin
2 teaspoons unsweetened
  cocoa powder
2 cans (14 ounces each)
  crushed plum tomatoes
1/4 cup tarragon vinegar
2 tablespoons strong brewed
  coffee
1 to 2 teaspoons cayenne
  (red pepper)
1/4 teaspoon salt
2 cups cooked and drained
  black beans

i n Dutch oven or large kettle heat oil over medium high heat. Add onion, garlic, and bell pepper. Saute 5 minutes. Add turkey. Saute additional 5 minutes, breaking up any lumps with back of spoon. Reduce heat to low.

Stir in chili powder, flour, cumin and cocoa powder. Cook and stir 3 minutes. Add tomatoes, vinegar, coffee, cayenne and salt. Bring to boil over medium heat. Cover and simmer 40 to 45 minutes or until thick and turkey is tender, stirring occasionally. Add beans. Cook 5 minutes or until beans are heated through. Ladle into deep serving bowls. Serve immediately. (Chili may be made up to 3 days ahead. Cover and refrigerate until ready to reheat.)

SERVES 6

spicy beef pot roast

6 large ancho chiles, seeds removed and sliced into 1-inch strips
Boiling water
8 cloves garlic
3 tablespoons red wine vinegar
1 tablespoon salt
1 teaspoon cinnamon
10 black peppercorns
1/4 teaspoon dried thyme
1/4 teaspoon dried marjoram
1/4 teaspoon dried oregano
2-1/2 cups water
2 thick slices bacon, cut into 1/4-inch strips
4-pound beef rump roast, fat trimmed
1/2 cup currants

Preheat oven to 325 degrees. Heat large skillet over medium heat. Add chiles. Roast 3 minutes or until darkened and pungent, turning occasionally. Transfer to large bowl. Cover with boiling water. Let stand 20 minutes.

Meanwhile, in blender or food processor combine garlic, vinegar, salt, cinnamon, peppercorns, thyme, marjoram and oregano. Add 2-1/2 cups water. Drain chiles and add to garlic mixture. Blend or process 1 minute or until smooth. Set aside. Place bacon in large, flame-proof casserole dish over medium-low heat. Cover and cook 5 minutes or just until lightly browned. Add beef. Cook 3 to 4 minutes per side or until browned. Transfer to large platter. Drain bacon, discarding fat. Return bacon to dish. Add chile mixture. Cook and stir over medium-low heat 5 minutes. Return beef to dish, spooning chile sauce over top. Cover with double thickness of aluminum foil and replace lid to seal tightly. Bake 1-1/2 hours. Turn meat. Baste with chile sauce. Add currants. Replace foil and lid. Bake additional 1-1/2 hours or until meat is very tender. Slice thin enough to make 10 slices, about 1/4- to 1/2-inch thick. Serve immediately with chile sauce from dish. (If sauce is too thick, add small amount of water. If too thin, cook and stir over medium heat until reduced and thickened to desired consistency.)

SERVES   10

sesame sirloin

1/2 cup vegetable oil
·1/3 cup sesame seeds
1 medium onion, thinly sliced
1/2 cup soy sauce
1/4 cup fresh lemon juice
1 tablespoon sugar
1/4 teaspoon freshly-ground
    black pepper
2 cloves garlic, crushed
2-1/2- to 3-pound boneless
    top sirloin steak, 1- to
    1-1/2 inches thick

i n saute pan combine oil and sesame seeds. Cook over medium heat until sesame seeds are golden. In 13 x 9-inch glass baking dish combine sesame seeds, onion, soy sauce, lemon juice, sugar, pepper and garlic. Add steak, turning to coat with mixture. Cover and refrigerate several hours or overnight to marinate. Remove steak from marinade. Grill or broil a few inches from heat 12 minutes per side or to desired doneness. Baste with marinade during cooking. Slice and serve immediately.

SERVES   6

steaks with wild mushroom sauce

2 tablespoons olive oil,
    divided
1 large shallot, minced
1/2 cup brandy
2 cups unsalted beef stock
1/2 cup heavy or whipping
    cream
1/2 pound fresh mushrooms
    such as chanterelle, morel
    or oyster, sliced
Salt and freshly-ground black
    pepper, to taste
1 tablespoon butter
2 (8-ounces each) beef sirloin
    steaks

i n large skillet heat 1 tablespoon of the olive oil over medium-high heat. Add shallot. Saute 3 minutes. Remove skillet from heat. Add brandy. Ignite with match. When flames subside, return skillet to heat. Add beef stock. Bring to boil. Boil 15 minutes or until reduced to 1/2 cup, stirring occasionally. Whisk in cream. Return to boil. (Sauce may be prepared 1 day in advance to this point. Cover and refrigerate until ready to use. Bring to simmer before finishing.) Add mushrooms. Reduce heat and simmer 20 minutes or until tender, stirring occasionally. Salt and pepper to taste.

In medium skillet heat butter and remaining 1 tablespoon olive oil over medium-high heat. Add steaks and cook 2 minutes per side or just until browned. Reduce heat to medium. Cook 3 minutes per side for medium-rare, or to desired doneness. Transfer to serving plates and keep warm. Add mushroom mixture to beef cooking skillet. Bring to boil, scraping up any browned bits. Spoon over steaks. Serve immediately.

SERVES   2

roast tenderloin stuffed with lobster

5- to 6-pound beef tenderloin,
  fat trimmed
Meat from two lightly cooked
  lobster tails
3 tablespoons melted butter
2 cloves garlic, crushed
1/2 teaspoon dried basil
1/2 teaspoon dried oregano
1 teaspoon fresh lemon juice
Bearnaise Sauce
  (recipe follows)

Preheat oven to 375 degrees. Cut tenderloin lengthwise almost in half and pull open. Arrange lobster along fold. Close and secure with string at 1 inch intervals. In small bowl combine melted butter, garlic, herbs and lemon juice. Drizzle over meat. Bake 1 hour and 15 minutes or to desired doneness. Slice and serve immediately with Bearnaise Sauce.

bearnaise sauce:

In top of double boiler combine 1/4 cup dry white wine, 2 tablespoons tarragon vinegar, 1 tablespoon minced fresh onion, 2 crushed white peppercorns, 2 snipped sprigs fresh tarragon and 1 snipped sprig fresh chervil. Cook and stir over direct heat until reduced by about half. Cool to room temperature. Place over hot water. Gradually add 3 egg yolks and 3/4 cup melted butter, beating well after each addition. Continue beating until thickened. Salt and pepper to taste. Serve warm.

SERVES   6

beef tenderloin au poivre

1/4 cup butter, divided
1 red bell pepper, cut into
  very thin strips
1 yellow bell pepper, cut into
  very thin strips
1 orange bell pepper, cut
  into very thin strips
4 slices filet of beef, each
  1-1/2-inches thick
Salt, to taste
1-1/2 tablespoons cracked
  black peppercorns
1 tablespoon olive oil
2 tablespoons brandy
1/2 cup heavy or whipping
  cream

In large skillet melt 2 tablespoons of the butter over medium-high heat. Add bell peppers. Saute just until tender but not soft. Set aside.

Sprinkle both sides of beef with salt and cracked peppercorns. In another skillet heat 1 tablespoon of the remaining butter and olive oil over medium-high heat. Add beef filets. Saute 5 minutes per side. Remove from skillet and keep warm. To same skillet add brandy, scraping up anybrowned bits from pan. Whisk in cream. Bring to boil and reduce slightly, whisking constantly. Add remaining 1 tablespoon butter, whisking until blended. Salt and pepper to taste. Arrange most of bell pepper strips on large serving platter. Place filets over top. Spoon brandy mixture over filets. Garnish with remaining bell pepper strips. Serve immediately.

SERVES   4

filet mignon with peppercorn sauce

2 filet mignon, each 1-1/2 inches thick
Salt and freshly-ground black pepper
1 tablespoon butter
3 tablespoons brandy
1/2 cup heavy or whipping cream
2 teaspoons cracked green peppercorns in brine
1 teaspoon Dijon mustard

Season steaks with salt and generous amount of pepper. In large skillet melt butter over medium-high heat. Add steaks. Cook 4 minutes per side for rare, or to desired doneness. Transfer to dinner plates. Keep warm. To same skillet add brandy. Ignite with match. Return skillet to medium-high heat. Bring to boil, scraping browned bits from skillet into brandy. Whisk in cream and peppercorns. Return to boil. Boil and stir 2 minutes or until reduced to desired sauce consistency. Spoon over steaks. Serve immediately.

SERVES   2

flaming filet mignon

6 filet mignon, each 1-inch thick
9 slices bacon
2 cups diced fresh mushrooms
1/2 cup snipped fresh parsley
1/4 cup minced fresh onions
1/4 cup butter
1 teaspoon salt
1/8 teaspoon freshly-ground black pepper
6 very large mushroom caps
1/2 to 3/4 cup warm brandy

Wrap each steak with bacon slice. Secure with toothpicks. Dice remaining 3 slices bacon. Place in large skillet. Cook over medium-high heat until crisp. Drain fat. Add mushrooms, parsley, onions and butter. Saute until lightly browned. Add salt and pepper. Keep warm. Grill or broil steaks a few inches from heat to desired doneness, turning once. Transfer to large serving platter. Top with mushroom mixture. Place mushroom cap, upside down, on each steak. Fill with warm brandy. Ignite brandy and serve immediately.

SERVES   6

grilled peppered steaks

3/4 cup olive oil
1/3 cup red wine vinegar
4-1/2 tablespoons Dijon mustard
1/4 cup packed brown sugar
1 tablespoon plus 1 teaspoon coarsely-ground black pepper
1 tablespoon snipped fresh rosemary
1 tablespoon snipped fresh thyme
1 teaspoon salt
4 cloves garlic, minced
2 large shallots, chopped
3 (1-1/4 pounds each) flank steaks
Freshly-ground black pepper, to taste
Fresh thyme and rosemary sprigs

i n large shallow baking dish combine olive oil, vinegar, mustard, brown sugar, pepper, rosemary, thyme, salt, garlic and shallots. Add steaks, turning to coat with mixture. Cover and refrigerate overnight to marinate. Remove steaks from marinade. Season with pepper to taste. Grill 4 minutes per side for medium-rare, or to desired doneness. Thinly slice across grain. Arrange on large serving platter. Garnish with fresh thyme and rosemary sprigs. Serve immediately.

SERVES 8

cold pepper steak

1/4 cup water
1/4 cup red wine vinegar
1/4 cup vegetable oil
2 tablespoons freshly-ground black pepper
2 teaspoons dried thyme
3-pound London broil, 1-3/4 inches thick
Hard rolls, sliced in half
Brown mustard
Freshly grated horseradish

i n large shallow baking dish combine water, vinegar, oil, pepper and thyme. Add meat, turning to coat with mixture. Cover and refrigerate 8 hours to marinate, turning occasionally. Remove meat from marinade. Place on lightly greased broiler rack over pan. Broil 4 inches from heat 14 minutes. Turn and broil additional 14 minutes or to desired doneness. Transfer to large serving platter. Cover and refrigerate up to 2 days. Slice thin. Serve cold on hard rolls with brown mustard and freshly grated horseradish.

SERVES 10 - 12

festive chili

1 pound smoked bacon, cut into 3/8-inch pieces
4 pounds round steak, cut into 1/4-inch cubes
2 cans (28 ounces each) whole tomatoes, chopped, with liquid
1 can (15 ounces) tomato sauce
1 can (7 ounces) diced green chiles
1 can (6 ounces) tomato paste
2 tablespoons diced jalapeno peppers, optional
1 tablespoon olive oil
2 cups chopped onions
2 cups chopped green bell pepper
1 cup snipped fresh parsley
2 teaspoons ground coriander
3 cloves garlic
2 tablespoons plus 2 teaspoons ground cumin
2 tablespoons mild chili powder
1 tablespoon fresh lemon juice
2 teaspoons salt
1 teaspoon cayenne (red pepper)
1 teaspoon freshly-ground black pepper
1/2 teaspoon medium-hot chili powder
1/4 teaspoon dried oregano
1/4 teaspoon paprika
1/2 cup corn flour
Sour cream, shredded Monterey Jack and Cheddar cheeses

in large skillet brown bacon. Drain and set aside. In same skillet brown round steak. Place bacon and steak in Dutch oven or large kettle. Stir in whole tomatoes with liquid, tomato sauce, green chiles, tomato paste and if desired, jalapeno peppers. Heat to simmering.

In skillet heat olive oil over medium-high heat. Add onions and bell pepper. Saute just until onions are transparent. Add to mixture in Dutch oven. Stir in parsley, coriander, garlic, cumin, chili powders, lemon juice, salt, cayenne, black pepper, oregano and paprika. Cook over low heat 1 hour, stirring occasionally. Stir in corn flour. Cover and simmer 2-1/2 hours, stirring occasionally. Ladle into deep serving bowls. Top with sour cream, Monterey Jack and Cheddar cheeses. Serve immediately.

SERVES   10

sally's sherried pork

4- to 5-pound boned and rolled pork roast, fat trimmed
2 tablespoons dry mustard
2 teaspoons dried thyme
1/2 cup dry sherry
1/2 cup soy sauce
2 cloves garlic, minced
1 teaspoon ginger
Sherry Sauce (recipe follows)

rub pork with mustard and thyme. In large shallow baking dish combine sherry, soy sauce, garlic and ginger. Add pork, turning to coat with mixture. Cover and refrigerate at least 3 hours or overnight to marinate. Preheat oven to 325 degrees. Transfer pork to rack over roasting pan. Bake 2-1/2 to 3 hours or until tender and done. Slice and serve with warm Sherry Sauce.

sherry sauce:

In small saucepan melt 1 jar (10 ounces) currant jelly over low heat, stirring constantly. Whisk in 2 tablespoons dry sherry. Serve warm.

SERVES   8 - 10

pork chops with apple and onion

1 tablespoon vegetable oil
2-1/2 pounds pork chops, fat trimmed
1 tablespoon butter
1 onion, chopped
1 Golden Delicious apple, peeled and thinly sliced
2 cloves garlic, minced
1/2 teaspoon dried rosemary
1/2 cup apple cider
1/4 cup dry white wine

in large skillet heat oil over medium-high heat. Add pork chops. Brown 2 minutes per side. Remove from skillet and set aside. Melt butter in same skillet over medium-high heat. Add onion, apple and garlic. Saute 3 minutes. Reduce heat to medium-low. Return pork chops to skillet. Sprinkle with rosemary, cider and wine. Cover and cook 20 minutes or until tender and cooked through. Serve immediately.

SERVES   2

pork tenderloin with sesame sauce

1-1/4 pounds pork
    tenderloin, fat trimmed
Salt and freshly-ground black
    pepper, to taste
2 tablespoons sesame seeds
1/4 cup packed brown sugar
2 tablespoons Oriental
    sesame oil
2 tablespoons cider vinegar
2 tablespoons Dijon mustard
2 tablespoons water

rub pork with salt and pepper to taste. In small skillet toast sesame seeds over high heat, stirring frequently. In large shallow baking dish combine toasted sesame seeds, brown sugar, sesame oil, vinegar, mustard and water. Add pork, turning to coat with mixture. Cover and refrigerate at least 2 hours to marinate. Heat grill with rotisserie or preheat oven to 350 degrees. Grill on rotisserie with lid closed or cover and bake about 30 minutes per pound or until tender and done. Slice and serve immediately.

SERVES   4

fettuccine with sausage and sage

1/2 pound sweet Italian
    sausage
2 cloves garlic, minced
1-1/2 cups chicken stock or
    broth
8 sun-dried tomatoes,
    chopped
Sage Butter (recipe follows)
16 ounces fettuccine,
    uncooked
2 tablespoons salt
2 ounces cubed or crumbled
    goat cheese, room
    temperature

remove and discard casing from sausage. Heat large skillet over medium-high heat. Add sausage. Saute until cooked through and crumbled. Add garlic. Saute 2 minutes. Add chicken stock and tomatoes. Bring to simmer, stirring occasionally. Add 3 tablespoons of the Sage Butter. Cover and keep warm. Cook fettuccine according to package directions using 2 tablespoons salt in cooking water. Drain and return to cooking pot. Add sausage mixture. Lightly toss over low heat. Transfer to dinner plates or large serving bowl. Top with goat cheese. Serve immediately.

sage butter:

In small bowl cream 6 tablespoons butter until softened. Beat in 2 tablespoons snipped fresh sage. Shape into small loaf or cylinder. Wrap in plastic and refrigerate until ready to use. (Leftover butter can be refrigerated up to 3 days or frozen up to 1 month.)

SERVES   4

raspberry pork roast

2-pound boneless pork roast, fat trimmed
Salt and freshly-ground black pepper, to taste
1/2 cup raspberry preserves
2 tablespoons slivered almonds

Preheat oven to 350 degrees. Sprinkle roast with salt and pepper to taste. Place in shallow roasting pan. Fill pan with 1 inch of water. Bake 1 hour or until tender. Spoon raspberry preserves over top. Sprinkle with almonds. Bake additional 10 minutes. Slice and serve immediately with juices from pan.

SERVES 6 - 8

penne with eggplant, roasted peppers and sausage

1-1/2 pounds (about 6) Japanese eggplants, cut lengthwise into 1/4-inch slices
7 tablespoons olive oil, divided
1-1/2 teaspoons salt, divided
3/4 teaspoon freshly-ground black pepper, divided
1 pound Italian sausage
1 jar (4 ounces) roasted red peppers, drained, or 1 roasted fresh red bell pepper, peeled and seeded, coarsely chopped
1 medium tomato, peeled and diced
1/2 cup snipped fresh cilantro
2 tablespoons fresh lemon juice
1 clove garlic, minced
1 teaspoon balsamic vinegar
16 ounces penne or other macaroni, uncooked

Preheat oven to 350 degrees. Brush eggplant slices with 3 tablespoons of the olive oil. Sprinkle with 1 teaspoon of the salt and 1/2 teaspoon of the pepper. Arrange eggplant and sausage on large baking sheet. Cover with foil. Bake 20 minutes or until eggplant is tender. Remove eggplant from baking sheet. Dice and set aside.

Return sausage to oven. Bake, uncovered, additional 10 minutes or until cooked through. Cut into 1/4-inch thick slices. In large serving bowl lightly toss eggplant, sausage, roasted red peppers, tomato, cilantro, lemon juice, garlic, vinegar, remaining 1/2 teaspoon salt and 1/4 teaspoon pepper. Cook pasta according to package directions. Drain and transfer to large serving bowl. Lightly toss with remaining 4 tablespoons olive oil and sausage mixture. Serve immediately or let stand at room temperature up to 1 hour before serving.

SERVES 4 - 6

veal blanquette with dill

1/2 cup butter, divided
4-1/2 pounds veal, cut into
   1-1/2-inch cubes
Salt and freshly-ground black
   pepper, to taste
1 cup finely chopped onion
2 tablespoons snipped fresh
   dill or 2 teaspoons dried
   dill
1 clove garlic, minced
1/3 cup all-purpose flour
1/2 teaspoon nutmeg
1-1/2 cups chicken stock or
   broth
1/2 cup water
3 carrots, thinly sliced or
   julienned
2 leeks, thinly sliced or
   julienned
1 cup heavy or whipping
   cream
Fresh dill
Baked rice or mashed
   potatoes

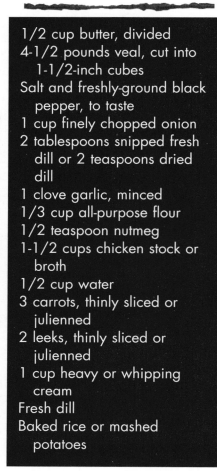

Preheat oven to 375 degrees. In large, deep flame-proof casserole dish melt 4 tablespoons of the butter over medium heat. Add veal. Salt and pepper to taste. Stir in onion, dill and garlic. Cook and stir 5 minutes without browning. Sprinkle with flour and nutmeg. Add chicken broth or stock and water. Bring to boil. Remove from heat. Cover and bake 1 hour.

In large skillet melt remaining 4 tablespoons butter over medium heat. Add carrots and leeks. Cook and stir until soft. Add half of carrots and leeks to veal. Stir in cream. Bring to boil, stirring constantly. Garnish with fresh dill and remaining carrots and leeks. (Freezes well.) Serve immediately with baked rice or mashed potatoes.

SERVES   8 - 10

veal with mushroom cream sauce

1 pound veal
2 tablespoons butter
1 onion, minced
6 large mushrooms, sliced
1 clove garlic, minced
1/2 cup dry white wine
1 cup heavy or whipping
   cream
1/4 teaspoon salt
2 tablespoons snipped fresh
   parsley

Pound veal 1/4-inch thick. Cut into 2-inch strips. In large skillet melt butter over medium-high heat. Add veal. Saute 1 minute. Using slotted spoon transfer veal to large serving platter. To same skillet add onion, mushrooms and garlic. Saute 30 seconds. Add wine. Boil and stir until reduced by half. Whisk in cream, salt, parsley and any juices from veal platter. Cook and stir until thickened. Return veal to skillet. Heat through. Serve immediately.

SERVES   4

veal princess

1/2 pound veal medallions
1/2 cup all-purpose flour
2 tablespoons clarified butter
1/2 pound fresh bay scallops
1/4 cup sherry
1 cup heavy or whipping
   cream
Pinch dried tarragon
Salt and freshly-ground black
   pepper, to taste

Pound veal 1/4-inch thick. Dredge through flour. In large skillet melt butter over medium-high heat. Add veal. Saute 1 minute. Turn and add scallops. Cook additional 2 minutes. Remove veal and scallops from skillet. Set aside and keep warm. Whisk sherry into pan drippings and deglaze by scraping any browned bits from skillet into sherry. Whisk in cream and tarragon. Cook and stir until slightly thickened. Salt and pepper to taste. Arrange veal and scallops on serving plates. Top with sherry mixture. Serve immediately.

SERVES   2

veal chops with fennel butter

1/4 cup plus 2 tablespoons
   dry red wine
2 cloves garlic, crushed
1 teaspoon ground thyme
1 teaspoon dried rosemary
3/4 teaspoon Dijon mustard
1/4 teaspoon salt
1/8 teaspoon freshly-ground
   black pepper
1 cup olive oil
4 (8-ounce) rib or loin veal
   chops, 1-inch thick, fat
   trimmed
Fennel Butter (recipe follows)
1 teaspoon fennel seeds
Fresh fennel tops

In large shallow baking dish combine wine, garlic, thyme, rosemary, mustard, salt and pepper. Whisk in olive oil. Add veal, turning to coat with mixture. Cover and refrigerate 24 hours to marinate, turning occasionally. Let stand at room temperature 30 minutes. Remove from marinade and pat dry. Grill or broil a few inches from heat 5 minutes per side for medium or to desired doneness. Arrange on serving plates. Top with dollops of Fennel Butter. Sprinkle with fennel seeds and garnish with fennel tops. Serve immediately.

fennel butter:

   In small bowl beat 1/2 cup butter until softened. Beat in 1/2 chopped fresh fennel bulb. Salt and pepper to taste. Cover and refrigerate until ready to use.

SERVES   4

veal in caper sauce

1 pound veal medallions
3/4 cup all-purpose flour
1/4 cup butter, divided
2 tablespoons olive oil
Salt and freshly-ground black
    pepper, to taste
2 tablespoons snipped fresh
    parsley or parsley flakes
1 tablespoon fresh lemon
    juice
1 teaspoon drained capers
Lemon slices

pound veal 1/4-inch thick. Dredge through flour. In large skillet melt 2 tablespoons of the butter with olive oil over medium-high heat. Add veal and brown lightly on both sides. Cook just until tender. Remove skillet from heat and transfer veal to warm serving platter. Salt and pepper to taste. Keep warm. To same skillet add parsley, lemon juice, capers and remaining 2 tablespoons butter. Cook and stir over low heat just until butter is melted and warmed. Drizzle over veal. Garnish with lemon slices. Serve immediately.

SERVES   4

breaded veal with lemon and capers

1 pound veal medallions
Salt and freshly-ground black
    pepper, to taste
All-purpose flour
2 eggs, slightly beaten
3 tablespoons water
1 cup fresh bread crumbs
1/4 cup vegetable oil
6 tablespoons butter
1/2 to 1 tablespoon fresh
    lemon juice
4 thin lemon slices
1/4 cup drained capers
1/4 cup snipped fresh
    parsley

pound veal 1/4-inch thick. Salt and pepper to taste. Dredge through flour. In shallow bowl beat together eggs and water. Salt and pepper to taste. Dip veal into egg mixture, coating well. Dip into bread crumbs.

In large skillet heat oil over medium-high heat. Add veal and brown lightly on both sides. Cook just until tender. Remove veal to warm serving platter. In same skillet melt butter over medium heat. Add lemon juice, scraping any browned bits from skillet into butter mixture. Drizzle over veal. Garnish with lemon slices, capers and parsley. Serve immediately.

SERVES   4

roast stuffed leg of lamb

1/2 cup chopped golden
raisins
1/4 cup chopped pine nuts
1/4 cup minced prosciutto
1/4 cup fresh bread crumbs
1/4 cup snipped mixed fresh
herbs such as parsley,
thyme, chives, mint and
oregano
2 tablespoons plus 1
teaspoon olive oil, divided
1 tablespoon minced garlic
2 teaspoons freshly grated
lemon peel
1 teaspoon balsamic vinegar
1/2 teaspoon freshly-ground
black pepper
1/4 teaspoon kosher salt
5- to 6-pound leg of lamb,
butterflied
Salt and freshly-ground black
pepper, to taste

In medium bowl combine raisins, pine nuts, prosciutto, bread crumbs, mixed herbs, 2 tablespoons of the olive oil, garlic, lemon peel, vinegar, 1/2 teaspoon pepper and 1/4 teaspoon salt. Spread open lamb. Fill evenly with herb mixture. Close lamb. Secure with string at 2-inch intervals. Cover and refrigerate at least 4 hours or overnight. Bring to room temperature.

Preheat oven to 450 degrees. Rub lamb with remaining 1 teaspoon olive oil. Salt and pepper to taste. Place lamb on rack over roasting pan. Roast 12 to 15 minutes per pound for rare to medium-rare, or to desired doneness. (Meat thermometer may be used.) Let stand 20 minutes. Remove strings. Slice and serve immediately.

SERVES   6 - 8

parsleyed rack of lamb

2 racks (about 2-1/2 pounds)
lamb, fat trimmed
1/4 cup butter, divided
1/2 cup fresh bread crumbs
3 tablespoons snipped fresh
parsley
1 shallot, minced
1 clove garlic, minced
1 teaspoon olive oil

Preheat broiler to 500 degrees. Butter large baking dish. Place lamb in single layer, meat side down, in prepared dish. Dot with 2 tablespoons of the butter. Broil a few inches from heat 2 to 3 minutes. Turn, meaty side up, and broil additional 2 to 3 minutes. Meanwhile, in small bowl combine bread crumbs, parsley, shallot, garlic and olive oil. Sprinkle over meaty side of lamb. Melt remaining 2 tablespoons butter. Drizzle over lamb. Bake at 400 degrees 8 to 10 minutes or to desired doneness. Serve immediately.

SERVES   6

venison chateaubriand

3 pounds venison steaks*,
   1-1/2 inches thick
1/2 cup Burgundy wine or
   Cabernet Sauvignon
1/4 cup extra-virgin olive oil
1/4 cup snipped fresh basil
4 cloves garlic, minced
1/2 teaspoon salt
Freshly-ground black pepper,
   to taste
4 portobello mushrooms,
   sliced
Fresh basil sprigs

arrange venison in large shallow baking dish. In jar place wine, olive oil, basil, garlic, salt and pepper, to taste. Tightly fit lid on jar. Shake well and pour over venison. Pierce with fork while spooning marinade over meat. Cover and refrigerate 1 hour. Turn meat and pierce with fork again while spooning with marinade. Continue to marinade in refrigerator 6 hours, turning twice. Remove venison from pan and transfer marinade to small saucepan. Bring to boil. Reduce heat to medium. Stir in mushrooms. Cook and stir just until soft. Pour marinade into bowl, leaving the mushrooms and small amount of marinade in pan to keep warm.

Grill venison a few inches from heat 10 to 15 minutes or until rare to medium, basting occasionally with marinade from bowl. (To avoid toughness, do not cook to well done.) Slice 1/4-inch thick. Arrange on large serving platter. Top with warm marinade-mushroom mixture. Garnish with basil sprigs. Serve immediately.

*Venison tenderloin may be substituted. Ask butcher to bone both loins, keeping intact. Remove silvery white sheath of muscle from surface with fillet knife.

SERVES   6

tom's venison chili

2 pounds ground venison
1/2 medium onion, chopped
8-inch stick pepperoni, diced
3 tablespoons Worcestershire
  sauce
1 teaspoon freshly-ground
  black pepper
1/2 teaspoon seasoned salt
No. 10 can (4 pounds)
  kidney beans
3 cups water
3 cans (6 ounces each)
  tomato paste
1/4 cup chili powder, or
  to taste
1/4 cup sugar
2 tablespoons cider vinegar
Hot red pepper flakes,
  to taste
Cayenne (red pepper),
  to taste
1 large green bell pepper,
  chopped
Cheddar cheese, optional

i n large stock pot brown meat in 1/4-inch water. Add onion, pepperoni, Worcestershire sauce, pepper and seasoned salt. Cook over medium heat 10 minutes, stirring occasionally. Add beans, water, tomato paste, chili powder, sugar, vinegar, red pepper flakes and cayenne to taste. Bring to boil, stirring frequently. Reduce heat. Add bell pepper. Simmer, uncovered, 1-1/2 hours or to desired consistency, stirring occasionally. Ladle into deep serving bowls. Sprinkle with Cheddar cheese, if desired. Serve immediately.

SERVES   8 - 10

vegetable tortilla lasagna

2 tablespoons vegetable oil
1 large zucchini, cut into
   1/4-inch slices
3/4 cup frozen, thawed corn
   kernels
Salt and freshly-ground black
   pepper, to taste
1-1/4 cups shredded
   Monterey Jack cheese,
   divided
1/4 cup ricotta cheese
1/2 teaspoon ground cumin
1 cup bottled salsa
Six 6-inch corn tortillas
1 jar (7 ounces) roasted red
   peppers, drained and
   patted dry
3 tablespoons snipped fresh
   cilantro
Lime wedges

Preheat oven to 500 degrees. Brush 2 large shallow pans with oil. Arrange zucchini in single layer in one of the prepared pans and in half of the second pan. Arrange corn in other half of second pan. Salt and pepper to taste. Place pans on two racks in oven. Roast 5 minutes. Stir corn and reverse pans. Roast additional 5 minutes or until lightly browned.

Meanwhile, in small bowl combine 1 cup of the Monterey Jack cheese, ricotta cheese and cumin. Salt and pepper to taste. Set aside. Place salsa in fine sieve. Drain 3 seconds. (Do not press on solids.) Set aside. Lightly grease a loaf pan, about 9 x 5 inches. Cut tortillas into six 5 x 3-3/4-inch rectangles. Arrange two of the tortillas on bottom of loaf pan, overlapping in middle. Spread with 1/4 cup of the drained salsa. Top with half of the ricotta cheese mixture, half of the zucchini, half of the red peppers, half of the corn and 1 tablespoon of the cilantro. Repeat layers one more time. Top with remaining 2 tortillas, 1/2 cup salsa, 1/4 cup Monterey Jack cheese and 1 tablespoon cilantro. Cover with foil. Bake 12 minutes or until heated through and cheese melts. Let stand, covered, 5 minutes. Serve with lime wedges.

SERVES 8 - 10

boogie-woogie barbeque sauce

2 tablespoons butter
1 onion, chopped
2 cloves garlic, minced
1-1/2 cups ketchup
1/4 cup packed brown sugar
1/4 cup white vinegar
1/4 cup Worcestershire
   sauce
1 tablespoon chili powder
1/4 teaspoon salt
Dash Tabasco sauce

In medium saucepan melt butter over medium-high heat. Add onion and garlic. Saute just until tender. Stir in ketchup, brown sugar, vinegar, Worcestershire sauce, chili powder, salt and Tabasco sauce. Cook over low heat 30 minutes, stirring occasionally. Brush on chicken, pork or beef during grilling.

MAKES 1-1/2 CUPS

back-slappin' bohemian barbeque sauce

- 3 bottles Heinz Thick n' Rich cajun barbecue sauce
- 3 bottles Durkee's pepper sauce
- 1 can (24 ounces) V-8 juice
- 1 cup chopped habanero or jalapeno peppers
- 1/3 cup Worcestershire sauce
- 1/2 cup Shirachachili sauce
- 3 large onions, chopped
- 1 whole bulb (about 8 cloves) garlic, crushed
- 2 tablespoons freshly-ground black pepper

In large kettle combine all ingredients. Bring to boil. Reduce heat and simmer, uncovered, until sauce reaches desired consistency. Stir occasionally during cooking. Brush on beef, poultry or fish during grilling, or use as a spicy dipping sauce. Cover and refrigerate or freeze leftovers. Reheat.

MAKES   3 - 4 QUARTS

the very best barbeque rub

- 2 teaspoons dried basil, ground
- 2 teaspoons dried rosemary, ground
- 2 teaspoons dried tarragon, ground
- 2 teaspoons paprika
- 2 teaspoons dry mustard
- 2 teaspoons onion powder
- 2 teaspoons salt
- 1 teaspoon garlic powder
- 1 teaspoon chili powder
- 1 teaspoon cayenne (red pepper)

Combine all ingredients. Rub on poultry or pork before grilling. (Recipe may be made in larger quantities and stored in an air-tight container until ready to use.)

MAKES   1/2 CUP

Vegetables and sides

i n a war which pitted brother against brother, this
legendary Adams County battlefield hosted the most
casualty-laden battle ever waged on North American
soil - even to this day. While war ravaged on, civilians
for the most part remained unaffected. Bountiful spreads
were the order of the day for civilian tables, in decided
contrast to dwindling food rations for the soldiers, which
included (at best) hard bread, salt pork, and coffee. In
the war's aftermath, however, shortages and more
carefully controlled portions were widespread until the
reunited country returned to normalcy.

green beans with almonds and basil

1 pound fresh green beans, washed and trimmed

3 tablespoons butter

3 tablespoons slivered blanched almonds

1-1/2 tablespoons snipped fresh parsley

1 teaspoon snipped fresh basil

place green beans in large saucepan. Add small amount of water. Cover and bring to boil. Reduce heat and cook 10 to 12 minutes or until crisp-tender. Drain and transfer to large serving dish. Keep warm. In small skillet melt butter over medium-high heat. Add almonds. Saute until lightly browned. Stir in parsley and basil. Pour over green beans. Toss gently. Serve hot.

SERVES 4

green beans in yellow pepper butter

7 tablespoons butter or margarine, divided

1 medium yellow bell pepper, shredded

1/4 cup pine nuts

1 tablespoon fresh lemon juice

1/4 teaspoon salt

1/8 teaspoon freshly-ground black pepper

1-1/2 pounds fresh green beans, washed and trimmed

1 large yellow bell pepper, cut into julienne strips

Salt, to taste

in small saucepan melt 1 tablespoon of the butter or margarine over medium-high heat. Add shredded bell pepper. Saute 5 minutes or until crisp-tender. Set aside.

In food processor or blender soften remaining 6 tablespoons butter. Add pine nuts. Cover and process until almost smooth. Add sauteed bell pepper, lemon juice, salt and black pepper. Cover and process until almost smooth. Set aside.

Place green beans in large saucepan. Add small amount of water. Cover and bring to boil. Reduce heat and cook 10 to 12 minutes or until crisp-tender. Place bell pepper julienne strips in small saucepan. Add small amount of water. Cover and bring to boil. Reduce heat and cook 3 minutes. Salt to taste. Place cooked beans and bell pepper julienne strips in large serving dish. Pour butter-bell pepper sauce over all. Toss to coat. Serve immediately.

SERVES 8

brussels sprouts with walnut cream sauce

2-1/2 pounds fresh brussels sprouts, washed and stems removed
3 tablespoons butter or margarine
3 tablespoons all-purpose flour
2 cups heavy or whipping cream
2 cloves garlic, minced
1/4 teaspoon ground bay leaves
Salt, to taste
White pepper, to taste
2/3 cup half-and-half
3 tablespoons grated Parmesan cheese
1 cup walnuts, ground

Place brussels sprouts in large saucepan. Add water to partially cover. Cover and bring to boil. Reduce heat. Cook 10 to 12 minutes or until tender. Drain and transfer to large serving dish. Keep warm.

In large saucepan melt butter or margarine over low heat. Add flour, stirring until smooth. Cook 1 minute, stirring constantly. Gradually add heavy or whipping cream. Cook over medium heat, stirring constantly, until mixture is thickened and bubbly. Add garlic and bay leaves. Salt and pepper, to taste. Cook, stirring constantly, additional 3 minutes. Remove from heat. Using wire whisk, beat in half-and-half and Parmesan cheese. Stir in walnuts. Return to low heat. Heat through. (Do not boil.) Pour warm sauce over brussels sprouts. Toss gently. Serve immediately.

SERVES 8 - 10

lemon broccoli with pecans

1-1/2 pounds fresh broccoli, washed and trimmed
1 tablespoon butter
1/3 cup chopped pecans
1 tablespoon sugar
2 teaspoons cornstarch
1/2 cup chicken broth
1/4 cup fresh lemon juice
1 tablespoon freshly-grated lemon peel
1/4 teaspoon freshly-ground black pepper

Cut broccoli into spears. Steam until crisp-tender. Meanwhile, in large skillet melt butter over medium-high heat. Add pecans. Saute until lightly browned. Set aside.

In medium saucepan thoroughly combine sugar and cornstarch. Stir in chicken broth, lemon juice, lemon peel and pepper. Bring to boil over medium heat, stirring constantly. Cook, stirring constantly, until thickened. Place cooked broccoli in large serving dish. Pour lemon sauce over top. Sprinkle with pecans. Serve immediately.

SERVES 4 - 6

mediterranean pasta

8 slices bacon, diced
1 large onion, chopped
1 small eggplant, peeled and cubed
2 cups chopped fresh tomatoes or 1 can (14-1/2 ounces) chopped tomatoes
4 cloves garlic, minced
1 tablespoon red wine vinegar
1 teaspoon dried thyme
1/3 cup drained and rinsed capers, optional
Salt, to taste
Freshly-ground black pepper, to taste
1 pound penne or ziti pasta, uncooked
2 tablespoons olive oil
1-1/2 cups crumbled feta cheese
Snipped fresh parsley

in large skillet fry bacon until crisp. Set aside bacon on paper towels to drain. Add onion and eggplant to drippings in skillet. Saute 15 minutes or until eggplant is tender and golden brown. Add tomatoes, garlic, vinegar and thyme. Reduce heat. Cook 5 minutes, stirring occasionally. Add capers, if desired. Salt and pepper to taste. Remove from heat and set aside. Cook pasta according to package directions. Transfer to large serving bowl. Toss with olive oil. Add eggplant mixture, bacon and feta cheese. Gently toss to coat. Garnish with parsley. Serve immediately.

SERVES 4 - 6

pasta and broccoli with gorgonzola sauce

1 pound capellini, uncooked
1/2 cup butter or
  margarine, divided
1/4 cup grated Parmesan
  cheese
1/4 cup snipped fresh
  parsley
2 pounds fresh broccoli,
  washed and trimmed
1 cup heavy or whipping
  cream
8 ounces crumbled
  Gorgonzola cheese

Cook capellini according to package directions. Toss with 1/4 cup of the butter or margarine, Parmesan cheese and parsley. Set aside.

Cut broccoli into florets. (Do not use stems.) Blanch in small amount of boiling water 2 to 3 minutes or until bright green but still firm. Transfer to colander. Rinse under cold water and drain. Toss with pasta mixture. Set aside.

In medium saucepan melt remaining 1/4 cup butter or margarine. Add cream. Bring to boil. Reduce heat and cook 5 minutes, stirring constantly. Add Gorgonzola cheese, stirring until melted. Pour over pasta mixture. Gently toss to coat. Serve immediately.

SERVES   6

greek spaghetti

3 tablespoons olive oil
1 onion, chopped
2 cloves garlic, minced
2 jars (6 ounces each)
  marinated artichoke hearts
24 pitted Greek black olives
Juice of 1 lemon
1 teaspoon dried oregano
1 pound spaghetti, uncooked
2/3 cup grated Parmesan
  cheese
6 ounces feta cheese,
  crumbled

In large skillet heat olive oil over medium-high heat. Add onion and garlic. Saute 2 to 3 minutes. Drain and halve artichoke hearts, reserving liquid. Add reserved liquid to skillet with olives, lemon juice and oregano. Heat through. Add artichoke hearts. Cover and keep warm. Cook spaghetti according to package directions. Toss with artichoke mixture, Parmesan and feta cheeses. Serve immediately.

SERVES   4 - 6

portofino primavera

2 tablespoons olive oil
1 cup chopped onion
2 cloves garlic, minced
1 can (14-1/2 ounces) diced
  tomatoes in juice
1 can (6 ounces) tomato
  paste
1 cup chicken broth
1 cup sliced zucchini
1 cup sliced black olives
1 cup sliced canned
  artichoke hearts
2 tablespoons capers
1/2 teaspoon salt
1 pound linguine, uncooked

i n medium saucepan heat oil over medium-high heat.
Add onion and garlic. Saute 1 minute. Add tomatoes with juice, tomato paste, chicken broth, zucchini, olives, artichoke hearts, capers and salt. Bring to boil, stirring occasionally. Reduce heat and simmer, uncovered, 15 to 20 minutes. Cook linguine according to package directions. Serve with sauce.

SERVES   6 - 8

risotto with spinach, fontina and prosciutto

2 cups water
1-1/2 cups chicken broth
1 tablespoon olive oil
1 small onion, minced
1 cup arborio rice,
  uncooked
1/2 cup dry white wine
1 cup frozen, thawed
  spinach
1 cup freshly grated fontina
  cheese
3 ounces thinly sliced
  prosciutto, cut into 1/2-
  inch strips
1/2 teaspoon freshly-ground
  black pepper

i n medium saucepan bring water and chicken broth to
boil. Cover and keep warm over lowest heat. In large saucepan heat olive oil over medium-high heat. Add onion. Saute 3 minutes or just until tender. Stir in rice. Saute 1 minute. Add wine. Simmer over medium-high heat 2 minutes or until wine is reduced to 1/4 cup. Stir in 1/2 cup of the warm chicken broth-water mixture. Simmer 1 minute or until rice absorbs all of the liquid, stirring constantly. Repeat with another 1/2 cup warm broth mixture, stirring until absorbed. Repeat with remaining broth, adding 1/2 cup at a time. Cook 20 minutes or until rice is creamy and tender, stirring frequently. Squeeze excess moisture from spinach. Add spinach to rice. Heat through. Remove from heat. Stir in fontina cheese, prosciutto and pepper. Serve immediately.

SERVES   4

fettuccine with fennel, prosciutto and goat cheese

2 tablespoons olive oil
1 large fennel bulb, halved lengthwise, cored and sliced thin
1 clove garlic, minced
1/4 teaspoon hot red pepper flakes
1/2 cup heavy or whipping cream
1/4 teaspoon salt
1/4 teaspoon freshly-ground black pepper
1 pound fettuccine, uncooked
4 ounces thinly sliced prosciutto, cut into 1/2-inch strips
3 ounces goat cheese, crumbled

i n large skillet heat oil over medium-high heat. Add fennel. Saute 8 minutes or just until tender. Add garlic and red pepper flakes. Saute 30 seconds or just until fragrant. Reduce heat. Stir in cream. Heat 2 minutes. (Do not boil.) Add salt and pepper. Cover and keep warm. Cook fettuccine according to package directions. Transfer to large serving bowl. Add fennel mixture. Gently toss to coat. Sprinkle with prosciutto and goat cheese. Serve immediately.

SERVES   4 - 6

spinach pasta with vodka sauce

1 pound fresh spinach pasta, uncooked
3/4 cup sweet (unsalted) butter
2 large tomatoes, peeled and chopped
6 tablespoons vodka
1/4 cup snipped fresh parsley
1 cup heavy or whipping cream
Salt, to taste
Freshly-ground black pepper
1-1/2 cups freshly grated Parmesan cheese

C ook pasta according to package directions. Set aside. In large skillet melt butter over medium-high heat. Add tomatoes, vodka and parsley. Saute 6 minutes or until thickened, stirring constantly. Add cream. Cook 3 to 5 minutes, stirring constantly. Remove from heat. Add pasta. Gently toss to coat. Salt and pepper to taste. Add Parmesan cheese. Serve immediately.

SERVES   8

four-cheese pasta
with fresh tomato sauce

3 pounds plum tomatoes,
   diced
1/2 cup snipped fresh basil
1-1/2 teaspoons kosher salt
3 cloves garlic, minced
1 cup ricotta cheese, room
   temperature
2 tablespoons heavy or
   whipping cream
1/4 teaspoon nutmeg
Freshly-ground black pepper,
   to taste
1/2 cup fontina cheese,
   finely diced
1/2 cup mozzarella cheese,
   finely diced
1 pound ridged mostacelli,
   uncooked
3 tablespoons extra-virgin
   olive oil
Freshly-grated Parmesan
   cheese

i n medium bowl combine tomatoes, basil, salt and garlic. Let stand at room temperature 1 to 2 hours to blend flavors, stirring occasionally. Drain and discard any excess liquid.

In separate bowl fluff ricotta cheese with fork. Stir in cream, nutmeg and pepper, to taste. Add fontina and mozzarella cheeses. Set aside at room temperature. Meanwhile, cook mostacelli according to package directions. Transfer to large heated bowl. Toss with olive oil. Add ricotta cheese mixture. Gently toss to coat. Place on warm serving dishes. Spoon tomato mixture on top. Sprinkle with Parmesan cheese. Serve immediately with additional Parmesan.

SERVES   4 - 6

bow ties with arugula, bacon and parmesan

6 slices bacon, diced
1 clove garlic, minced
1/2 cup dry white wine
1/4 cup heavy or whipping cream
8 ounces fresh arugula, rinsed, stemmed and halved crosswise
4 quarts water
2 teaspoons salt
12 ounces pasta bow ties, uncooked
1/2 cup grated Parmesan cheese
1/2 teaspoon freshly-ground black pepper

i n medium skillet fry bacon until crisp. Remove and discard all but 2 tablespoons of the bacon drippings. Set aside bacon on paper towels to drain.

Add garlic to drippings in skillet. Saute 3 minutes or just until softened. Add wine. Bring to boil. Reduce heat and simmer 3 minutes or until reduced to 1/4 cup. Add cream and arugula. Bring to simmer. Remove from heat and set aside. In Dutch oven or large kettle bring 4 quarts water to boil with salt. Add pasta. Cook 10 minutes or just until tender. Drain, reserving 1/2 cup of the cooking water. Return pasta to kettle. Add bacon, arugula mixture, reserved cooking water and cheese. Gently toss to coat. Sprinkle with pepper. Serve immediately.

SERVES   4 - 6

linguine with sun-dried tomatoes, broccoli and romano

1 pound fresh broccoli, washed and trimmed
6 quarts water
1 tablespoon salt
12 ounces linguine, uncooked
1 jar (3-1/2 ounces) sun-dried tomatoes in olive oil
3 tablespoons olive oil
2 cloves garlic, minced
1/4 teaspoon hot red pepper flakes
1/4 cup grated Romano cheese, divided
Salt, to taste

C ut broccoli into florets and slice stems. In Dutch oven or large kettle bring 6 quarts water to boil with 1 tablespoon salt. Add broccoli. Blanch 3 minutes or just until bright green but still firm. Remove and transfer with slotted spoon to colander. Rinse under cold water and drain. Return cooking water to boil. Add pasta. Cook 9 minutes or just until tender. Drain. Drain and reserve olive oil from sun-dried tomatoes. Slice tomatoes and set aside. In large skillet heat olive oil and reserved oil from tomatoes over medium-high heat. Add garlic. Saute 30 seconds or just until fragrant. Add drained broccoli, tomatoes and red pepper flakes. Saute 2 minutes or just until heated through. Transfer linguine to large serving bowl. Add broccoli mixture and 2 tablespoons of the cheese. Gently toss to coat. Salt, to taste. Sprinkle with remaining cheese. Serve immediately.

SERVES   4

risotto with roasted asparagus and walnuts

4-1/2 to 5 cups low-salt chicken broth

1 tablespoon extra-virgin olive oil, divided

1/3 cup chopped onion

1-1/4 cups arborio rice or other medium-grain white rice

1/2 cup dry white wine

1 pound fresh asparagus, washed and trimmed

1 clove garlic, thinly sliced

Salt, to taste

Freshly-ground black pepper, to taste

1/4 cup finely chopped toasted walnuts

2 tablespoons freshly grated Parmesan cheese

Preheat oven to 450 degrees. In medium saucepan bring chicken broth to boil.   Cover and keep warm over lowest heat. In medium saucepan heat 1 teaspoon of the olive oil over medium-high heat. Add onion. Saute 4 minutes or until golden brown. Stir in rice. Saute 1 minute. Add wine, stirring constantly until evaporated. Stir in 1/2 cup of the warm chicken broth. Simmer 1 minute or until rice absorbs all of the liquid, stirring constantly. Repeat with another 1/2 cup warm broth, stirring until absorbed. Repeat with remaining broth, adding 1/2 cup at a time. Cook 25 minutes or until rice is creamy and tender, stirring frequently.

Meanwhile, place asparagus and garlic in shallow baking dish. Drizzle with remaining 2 teaspoons olive oil. Salt and pepper to taste. Gently toss asparagus to coat with oil. Bake 16 minutes or until tender, turning occasionally. Stir walnuts and Parmesan cheese into rice mixture. Salt and pepper to taste. Arrange asparagus on individual serving plates. Top with risotto. Serve immediately.

SERVES   4 - 6

penne with asparagus and brie

1 pound fresh asparagus, washed, trimmed and cut into 2-inch pieces

2-1/2 pounds tomatoes, cubed

1 pound Brie cheese, cubed

1 cup extra-virgin olive oil

1/4 cup snipped fresh parsley

2 cloves garlic, crushed

1/2 teaspoon salt

Freshly-ground black pepper, to taste

1 pound penne, uncooked

Steam asparagus until crisp-tender. In large bowl combine asparagus with tomatoes, cheese, olive oil, parsley, garlic, salt and pepper.   Let stand 1 hour at room temperature to blend flavors. Cook penne according to package directions. Toss with asparagus mixture. Serve immediately.

SERVES   4 - 6

bacon, tomato and ricotta rigatoni

6 slices bacon, diced
4 medium plum tomatoes, diced
1 pound rigatoni, uncooked
1 cup ricotta cheese
1/4 cup grated Parmesan cheese
1/2 cup snipped fresh parsley
1/2 teaspoon freshly-ground black pepper

i n medium skillet fry bacon until crisp. Remove and discard all but 1 tablespoon of the bacon drippings. Add tomatoes to bacon and drippings in skillet. Cook until heated through, stirring occasionally. Cover and keep warm. Cook rigatoni according to package directions. Transfer to large serving bowl. Add ricotta and Parmesan cheeses, parsley and pepper. Gently toss to coat. Serve immediately.

SERVES   4 - 6

wilted spinach penne

6 tablespoons olive oil, divided
1/4 cup fine dry Italian bread crumbs
1 large onion, chopped
3 cloves garlic, minced
2 teaspoons hot red pepper flakes
1 pound fresh spinach, rinsed and drained well*
1 small jar pimientos or roasted red peppers, drained and cut into strips
1 pound penne, uncooked
Grated Parmesan or Asiago cheese

i n large skillet heat 2 tablespoons of the olive oil over medium-high heat. Add bread crumbs. Saute until browned. Remove from pan and set aside. Wipe pan clean with paper towels. Add remaining 4 tablespoons olive oil. Heat over medium-high heat. Add onion, garlic and red pepper flakes. Saute 6 to 7 minutes or until onion is tender but not browned. Add spinach. Cook 1 to 2 minutes or just until wilted. Remove from heat. Stir in pimientos or red pepper strips. Set aside. Cook penne according to package directions. Toss with spinach mixture. Sprinkle with browned bread crumbs and Parmesan or Asiago cheese. Serve immediately.

*One package (10 ounces) frozen spinach may be substituted for fresh spinach; thaw and squeeze out excess moisture before using.

SERVES   4 - 6

brown rice pilaf with raisins

2 tablespoons butter
1 tablespoon vegetable oil
1/4 cup chopped onion
1 cup brown rice, uncooked
2-1/2 cups chicken broth or water
1/4 teaspoon freshly-ground black pepper
1/2 cup golden raisins
1/2 cup dry white wine
3/4 cup toasted sliced almonds

in large skillet melt butter with oil over medium-high heat. Add onion. Saute until transparent. Reduce heat. Add rice. Cook 3 minutes or until lightly browned, stirring constantly. Add chicken broth or water and pepper. Bring to boil. Cover and reduce heat. Simmer 45 minutes. Meanwhile, in small bowl combine raisins and wine. Set aside 45 minutes to plump. Drain. Add with almonds to cooked rice. Serve immediately.

SERVES   4 - 6

pecan rice pilaf

1/2 cup butter, divided
1 cup chopped pecans
1/2 cup chopped onions
2 cups long-grain white rice, uncooked
2 cups chicken broth
2 cups water
1/2 teaspoon salt
1/4 teaspoon dried thyme
1/8 teaspoon freshly-ground pepper
3 tablespoons snipped fresh parsley, divided

in large skillet melt 3 tablespoons of the butter over medium-high heat. Add pecans. Saute 2 to 3 minutes or until lightly browned. Using slotted spoon transfer pecans to small bowl. Cover and set aside.

In same skillet melt remaining 5 tablespoons butter over medium-high heat. Add onions. Saute 5 minutes or just until tender. Add rice. Gently toss to coat.

Meanwhile, in large saucepan combine chicken broth, water, salt, thyme, pepper and 2 tablespoons of the parsley. Bring to boil. Add rice mixture. Reduce heat. Cover and simmer 20 minutes or until liquid is absorbed. Stir in pecans and remaining 1 tablespoon parsley. Fluff with fork. Serve immediately.

SERVES   6 -8

barley, shitake and spinach pilaf

4 cups vegetable broth or water
1 cup pearled barley
2 teaspoons dark Oriental sesame oil
1 teaspoon canola oil
1 medium onion, chopped
3 cups sliced button mushrooms
1-1/2 cups sliced shiitake mushrooms
2 cloves garlic, minced
2 cups torn fresh spinach
1 teaspoon sesame seeds
1 teaspoon low-sodium tamari or soy sauce
1/2 teaspoon cayenne (red pepper)

i n large saucepan combine vegetable broth or water and barley. Bring to boil. Reduce heat and cover. Simmer 45 minutes or until barley is tender and liquid is absorbed.

Meanwhile, in large non-stick skillet heat sesame and canola oils over medium-high heat. Add onion. Saute 5 to 7 minutes or until well-browned. (Add a splash of water to pan, as needed to prevent sticking.) Add mushrooms and garlic. Saute 3 minutes. Add cooked barley, spinach and sesame seeds. Cook 3 minutes or just until spinach is wilted and heated through. Add tamari or soy sauce and cayenne. Serve immediately.

SERVES   6 - 8

carrots in cognac

1/2 cup butter
1/2 teaspoon salt
1/2 teaspoon confectioners' sugar
1 pound fresh carrots, peeled and thinly sliced
2 tablespoons Cognac

i n large skillet melt butter over medium-high heat. Blend in salt and confectioners' sugar. Add carrots and Cognac. Cover tightly. Cook over lowest heat 45 minutes to 1 hour or just until crisp-tender. (Do not remove lid or stir during cooking.) Serve hot.

SERVES   8

baked eggplant extraordinaire

1 large eggplant, peeled and cut into 12 slices

2 medium tomatoes, cut into 12 slices

1 large onion, cut into 12 slices

1/2 cup melted butter or margarine, divided

1/2 teaspoon salt

1/2 teaspoon dried basil

1 package (8 ounces) sliced mozzarella cheese

1/2 cup seasoned dry bread crumbs

2 tablespoons grated Parmesan cheese

P reheat oven to 450 degrees. Arrange eggplant slices in large shallow pan such as a jelly roll pan. Place tomato and onion slice on top of each eggplant slice. Drizzle with 1/4 cup of the melted butter or margarine. Combine salt and basil. Sprinkle over vegetables. Bake, uncovered, 20 minutes. Remove from oven. Top with cheese slices. Combine remaining 1/4 cup melted butter and bread crumbs. Sprinkle over vegetables and cheese. Sprinkle with Parmesan cheese. Bake, uncovered, 5 minutes or just until cheese melts. Serve immediately.

SERVES   8 - 10

eggplant, zucchini and bell pepper saute

1 small eggplant

1 small red bell pepper

1 small zucchini

3-1/2 tablespoons olive oil

2 tablespoons snipped fresh basil or parsley

1 tablespoon butter

Salt and freshly-ground black pepper, to taste

S lice eggplant, bell pepper and zucchini into 2-1/2- x 1/3-inch strips. In large skillet heat 1-1/2 tablespoons of the olive oil over medium-high heat. Add eggplant. Saute 3 minutes or until lightly browned and soft. Remove from skillet and set aside.

In same skillet heat additional 1 tablespoon olive oil. Add bell pepper. Saute 1 minute. Add remaining tablespoon olive oil and zucchini. Saute 1 minute more. Return eggplant to same skillet. Heat through. Salt and pepper to taste. Serve immediately.

SERVES   2 - 4

saffron rice with sun-dried tomatoes

2 cups chicken stock or broth
Pinch saffron
1 cup rice, uncooked
1/4 cup olive oil
1/2 green bell pepper,
    seeded and chopped
1/2 red bell pepper,
    seeded and chopped
1 jalapeno pepper,
    seeded and chopped
1/2 stalk celery, chopped
2 small green onions,
    chopped
1 clove garlic, minced
1 teaspoon snipped fresh
    thyme or 1/4 teaspoon
    dried thyme
2 tablespoons (about 4)
    sun-dried tomatoes,
    chopped
Salt and freshly-ground
    black pepper, to taste

i n large saucepan combine chicken stock or broth and saffron. Bring to boil. Stir in rice. Reduce heat. Cover and cook 20 minutes or until tender. Remove from heat and set aside.

In large skillet heat olive oil over medium-high heat. Add bell pepper, jalapeno pepper, celery, green onions, garlic and thyme. Saute 5 minutes or until vegetables are soft. Stir in tomatoes. Cook 10 minutes or until rehydrated. Stir in cooked rice. Salt and pepper to taste. Serve immediately. (Recipe may be made several hours in advance. Cover and refrigerate until ready to use. Reheat over medium heat about 15 minutes.)

SERVES 4

the wildest wild rice

1/2 cup wild rice, uncooked
2 tablespoons butter
1 cup chopped onion
1 cup chopped green bell
  pepper
3/4 cup sliced mushrooms
1 cup condensed cream of
  mushroom soup
  (Do not dilute)
1/2 cup heavy or whipping
  cream
1/4 teaspoon salt
1/4 teaspoon curry powder
1/8 teaspoon freshly-ground
  black pepper
1/8 teaspoon dried
  marjoram
Dash dried basil
Dash dried tarragon
Snipped fresh dill

Cook rice according to package directions using chicken broth in place of water. Set aside. Meanwhile, in large skillet melt butter over medium-high heat. Add onion. Saute just until tender. Add green pepper and mushrooms. Saute additional 5 minutes. Stir in mushroom soup, cream, salt, curry powder, pepper, marjoram, basil and tarragon. Cook 10 minutes, stirring occasionally. Add cooked rice. Heat through. Top with fresh dill. Serve immediately.

SERVES   4 - 6

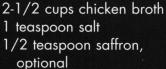

avocado rice

3 tablespoons butter
1 onion, chopped
1 clove garlic, minced
1 cup white rice, uncooked
2-1/2 cups chicken broth
1 teaspoon salt
1/2 teaspoon saffron,
  optional
Dash freshly-ground black
  pepper
2 avocados, peeled and
  chopped

In large skillet melt butter over medium-high heat. Add onion and garlic. Saute 2 to 3 minutes or just until tender. Add rice. Saute until slightly browned. Stir in chicken broth, salt, saffron and pepper. Bring to boil. Cover and reduce heat. Simmer 20 minutes or until rice is tender. Add avocados. Serve immediately.

SERVES   6 - 8

rice with fennel and fontina

1-1/2 cups short-grain white rice, uncooked
1 teaspoon salt
3 tablespoons butter, divided
1 tablespoon olive oil
1 medium onion, minced
2 small fennel bulbs, halved, cored and coarsely chopped
2 tablespoons minced fresh fennel leaves, divided
2 tablespoons snipped fresh parsley, divided
1/2 teaspoon fennel seeds
1/2 cup dry white wine
3/4 cup water
1/2 teaspoon salt
1/4 teaspoon freshly-ground black pepper
3/4 cup finely diced fontina cheese
1/2 cup freshly grated Parmesan cheese

Cook rice with 1 teaspoon salt according to package directions. Keep warm. Meanwhile, in large skillet heat 2 tablespoons of the butter and olive oil over medium-high heat. Add onion, fennel bulbs, 1 tablespoon of the fennel leaves, 1 tablespoon of the parsley and fennel seeds. Saute 3 minutes or until vegetables are tender. Add wine. Simmer over medium-high heat 2 minutes or until wine is reduced to 1/4 cup. Add water. Simmer 5 minutes or until fennel is tender and liquid is reduced to 1/2 cup. Stir in remaining 1 tablespoon butter, salt and pepper. Transfer rice to large serving bowl. Add fontina and Parmesan cheeses. Stir in fennel mixture. Sprinkle with remaining fennel leaves and parsley. Serve immediately.

SERVES 4

paxtang potatoes

2 green onions, minced
2 cloves garlic, minced
2 teaspoons snipped fresh
   thyme or 1 teaspoon dried
   thyme
1-3/4 teaspoons salt
1/2 teaspoon nutmeg
1/2 teaspoon white pepper
4-1/2 pounds potatoes,
  washed
3 to 3-1/2 cups half-and-half
   or light cream
2 tablespoons sweet
   (unsalted) butter

preheat oven to 300 degrees. In small bowl combine green onions, garlic, thyme, salt, nutmeg and pepper. Set aside.

Peel and cut potatoes into paper-thin slices. Rinse in cold water and drain. Arrange a third of the potato slices in buttered 3- to 4-quart casserole dish. Top with half of the green onion mixture. Top with another third of potatoes and remaining onion mixture. Finish with remaining potatoes. Pour just enough half-and-half or light cream over top to cover potatoes. Cover and set over very low heat 20 minutes. Dot with butter. Bake, uncovered, 2-1/2 hours or until potatoes are tender. Serve immediately.

SERVES   8

sweet potatoes in orange cups

8 medium sweet potatoes
1 cup light cream
3/4 cup packed brown
   sugar
1/2 cup butter
4 eggs, slightly beaten
1 teaspoon salt
1/4 teaspoon cinnamon
1/8 teaspoon allspice
1/2 cup sherry
1/4 cup chopped pecans
4 large oranges,
   washed and halved

preheat oven to 350 degrees. Bake potatoes 1 hour or until soft. Peel and mash until smooth. While potatoes are still hot, add cream, sugar, butter, eggs, salt, cinnamon and allspice, mixing well. Stir in sherry and pecans, reserving a few pecans for garnish. To make "cups," scoop out pulp from orange halves. Spoon sweet potato mixture into orange cups. Garnish with pecans. Place on baking sheet. Bake at 350 degrees for 20 minutes or until tops are browned. Serve immediately.

SERVES   8

mashed potatoes
with roasted shallot hollandaise

4 shallots (Do not peel)
1 tablespoon olive oil
1 tablespoon salt
4 large (about 2 pounds)
    potatoes, peeled and
    quartered
Hollandaise Sauce
    (recipe follows)
1/3 cup heavy or whipping
    cream
1/3 cup milk
3 tablespoons butter
Salt and freshly-ground
    black pepper

Preheat oven to 500 degrees. Toss unpeeled shallots with olive oil and 1 tablespoon salt. Arrange in baking pan. Roast 25 minutes or until soft, stirring occasionally. Cool, skin and mince. Set aside.

In medium saucepan cover potatoes with cold, lightly salted water. Bring to boil. Cook 20 minutes or until tender. Drain. Meanwhile prepare Hollandaise Sauce and add minced roasted shallots. Mash potatoes and transfer to saucepan with cream, milk and butter. Salt and pepper to taste. Heat through over medium-low heat, stirring constantly. Serve immediately, topped with Hollandaise.

hollandaise sauce:

In small saucepan slowly melt 1/2 cup butter. Keep warm. In separate saucepan heat 1-1/2 tablespoons fresh lemon juice or dry sherry just until warm. In top of double boiler over hot, not boiling water, beat 3 egg yolks with wire whisk until slightly thickened. Whisk in 1/4 cup boiling water, 1 tablespoon at a time, beating well after each addition. Whisk in the warm lemon juice or sherry. Remove from heat. Beat with wire whisk while slowly adding warm butter, 1/4 teaspoon salt and pinch cayenne (red pepper). Beat until thick.

SERVES   4

spicy roast potatoes

2 pounds red potatoes,
  washed (Do not peel)
2 tablespoons olive oil
1/4 teaspoon cayenne
  (red pepper)
Salt, to taste
Freshly-ground black pepper,
  to taste
Vegetable oil cooking spray

Preheat oven to 450 degrees. Line large baking sheet with foil. Lightly coat with cooking spray. Slice potatoes into 1/4-inch French fries.

In large bowl combine oil and cayenne. Add potatoes. Toss to coat with oil mixture. Arrange in single layer on prepared baking sheet. Bake 10 minutes. Remove from oven and turn. Salt and pepper to taste. Bake additional 10 minutes. Salt and pepper, again, if desired. Serve immediately.

SERVES   4

perfect potatoes with dill

2 tablespoons butter
1 small onion, halved and
  thinly sliced
1-1/2 pounds new red
  potatoes, washed and cut
  into 1/4-inch slices
  (Do not peel)
1-1/2 cups chicken broth
1 bay leaf
Salt, to taste
Freshly-ground black pepper,
  to taste
1 tablespoon snipped fresh
  dill

In large saucepan melt butter over medium-high heat. Add onion. Saute until translucent. Add sliced potatoes, chicken broth and bay leaf. Cover and bring to boil. Reduce heat. Simmer 5 minutes. Uncover and continue cooking until liquid evaporates. Remove and discard bay leaf. Salt and pepper to taste. Transfer to large serving dish. Sprinkle with dill. Serve immediately.

SERVES   4

spanish potatoes

1/4 cup olive oil
1/4 cup fine dry bread
   crumbs
2 cloves garlic, minced
1 tablespoon finely chopped
   black olives
2 teaspoons paprika
1 teaspoon salt
4 large baking potatoes,
   washed (Do not peel)

preheat oven to 375 degrees. In small bowl combine olive oil, bread crumbs, garlic, black olives, paprika and salt. Slice potatoes in half lengthwise. Score cut sides of potato halves. Top each with half tablespoonful of bread crumb mixture. Place on baking sheet. Bake 40 to 50 minutes or until potatoes are crisp on top and tender inside. Serve immediately.

SERVES   8

grilled sweet potatoes
with garlic and thyme

1-1/2 pounds sweet
   potatoes, peeled and cut
   into small chunks
12 cloves garlic
12 sprigs fresh thyme
1/3 cup butter, sliced
Salt and freshly-ground
   black pepper, to taste
6 large pieces aluminum
   foil, folded in half to
   make double layers

divide sweet potatoes evenly among double layers of foil. To each add 2 cloves garlic, 2 sprigs thyme and slices of butter. Salt and pepper to taste. Pull foil up and around mixtures, sealing closed. Place over medium-hot coals. Grill 20 to 25minutes or until potatoes are tender. Serve in foil.

SERVES   6

mashed potatoes with pesto

6 medium (about 2-1/2 pounds) baking potatoes, peeled and quartered
1/2 cup firmly-packed snipped fresh basil leaves
1/4 cup extra-virgin olive oil
1/4 cup freshly grated Parmesan cheese
1 clove garlic
1/2 cup sour cream
6 tablespoons butter
White pepper, to taste

In large saucepan cover potatoes with cold, lightly salted water. Bring to boil. Cook 20 minutes or until tender. Drain. Meanwhile, in food processor combine basil leaves, olive oil, Parmesan cheese and garlic. Process until smooth to make pesto. Set aside.

Mash potatoes with sour cream, butter and white pepper, to taste. Add pesto mixture, blending well. Serve immediately.

SERVES   6 - 8

sun-dried tomato potatoes

2 baking potatoes, washed and pricked with fork
2 cloves garlic, minced
4 sun-dried tomatoes in oil, well-drained
1 tablespoon capers
Salt, to taste
Freshly-ground black pepper, to taste
1/4 cup shredded mozzarella cheese
Vegetable oil cooking spray

Preheat oven to 400 degrees. Bake potatoes 45 minutes or until tender. (Potatoes may also be baked in microwave.) Meanwhile, coat small nonstick skillet with cooking spray. Heat over medium-high heat. Add garlic. Saute until lightly browned. Add tomatoes and capers. Stir until heated through. Salt and pepper to taste. Remove from heat and set aside until potatoes are baked. Split potatoes. Top with sauteed tomato mixture. Sprinkle with cheese. Place on baking sheet. Broil just until cheese melts. Serve immediately.

SERVES   2

stir-fried broccoli and carrots

1/3 cup light corn syrup
3 tablespoons cider vinegar
2 tablespoons cornstarch
2 tablespoons soy sauce
1/2 teaspoon ground ginger
1 pound fresh broccoli,
   washed and trimmed
2 tablespoons vegetable oil
2 medium carrots, peeled
   and cut into julienne strips
2 medium onions, cut into
   wedges
1 can (8 ounces) water
   chestnuts, drained and
   sliced
1/4 cup chopped roasted
   cashews

i n small bowl combine corn syrup, vinegar, cornstarch, soy sauce and ginger. Set aside. Cut broccoli into small florets and set aside.

Slice broccoli stems and set aside. In large skillet heat oil over medium-high heat. Add broccoli stems, carrot strips and onion wedges. Stir-fry 2 minutes or until crisp-tender. Add broccoli florets and water chestnuts. Stir-fry additional minute or until crisp-tender. Pour soy sauce mixture over vegetables, tossing to coat. Cook 1 to 2 minutes or just until sauce thickens. Sprinkle with cashews. Serve immediately.

SERVES 4 - 6

roasted cauliflower with rosemary

3 pounds (about 1-1/2
   heads) fresh cauliflower,
   cut into 1-inch florets
2 tablespoons olive oil
2 tablespoons snipped
   fresh rosemary or 1
   teaspoon dried rosemary
Salt and freshly-ground
   black pepper, to taste

p reheat oven to 500 degrees. In 15-1/2- x 10-1/2-inch jelly roll pan toss cauliflower with olive oil and rosemary, coating well. Salt and pepper to taste. Roast in middle of oven 12 to 15 minutes or until browned in spots and tender. Serve immediately.

SERVES 8

garden medley

3 cups chicken broth
1 cup brown rice, uncooked
1 teaspoon salt
1/2 teaspoon dried basil
1/2 teaspoon dried thyme
2 tablespoons vegetable oil
1-1/2 cups diced peeled
 eggplant
1/2 cup chopped onion
1 clove garlic, crushed
1 cup sliced zucchini
1/2 cup chopped green
 bell pepper
1 large tomato, diced
1 cup shredded Swiss
 cheese
1 cup shredded Monterey
 Jack cheese
Vegetable oil cooking spray

in large saucepan bring broth to boil. Add rice, salt, basil and thyme. Cover and reduce heat. Simmer 50 minutes or until rice is tender and liquid is absorbed. Meanwhile, preheat oven to 325 degrees.

In large skillet heat oil over medium-high heat. Add eggplant, onion and garlic. Saute until tender. Add eggplant mixture, zucchini, bell pepper and tomato to cooked rice. Spoon half of mixture into 2-quart casserole dish which has been lightly coated with cooking spray. Combine Swiss and Monterey Jack cheeses. Sprinkle 1-1/2 cups over vegetable-rice mixture in pan. Top with remaining vegetable-rice mixture. Sprinkle with remaining 1/2 cup cheese mixture. Bake 25 minutes or until heated through. Serve immediately.

SERVES 6 - 8

glazed acorn squash

1 large acorn squash
1/3 cup orange juice
1/2 cup firmly packed
 brown sugar
1/4 cup light corn syrup
1/4 cup butter or margarine
2 teaspoons freshly-grated
 lemon peel
1/8 teaspoon salt
Vegetable oil cooking spray

preheat oven to 350 degrees. Wash and cut squash into 3/4-inch slices. Remove and discard seeds and membrane. Arrange squash in shallow baking dish which has been lightly coated with cooking spray. Pour orange juice over top. Cover and bake 30 minutes.

In small saucepan combine brown sugar, corn syrup, butter or margarine, lemon peel and salt. Bring to boil, stirring constantly. Reduce heat and simmer 5 minutes or until slightly thickened, stirring occasionally. Spoon over baked squash. Bake, uncovered, additional 15 to 20 minutes or until squash is tender, basting occasionally with liquid from pan. Serve immediately.

SERVES 2 - 4

curried tomatoes

3/4 cup minced fresh onion
1/2 teaspoon salt
1/4 teaspoon sugar
1/4 teaspoon curry powder
6 medium tomatoes, halved
1/4 cup butter, divided
2 tablespoons snipped fresh
   parsley

i n small bowl combine onion, salt, sugar and curry powder. Spread over tomato halves. Top each with 1 teaspoon butter. Place on broiler rack over pan. Broil about 6 inches from heat 8 to 10 minutes or until tomatoes are tender. Sprinkle with parsley. Serve immediately.

SERVES   12

artichoke stuffed tomatoes

6 tomatoes
1 cup shredded Monterey
   Jack cheese
1 cup chopped canned
   artichoke hearts
   (not marinated)
1/4 cup butter, softened
1/8 teaspoon garlic powder
Salt, to taste
Freshly-ground black pepper,
   to taste
Parmesan cheese

p reheat oven to 350 degrees. Scoop out and reserve inside of tomatoes. Arrange tomatoes in baking dish. Set aside.

In medium bowl combine Monterey Jack cheese, artichoke hearts, butter and garlic powder, adding some of the reserved tomato pulp for desired moistness. Salt and pepper to taste. Spoon into tomatoes and return to baking dish. Sprinkle with Parmesan cheese. Bake 30 minutes or until tomatoes are tender and bubbly. Serve immediately.

SERVES   6

steamed asparagus with almond butter

2 pounds fresh asparagus, washed and trimmed
1/2 cup sweet (unsalted) butter, divided
3 tablespoons finely chopped shallots
1 large clove garlic, minced
3 tablespoons snipped fresh parsley
2 teaspoons fresh lemon juice
2 teaspoons freshly-grated lemon peel
1/4 cup sliced almonds
Salt, to taste
Freshly-ground black pepper, to taste

Steam asparagus until crisp-tender. Meanwhile, in large skillet melt 2 tablespoons of the butter over medium-high heat. Add shallots and garlic. Saute 5 minutes or just until tender. Remove from skillet and set aside. To skillet add remaining 6 tablespoons butter. Melt over medium heat. Whisk in parsley, lemon juice and lemon peel. Add almonds and reserved shallot mixture. Cook 3 minutes or until butter is browned, stirring occasionally. Add cooked asparagus, turning to coat with butter mixture. Salt and pepper, to taste. Serve immediately.

SERVES 8

spinach and white beans with garlic

1 tablespoon olive oil
1 clove garlic, minced
1/2 pound fresh spinach, cleaned, dried and coarsely chopped
1 can (about 16 ounces) white beans, rinsed and drained well
1 tablespoon balsamic vinegar
Salt and freshly-ground black pepper, to taste

In large skillet heat oil over medium heat. Add garlic. Saute until pale golden color. Add spinach. Cook and stir until wilted. Add beans and vinegar. Salt and pepper to taste. Simmer 2 minutes, stirring constantly. Serve immediately.

SERVES 2

baked cabbage with cheddar and dill

1 medium head cabbage, washed and cut into 8 wedges
1/4 cup butter or margarine
1/2 cup finely chopped green bell pepper
1/4 cup finely chopped onion
1/4 cup all-purpose flour
1/2 teaspoon salt
1/2 teaspoon freshly-ground black pepper
2 cups milk
1/2 cup mayonnaise or salad dressing
3/4 cup shredded Cheddar cheese
3 tablespoons chili sauce
2 tablespoons snipped fresh dill

Place cabbage wedges in Dutch oven or large saucepan. Add small amount of water and dash salt. Cover and bring to boil. Reduce heat. Cook 12 minutes or until tender. Drain and transfer to oblong baking dish. Set aside.

Preheat oven to 375 degrees. In medium saucepan melt butter or margarine over medium-high heat. Add bell pepper and onion. Saute just until tender but not browned. Stir in flour, salt and pepper. Add milk, mixing well. Cook over medium heat, stirring constantly, until thickened and bubbly. Pour over cabbage. Bake, uncovered, 20 minutes. In small bowl combine mayonnaise or salad dressing, cheese, chili sauce and dill. Spoon over cabbage. Bake additional 5 minutes. Serve immediately.

SERVES   8

santa fe summer vegetables

1/4 cup butter
1 bag (about 16 ounces)
  frozen corn, partially
  thawed
1/2 cup chopped onion
1 clove garlic, minced
4 medium zucchini, diced
  (Do not peel)
4 cans (4 ounces each)
  chopped green chiles
1/2 cup water
1 teaspoon salt
1/4 teaspoon freshly-ground
  black pepper
3/4 cup shredded Monterey
  Jack or Cheddar cheese

i n large skillet melt butter over medium-high heat. Add corn. Saute 2 minutes. Add onion and garlic. Saute additional 2 minutes or just until tender, stirring occasionally. Add zucchini, green chilies, water, salt and pepper. Cook, uncovered, 15 minutes or until zucchini is tender. Sprinkle with cheese. Serve immediately.

SERVES   8 - 10

sesame snow peas

3 tablespoons sesame oil
1 pound fresh snow peas,
  washed and trimmed
10 green onions, sliced
2 tablespoons pine nuts
1 tablespoon toasted sesame
  seeds
Salt, to taste
Freshly-ground black pepper,
  to taste

i n wok or large skillet heat oil over medium-high heat. Add snow peas and green onions. Stir-fry 3 minutes. Add pine nuts and sesame seeds. Stir-fry additional 2 to 3 minutes, stirring constantly. Salt and pepper, to taste. Serve immediately.

SERVES   4 - 6

vegetable kabobs
with herbed yogurt sauce

12 fresh pearl onions,
   peeled and halved
24 button mushrooms
2 red bell peppers,
   seeded and cut into 12
   pieces
2 yellow bell peppers,
   seeded and cut into 12
   pieces
4 large zucchini, cut into 6
   x 1-inch slices
2/3 cup olive oil
1 tablespoon fresh lemon
   juice
1 tablespoon coriander
   seeds, crushed
2 teaspoons cumin seeds,
   crushed
2 fresh sprigs thyme,
   snipped
2 fresh sprigs sage,
   snipped
1 teaspoon fresh green
   peppercorns, crushed
Pinch freshly grated nutmeg
Herbed Yogurt Sauce
   (recipe follows)
24 bay leaves
Cold water

i n large bowl combine onions, mushrooms, bell peppers and zucchini. In small bowl whisk together olive oil and lemon juice. Pour over vegetables. Add coriander seeds, cumin seeds, thyme, sage, peppercorns and nutmeg. Toss gently to coat vegetables. Cover and refrigerate several hours or overnight to marinate.

About 30 minutes before cooking, soak bay leaves in cold water. Drain and pat dry with clean paper towels. Thread the marinated vegetables and bay leaves on 12 skewers. Grill over medium-hot coals 15 minutes or until lightly browned and tender, turning once and basting with leftover marinade. Serve immediately with Herbed Yogurt Sauce.

herbed yogurt sauce:

In small bowl combine 1-1/4 cups plain yogurt, 1 tablespoon fresh lemon juice, 1 tablespoon snipped fresh mint, 1 tablespoon snipped fresh dill, 1 teaspoon ground cumin and pinch cayenne (red pepper). Salt and pepper to taste. Cover and refrigerate until ready to serve.

SERVES   6

front street zucchini

2 cups zucchini grated and
   well drained
1 cup bread crumbs
   (unseasoned)
1 egg slightly beaten
1 teaspoon Old Bay
   seasoning
1/2 teaspoon garlic powder
1/2 teaspoon salt
Freshly ground pepper
   to taste
1-2 cups vegetable oil

i n small bowl combine zucchini, bread crumbs, egg, Old Bay seasoning, garlic powder, salt and pepper. Shape into 3 inch patties. Saute in vegetable oil 4 minutes per side. Add additional vegetable oil as needed. Serve immediately.

SERVES   4 - 6

zucchini with sun-dried tomatoes

1/2 cup sun-dried tomatoes
   with oil
4 medium zucchini, sliced
   (Do not peel)
1 tablespoon snipped fresh
   rosemary
1/4 teaspoon salt
1/8 teaspoon freshly-ground
   black pepper

d rain and reserve 2 tablespoons oil from tomatoes. Slice tomatoes into julienne strips. Set aside. Heat reserved oil in large skillet over medium-high heat. Add zucchini. Saute 5 minutes or until crisp-tender and lightly browned. Add tomato strips, rosemary, salt and pepper, tossing gently. Serve immediately.

SERVES   4

desserts

Nothing satisfies the cravings of a sweet tooth quite like chocolate. And while it takes but a few minutes (or less, on occasion) to consume a Hershey's milk chocolate bar, it takes 10 days - from cocoa beans through to finished product - to produce this classic confectionery. The smooth richness of this choco-holic palate pleaser is derived from wholesome milk, of which the Hershey Chocolate U.S.A. plant uses 700,000 quarts (1.5 million pounds) daily - enough to provide a city the size of Philadelphia with their daily consumption amount.

italian love cake

1 package (about 18 to 19 ounces) chocolate cake mix
2 pounds ricotta cheese
4 eggs
3/4 cup sugar
1 teaspoon vanilla extract
Chocolate Topping
(recipe follows)

Preheat oven to 325 degrees. Grease and flour a 13 x 9-inch oblong pan. Prepare cake batter according to package directions. Pour into prepared pan. In separate bowl combine ricotta cheese, eggs, sugar and vanilla extract, mixing well. Spread over cake batter in pan. Bake 1 hour and 15 minutes or until toothpick inserted comes out clean. Cool completely in pan. Frost with Chocolate Topping. Refrigerate until ready to serve.

chocolate topping:

In large bowl combine 1 package (4-serving size) instant chocolate pudding mix and 1 cup milk. Fold in 1 container (8 ounces) thawed frozen whipped topping.

variation:

For thinner cake, bake in a greased and floured jelly roll pan.

SERVES   10 - 12

nectarine shortcake

1/2 cup all-purpose flour
1/2 cup cake flour
1-1/2 tablespoons sugar
1 teaspoon baking powder
1 teaspoon baking soda
3 tablespoons sweet
   (unsalted) butter
About 1/3 cup buttermilk
Nectarine Sauce
   (recipe follows)
Sweetened whipped cream
Fresh mint leaves

Preheat oven to 450 degrees. In medium bowl combine flours, sugar, baking powder and baking soda. Cut in butter with pastry cutter or two forks until mixture forms coarse crumbs. Stir in just enough of the buttermilk to form soft dough. On lightly floured surface roll dough to 1-inch thickness. Using large biscuit cutter cut into 4 large rounds. Place on ungreased baking sheet. Bake 12 minutes or until lightly browned. Remove from baking sheet and cool completely on wire rack. Prepare Nectarine Sauce. Cut each shortcake in half crosswise. Place bottom halves on serving plates. Top with Nectarine Sauce. Cover with remaining shortcake halves. Garnish with sweetened whipped cream and mint leaves.

nectarine sauce:

Peel and slice 4 large nectarines, reserving skins. Place in bowl and set aside. In food processor puree reserved nectarine skins, 1/2 cup peach preserves and 1/4 cup fresh orange juice. Toss with sliced nectarines. Cover and refrigerate until ready to serve.

SERVES   4

chocolate velvet cake

3 squares (3 ounces)
  unsweetened baking
  chocolate
1 cup water
2-1/2 cups sifted cake flour
1-1/2 teaspoons baking soda
1/2 cup butter or regular
  stick margarine
2 cups sugar
3 eggs
1 teaspoon vanilla extract
1 cup buttermilk
Creamy Coffee Frosting
  (recipe follows)
1 square (1 ounce)
  unsweetened baking
  chocolate
1 teaspoon butter or regular
  stick margarine

Preheat oven to 350 degrees. Grease two 9-inch round cake pans. Line bottoms with wax paper. In small saucepan combine 3 squares baking chocolate and water. Bring to boil over medium heat, stirring constantly. Remove from heat and cool completely. Sift together flour and baking soda. Set aside.

In large bowl cream butter or margarine and sugar until light and fluffy. Add eggs, one at a time, beating well after each addition. Blend in vanilla extract. Add flour mixture alternately with buttermilk to creamed mixture, beating on low speed after each addition. Beat in cooled chocolate mixture. Pour into prepared pans. Bake 35 minutes or until toothpick inserted comes out clean. Cool 10 minutes in pans. Remove from pans and cool completely on wire racks.

Spread Creamy Coffee Frosting on top of one cake layer. Place second cake layer on top. Spread sides and top of cake with remaining frosting. In small saucepan melt 1 square baking chocolate and 1 teaspoon butter or margarine over very low heat, stirring occasionally. Cool slightly. Spoon around edge of cake, allowing to drip down sides.

creamy coffee frosting:

In small bowl combine 2 tablespoons hot water and 2 teaspoons instant coffee granules. In large bowl beat 3/4 cup butter or regular stick margarine until softened. Blend in 6 cups sifted confectioners' sugar, 1/4 cup milk, 1 teaspoon vanilla extract and coffee mixture. Beat until smooth and creamy.

SERVES   8 - 10

lemon lush cake

1 tablespoon melted butter
Confectioners' sugar
2 to 3 small lemons
1-1/4 cups sugar, divided
3/4 cup whole milk (Do not use low-fat or skim milk.)
1/2 cup butter or margarine
2/3 cup cake flour
6 eggs, separated
Dash salt
Lemon-Sour Cream Sauce (recipe follows)
Lemon slices, fresh daisies

preheat oven to 325 degrees. Brush a 12-cup Bundt pan with melted butter. Dust with confectioners' sugar, shaking out excess. Fill a 3-inch deep baking pan large enough to hold Bundt pan with 1 to 2 inches of water. Place in preheated oven while preparing cake batter. Remove peel from 2 of the lemons, being careful not to include white portion. Squeeze lemons to make 1/3 cup juice. Set aside.

Place lemon peel and 1/2 cup of the sugar in food processor. Process until peel is minced as finely as the sugar. Transfer to 2-quart microwave-proof bowl. Add milk and butter or margarine. Cover and microwave on high (full power) 2 to 3 minutes or until butter or margarine is melted. Return to food processor. Add flour. Process just until blended. With processor running, gradually add egg yolks. Add lemon juice and process a few seconds to blend. Set aside.

In large bowl beat egg whites with salt until soft peaks form. Gradually beat in remaining 3/4 cup sugar, 2 tablespoons at a time, until stiff but not dry peaks form. Fold in one-third of the egg yolk mixture, then remaining egg yolk mixture. Spoon and spread evenly in preheated Bundt pan. Bake in hot water bath 50 to 55 minutes or until top is golden brown and cracked. Cool 15 minutes in pan. (Cake will fall.) Run spatula around edge of warm cake. Invert onto serving plate. Serve warm or at room temperature with Lemon-Sour Cream Sauce. Garnish with lemon slices, daisies and mint leaves.

lemon-sour cream sauce:

In medium bowl combine 1 cup regular or light sour cream, 1/2 cup sugar, 3 to 4 tablespoons fresh lemon juice, to taste, and 2 tablespoons heavy or whipping cream. Cover and refrigerate until ready to serve.

SERVES 10 - 12

white chocolate frangelico cake

1 teaspoon baking soda
1 cup buttermilk
4 ounces white chocolate
1 cup sweet (unsalted) butter
2 cups sugar
4 eggs
1 teaspoon vanilla extract
Dash salt, optional
2-1/2 cups sifted cake flour
1 cup flaked coconut
Vegetable oil cooking spray
Frangelico Cream Cheese
   Frosting (recipe follows)

Preheat oven to 350 degrees. Lightly spray two 9-inch round cake pans with vegetable oil cooking spray. Line bottoms with parchment or wax paper. Stir baking soda into buttermilk. Set aside.

Melt white chocolate in top of double boiler over hot, not boiling, water, stirring constantly. Remove from heat. (Or, place chocolate in medium microwave-proof bowl. Microwave on high [full power] 1 minute or just until softened. Stir. If necessary, microwave on high an additional 30 seconds or just until melted.)

In large bowl cream butter, sugar and melted white chocolate. Add eggs, vanilla extract and if desired, salt, beating well. Add buttermilk-baking soda mixture alternately with flour to butter-sugar mixture in bowl, beating well after each addition. Stir in coconut. Pour into prepared pans. Bake 25 to 30 minutes. Cool 10 minutes in pans. Remove from pans and cool completely on wire racks. Frost with Frangelico Cream Cheese Frosting.

frangelico cream cheese frosting:

In large bowl beat 1 package (8 ounces) cream cheese and 1/2 cup sweet (unsalted) butter until softened. Blend in 5 cups unsifted confectioners' sugar and 2 to 3 tablespoons Frangelico liqueur. Beat until smooth and creamy. Adjust amount of liqueur, as needed, for spreading consistency.

SERVES   8 - 10

very berry lemon pound cake

2 eggs
2 egg yolks
3/4 cup sugar
1/3 cup fresh lemon juice
2 teaspoons freshly-grated
    lemon peel
3 tablespoons butter, cut
    into small pieces
1-1/2 cups chilled heavy
    or whipping cream
3 tablespoons sugar
3 tablespoons orange
    liqueur
1 package (12 ounces)
    pound cake
1 pint fresh raspberries or
    strawberries, hulled
    and sliced
Lemon peel curls

i n heavy saucepan beat eggs, egg yolks and 3/4 cup sugar with wire whisk until blended and slightly thickened. Add lemon juice, lemon peel and butter. Stir constantly over medium-low heat until mixture thickens and just begins to boil, about 5 minutes. Transfer to bowl. Cover and refrigerate several hours or overnight.

In large bowl whip cream until soft peaks form. Add 3 tablespoons sugar and orange liqueur. Continue whipping until cream is almost stiff. Cut cake horizontally into 4 layers. Place bottom layer on serving plate.

Top with 1/3 cup chilled lemon mixture. Arrange single layer of berries on top. Top with 1/3 cup whipped cream. Repeat layers twice. Top with remaining cake layer. Frost top and sides of cake with remaining whipped cream. Arrange remaining berries on top. Garnish with lemon curls. Cover and refrigerate at least 1 hour before serving.

SERVES   6

dessert cheese ball

1 cup raisins
1/2 cup rum
3 packages (8 ounces each)
    cream cheese
1-1/2 cups chopped toasted
    pecans*
1 cup semi-sweet chocolate
    chips
1 teaspoon cinnamon
Ginger snaps

s oak raisins in rum 24 hours. Drain well. In large bowl beat cream cheese until softened. Stir in drained raisins, toasted pecans, chocolate chips and cinnamon. Shape into ball. Cover and refrigerate several hours or overnight. Serve with ginger snaps.

*to toast pecans:

Preheat oven to 350 degrees. Arrange pecans in single layer on baking sheet. Bake 3 to 5 minutes or just until very lightly browned, stirring once during baking. Cool completely on baking sheet.

SERVES   20

banana cream cake

3 ripe bananas, mashed
1/2 cup buttermilk
1 teaspoon vanilla extract
2 cups cake flour
1 teaspoon baking powder
1 teaspoon baking soda
1/2 teaspoon salt
3/4 cup sweet (unsalted) butter
1-1/2 cups sugar
2 eggs
1 cup finely chopped walnuts, divided
1-1/2 cups heavy or whipping cream
2 teaspoons sugar
1 banana, sliced

Preheat oven to 350 degrees. Butter and flour two 8-inch round cake pans. In small bowl combine mashed banana, buttermilk and vanilla extract. Set aside. Sift together flour, baking powder, baking soda and salt.

In large bowl cream butter and 1-1/2 cups sugar until light and fluffy. Add eggs, one at a time, beating well after each addition. Beat in flour mixture alternately with banana mixture. Stir in 3/4 cup of the walnuts. Spoon into prepared pans. Bake 35 to 40 minutes or until toothpick inserted comes out clean. Cool 10 minutes in pans. Remove from pans and cool completely on wire racks.

In large bowl whip cream until soft peaks form. Add 2 teaspoons sugar. Continue whipping until cream is almost stiff. Top one cake layer with one-third of the whipped cream. Place second cake layer on top. Spread sides and top of cake with remaining whipped cream. Garnish with banana slices and remaining 1/4 cup walnuts. Refrigerate until ready to serve.

SERVES   10 - 12

spumoni dessert

2-1/2 cups lime sherbet, softened
2 tablespoons chopped pistachio nuts
1 can (8 ounces) unsweetened crushed pineapple, drained
1-1/2 cups vanilla ice cream, softened
2 cups raspberry sherbet, softened
Additional chopped pistachio nuts

Line a 9 x 5-inch loaf pan with wax paper. In large bowl combine lime sherbet and 2 tablespoons pistachio nuts. Spoon and spread evenly into prepared pan. Cover and freeze 30 minutes. Using paper towels squeeze excess moisture from pineapple. Stir into ice cream. Spoon and spread over sherbet in pan. Cover and return to freezer 30 minutes. Spoon and spread raspberry sherbet over ice cream in pan. Cover and freeze several hours or overnight. Invert onto serving plate. Remove wax paper. Garnish with additional pistachio nuts

SERVES   8

gingerbread cupcakes
with lemon-cream cheese frosting

1/4 cup sweet (unsalted) butter
1/2 cup sugar
1/2 cup molasses
1 egg
1 teaspoon baking soda
1/2 cup boiling water
1-1/4 cups all-purpose flour
1-1/2 teaspoons ginger
1 teaspoon cinnamon
1/2 teaspoon allspice
1/4 teaspoon cloves
1/4 teaspoon salt
Lemon-Cream Cheese Frosting (recipe follows)
Thinly sliced crystallized ginger

Preheat oven to 350 degrees. Paper-line standard-size muffin cups. In large bowl cream butter and sugar until light and fluffy. Add molasses and egg, beating well.

In small bowl combine baking soda and water, stirring until baking soda dissolves. Stir into molasses mixture. (Mixture will look curdled.) Combine flour, ginger, cinnamon, allspice, cloves and salt. Blend into molasses mixture. Fill prepared muffin cups 1/2 full with batter. Bake 20 minutes or until toothpick inserted comes out clean. Cool completely on wire rack. Frost with Lemon-Cream Cheese Frosting. Garnish with crystallized ginger.

lemon-cream cheese frosting:

In large bowl beat 1 package (8 ounces) cream cheese and 2 tablespoons butter until softened. Blend in 1-1/2 cups confectioners' sugar, 2 teaspoons fresh lemon juice, 1 teaspoon freshly-grated lemon peel and 1/2 teaspoon vanilla extract. Beat until smooth and creamy. Cover and refrigerate 30 minutes.

MAKES   1 DOZEN

shoofly cupcakes

1 tablespoon baking soda
2-1/4 cups boiling water
1 cup molasses
1 box (1 pound) light brown sugar
3/4 cup butter
4 cups all-purpose flour
1/4 teaspoon salt

Preheat oven to 375 degrees. Grease or paper-line standard-size muffin cups. In medium bowl stir baking soda into boiling water. Stir in molasses. Set aside.

In large bowl combine brown sugar and butter, using spoon to work out lumps. Combine flour and salt. Stir into brown sugar mixture. Measure out and set aside 1-1/2 cups of mixture. To remaining brown sugar-flour mixture in large bowl add molasses mixture, stirring well. (Batter will be slightly lumpy.) Fill prepared muffin cups 2/3 full with batter. Sprinkle with reserved 1-1/2 cups brown sugar mixture. Bake 20 to 25 minutes. Serve warm or at room temperature. (Cupcakes freeze well.)

MAKES   3 DOZEN

hungarian chocolate cake

10 egg yolks
2/3 cup sugar
10 tablespoons butter
8 ounces bittersweet or
   German-sweet baking
   chocolate
1 cup very finely ground
   pecans
8 egg whites
3/4 cup apricot preserves
2/3 cup chopped pecans
Chocolate Topping
   (recipe follows)

P reheat oven to 350 degrees. Grease and flour a 9-inch springform pan. In large bowl combine egg yolks and sugar. Set aside, stirring occasionally to dissolve sugar. (Do not beat.)

In top of double boiler, melt butter and baking chocolate over hot, not boiling, water. Stir occasionally until mixture is blended and smooth. Stir into egg yolk-sugar mixture. Add ground pecans.

In separate bowl beat egg whites until stiff but not dry. Stir one-fourth of the egg whites into the pecan mixture. Fold in remaining egg whites. Pour into prepared pan. Bake 50 to 60 minutes or until center springs back when lightly touched. Run spatula around edge of warm cake. Cool completely in pan. Remove side of pan and transfer cake to serving plate. Slice cross-wise and spread preserves on top of half layer. Top with second half of layer. Spread Chocolate Topping on top of cake. Garnish with chopped pecans. Refrigerate until ready to serve.

chocolate topping:

In small saucepan combine 1 cup semi-sweet chocolate chips and 1/2 cup heavy or whipping cream. Cook over low heat, stirring constantly, until chocolate is melted and blended with cream.

SERVES 8 - 10

frozen mocha pie

1 package (9 ounces)
   chocolate wafers
1/3 cup melted butter
1/2 gallon coffee ice
   cream, softened
1 jar (about 12 to 16
   ounces) hot fudge sauce
Chopped pecans

C rush chocolate wafers to make crumbs. Add melted butter, mixing well. Press onto bottom of a 13 x 9-inch oblong pan. Cover and freeze about 15 minutes. Spoon softened ice cream into crumb crust. Drizzle with fudge sauce. Garnish with pecans. Cover and freeze until ready to serve.

SERVES 10 - 12

italian cream cake

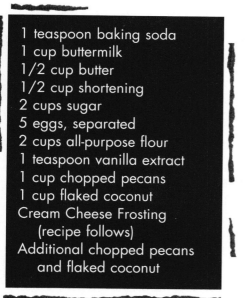

1 teaspoon baking soda
1 cup buttermilk
1/2 cup butter
1/2 cup shortening
2 cups sugar
5 eggs, separated
2 cups all-purpose flour
1 teaspoon vanilla extract
1 cup chopped pecans
1 cup flaked coconut
Cream Cheese Frosting
   (recipe follows)
Additional chopped pecans
   and flaked coconut

Preheat oven to 325 degrees. Grease three 9-inch round cake pans. Stir baking soda into buttermilk. Set aside.

In large bowl cream butter, shortening and sugar until light and fluffy. Add egg yolks, one at a time, beating well after each addition. Add buttermilk-baking soda mixture alternately with flour to butter-sugar mixture in bowl, beating well after each addition. Stir in vanilla extract.

In separate bowl beat egg whites until stiff. Fold into batter. Gently stir in pecans and coconut. Pour into prepared pans. Bake 30 minutes. Cool in pans 10 minutes. Remove from pans and cool completely on wire racks. Frost with Cream Cheese Frosting and garnish with additional chopped pecans and flaked coconut.

cream cheese frosting:

In large bowl beat 1 package (8 ounces) cream cheese and 1/2 cup butter until softened. Blend in a 1-pound box confectioners' sugar and 1 teaspoon vanilla extract. Beat until smooth and creamy.

SERVES   12

irish cream brownie pie

1 -9-inch pie crust, unbaked
1/2 cup sweet (unsalted)
   butter
2 squares (2 ounces)
   unsweetened baking
   chocolate
2 eggs
1 cup sugar
2 tablespoons Bailey's Irish
   Cream Liqueur
1 teaspoon vanilla extract
1/3 cup all-purpose flour
1/4 teaspoon salt
1 cup chopped pecans
Ice cream or sweetened
   whipped cream

Preheat oven to 350 degrees. Refrigerate pie crust while preparing filling. In small saucepan melt butter and chocolate over very low heat, stirring constantly. Set aside to cool slightly.

In large bowl beat eggs until foamy. Gradually beat in sugar. Blend in chocolate mixture on low speed. Add liqueur and vanilla extract. Stir in flour and salt. Sprinkle pecans over bottom of pie crust. Spoon chocolate mixture on top. Bake 35 minutes or until crust is golden and filling is set. Cool completely. Serve with ice cream or sweetened whipped cream.

SERVES   6 - 8

sweet potato pie

3 pounds fresh sweet
  potatoes
2 cups sugar
1-1/2 cups half & half
1 cup melted butter
1 cup drained, crushed
  pineapple
3 eggs, well beaten
1/4 cup clear vanilla
  extract
1-1/2 tablespoons
  cinnamon
1/2 tablespoon nutmeg
2 teaspoons lemon extract
Three 9-inch deep-dish pie
  crusts, unbaked

preheat oven to 350 degrees. Peel and quarter sweet potatoes. Place in large saucepan. Cover with water and boil, covered, until very soft. Mash or puree in food processor. Set aside. In large bowl combine sugar, half & half, melted butter, pineapple, eggs, vanilla extract, cinnamon, nutmeg and lemon extract. Add sweet potatoes, mixing well. Spoon into unbaked pie crusts. Bake 45 minutes or until crust is golden and filling is set. Cool completely.

SERVES   18 - 24

strawberry-chocolate tart

1 cup all-purpose flour
3 tablespoons sugar
1/4 teaspoon salt
1/3 cup walnuts
1/2 cup unsalted (sweet)
  butter, cut into small
  pieces
2 egg yolks
1/3 to 1/2 cup strawberry
  jam
3/4 cup plus 2 tablespoons
  heavy or whipping cream
6 squares (6 ounces)
  bittersweet or semi-sweet
  chocolate, chopped
Fresh strawberries

in food processor combine flour, sugar and salt. Add walnuts and process until finely chopped. Add butter and process a few seconds or until mixture resembles coarse meal. Add egg yolks and process just until clumps form. Shape dough into ball. Flatten to disk shape. Wrap in plastic wrap and refrigerate 30 minutes.

Preheat oven to 375 degrees. Butter a 9-inch diameter tart pan with removable bottom. Roll chilled dough between two sheets of wax paper to 11-inch round. Press dough into prepared pan, trimming edges, as needed. Cover and freeze 15 minutes. Bake 25 minutes or until golden. Spread bottom with jam. Bake additional 4 minutes or until jam sets. Cool completely on wire rack.

In small saucepan heat cream over medium-low heat until bubbles appear around edge of pan. Remove from heat. Add chocolate, stirring until melted. Cool to room temperature, about 50 minutes, stirring occasionally. (Cooled mixture should be thickened but pourable.) Pour into crust. Cover and refrigerate 1 hour or until filling is set. Garnish with strawberries just before serving.

SERVES   6 - 8

mrs. ridge's warm apple tarts

1-1/2 cups all-purpose flour
1/2 teaspoon salt
1/2 cup sweet (unsalted) butter, cut into pieces
1/4 cup ice water
3 to 4 large Granny Smith apples
1 tablespoon sweet (unsalted) butter
2-1/2 tablespoons sugar
1/4 teaspoon Chinese five-spice powder
1 egg, lightly beaten
Caramel Sauce
Creme Fraiche
Mint leaves

In medium bowl combine flour and salt. Cut in the butter using a pastry blender or 2 knives until mixture resembles large peas. Pour in ice water. Work in water until incorporated. Form the dough into an 8 inch log on a lightly floured pastry board. Knead dough for a minute or two. Wrap dough in plastic wrap and chill for 30 minutes or more.

Preheat oven to 350 degrees. Peel and core apples. Cut into eighths. Melt butter in a large saucepan over medium heat. Add apples and toss gently. Cook until apples are golden brown. Add 1/2 tablespoon sugar and five-spice powder. Cook for another 2 to 3 minutes. Cool.

Divide pastry into 4 balls. Roll each ball into a 1/4 inch thick circle. Divide the apples between each circle of pastry. Crimp the sides of each tart to form an edge. Brush tart dough with beaten egg. Sprinkle lightly with remaining sugar. Place tarts on baking sheet using a metal spatula. Bake for 15 to 20 minutes or until golden. Serve with your favorite Caramel Sauce and Creme Fraiche if desired. Garnish with fresh mint leaves.

SERVES 4

apricot-pear dessert

4 to 5 ripe pears, peeled
3 tablespoons sugar
2-1/2 teaspoons all-purpose flour
Pastry Shell (recipe follows)
1/2 to 3/4 cup apricot preserves
Whipped Cream

Preheat oven to 375 degrees. Slice pears and arrange in cooled pastry shell. In small bowl combine sugar and flour. Sprinkle over pears. Bake 20 minuts. In small saucepan heat apricot preserves until liquid, stirring occasionally. Brush over tart. Bake 20 minutes more. Serve warm with whipped cream.

pastry shell:

Preheat oven to 400 degrees. In large bowl combine 2 cups all-purpose flour, 1 tablespoon sugar and 1 teaspoon salt. Cut in 1/3 cup butter or 1/2 cup solid shortening. Add 1/4 cup milk, blending until dough forms. Roll out onto lightly floured surface into round large enough to fit bottom and side of 10-inch tart pan. Press onto bottom and side of pan. Prick with fork. Bake 7 minutes. Cool completely.

SERVES 6 - 8

white chocolate raspberry torte

1-1/4 cups finely chopped walnuts

3/4 cup sweet (unsalted) butter, divided

3 tablespoons sugar

1-1/2 cups all-purpose flour

1 teaspoon freshly-grated orange peel

1 egg

2-1/2 cups fresh raspberries

12 ounces white chocolate, chopped

1/2 cup heavy or whipping cream, heated (Do not boil.)

Sweetened whipped cream

Additional fresh raspberries

Preheat oven to 375 degrees. In large bowl combine walnuts, 1/2 cup of the butter, sugar, flour, orange peel and egg, beating well. Press onto bottom and up sides of 11-inch tart pan with removable bottom. Cover and freeze 15 minutes. Bake 25 to 30 minutes or until golden brown. Cool completely on wire rack.

Remove side of pan and transfer shell to large serving plate. Fill with 2-1/2 cups raspberries. Set aside. Melt white chocolate in top of double boiler over hot, not boiling, water. Remove from heat. (Or, place chocolate in medium microwave-proof bowl. Microwave on high [full power] 1 minute or just until soft. Stir. If necessary, microwave on high an additional 30 seconds or just until melted.) Whisk in warm cream and remaining 1/4 cup butter, whisking until melted and smooth. Spoon and spread over raspberries in shell. Cover and refrigerate several hours or overnight. Garnish with sweetened whipped cream and additional raspberries just before serving.

SERVES 8 - 10

fresh fruit cobbler

3 cups peeled, sliced fresh fruit such as apples, peaches or berries

3/4 cup sugar

2 tablespoons all-purpose flour

2 tablespoons butter, chopped

1 cup all-purpose flour

2 tablespoons sugar

1-1/2 teaspoons baking powder

1/2 teaspoon salt

1/3 cup shortening, softened

1/4 cup milk

1 egg

Preheat oven to 350 degrees. Arrange fruit in a 9-inch square pan. In small bowl combine 3/4 cup sugar and 2 tablespoons flour. Sprinkle over fruit in pan. Dot with butter. In large bowl combine 1 cup flour, 2 tablespoons sugar, baking powder and salt. Blend in shortening. Add milk and egg, stirring until blended. Drop by rounded tablespoonfuls onto fruit, arranging in a circle and leaving center open. Bake 40 minutes. Serve warm.

SERVES 6 - 8

jamaican blue mountain coffee flan

3/4 cup sugar
1/4 cup water
1-1/4 cups whole milk
   (Do not use low-fat or skim
   milk.)
1 cup heavy or whipping
   cream
2 teaspoons instant coffee
   granules
3 eggs
3 egg yolks
3/4 cup super-fine sugar
3 tablespoons coffee liqueur

Position rack in center of oven. Preheat to 325 degrees. Arrange six 1/2-cup ramekins or souffle dishes in large baking pan. Place pan in oven. Heat 10 minutes or until dishes are hot.

Meanwhile, in small saucepan combine 3/4 cup sugar and water. Bring to boil over medium heat, stirring constantly, until sugar dissolves. (Wash down any sugar crystals from sides of pan with wet pastry brush, as needed during cooking.) Continue boiling, without stirring, 10 minutes or until golden brown. Immediately divide hot mixture among heated ramekins, carefully tilting to coat sides. Cool completely on wire rack.

In medium saucepan bring milk and cream to boil. Remove from heat. Stir in instant coffee granules. Set aside. In large bowl whisk together eggs and egg yolks. Whisk in super-fine sugar and coffee liqueur. Gradually whisk in hot milk mixture. Strain. Divide among prepared ramekins. Return to large baking pan. Fill pan with water halfway up sides of ramekins. Bake 35 minutes or until filling is almost set. Remove from water and cool 15 minutes on wire rack. Run small sharp knife around edges to loosen. Cool completely. Cover and refrigerate overnight. Invert onto individual serving plates.

SERVES   6

peach flan

3 cups sliced fresh, sweet
   peaches
1 cup milk
1 cup light cream
3 eggs
1 to 2 tablespoons rum
1 teaspoon vanilla extract
1/4 cup all-purpose flour
1/4 cup sugar
Dash salt
Confectioners' sugar

Preheat oven to 375 degrees. Thoroughly butter a 1-1/2 quart baking dish. Dust with sugar. Spoon peach slices into dish. Set aside. In large bowl combine milk, cream, eggs, rum and vanilla extract. Blend in flour, sugar and salt. Pour over peach slices in pan. Bake 45 to 50 minutes. Serve warm, dusted with confectioners' sugar.

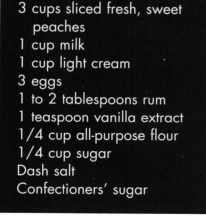

SERVES   6 - 8

bavarian apple torte

pastry:
1/2 cup butter or margarine
1/3 cup sugar
1/4 teaspoon vanilla extract
1 cup all-purpose flour

filling:
1 package (8 ounces) cream cheese
1/4 cup sugar
1 egg
1/2 teaspoon vanilla extract

topping:
1/3 cup sugar
1/2 teaspoon cinnamon
4 cups peeled and sliced tart apples (about 4 apples)
1/4 cup sliced almonds

pastry:
In medium bowl cream butter or margarine, sugar and vanilla extract until light and fluffy. Blend in flour. Spread on bottom and up sides of a 9-inch springform pan. Set aside.

filling:
In medium bowl beat cream cheese until softened. Add sugar, egg and vanilla extract, beating well. Pour into pastry-lined pan. Set aside.

topping:
Preheat oven to 400 degrees. Combine sugar and cinnamon. Toss with apple slices. Spoon over cream cheese mixture in pan. Sprinkle with almonds. Bake 10 minutes. Reduce heat to 375 degrees. Bake an additional 25 minutes. Cool completely on wire rack. Cover and refrigerate until ready to serve.

SERVES 8

low-fat chocolate amaretto cheesecake*

6 chocolate wafer cookies, finely crushed
1-1/2 cups (12 ounces) light cream cheese
1 cup low-fat cottage cheese
1 cup sugar
6 tablespoons unsweetened cocoa powder
1/4 cup all-purpose flour
1/4 cup Amaretto
1 teaspoon vanilla extract
1/4 teaspoon salt
1 egg
2 tablespoons semi-sweet chocolate mini chips
Chocolate curls, optional

Position rack in center of oven. Preheat to 300 degrees. Sprinkle chocolate wafer crumbs in bottom of a 7-inch springform pan. In food processor, process cream cheese, cottage cheese, sugar, cocoa powder, flour, Amaretto, vanilla extract and salt just until smooth and blended. Add egg and process just until blended. Stir in mini chips. Carefully pour over crumbs in pan. Bake 65 to 70 minutes or until set. Cool completely in pan. Cover and refrigerate several hours or overnight. Garnish with chocolate curls just before serving, if desired.

chocolate-mint variation:
Substitute 1/4 cup Creme-de-Menthe for the Amaretto and prepare as directed.

* 200 calories and 7 grams fat per serving

SERVES   12

raspberry cheesecake

2 cups graham cracker crumbs
1 cup slivered almonds, ground
1/4 cup melted butter
4 packages (8 ounces each) cream cheese
1/2 cup plus 2 tablespoons sugar
4 eggs
2 egg yolks
2 tablespoons all-purpose flour
1 teaspoon vanilla extract
8 ounces white chocolate, chopped
2 pints fresh raspberries
1 pint fresh raspberries, pureed
Additional fresh raspberries

Position rack in center of oven. Preheat to 325 degrees. In medium bowl combine graham cracker crumbs and ground almonds. Add butter, mixing well. Press onto bottom and half-way up side of 10-inch springform pan.

In large bowl beat cream cheese until softened. Beat in sugar. Add eggs and egg yolks, one at a time, beating well after each addition. Beat in flour and vanilla extract. Melt white chocolate in top of double boiler over hot, not boiling, water, stirring constantly. (Or, place white chocolate in medium microwave-proof bowl. Microwave on high [full power] 1 minute or just until softened. Stir. If necessary, microwave on high an additional 30 seconds or just until melted.) Gradually add to cream cheese mixture, beating well.

Spoon 2 pints raspberries into prepared pan. Pour cream cheese batter over top. Drizzle 1/4 cup of the pureed raspberries over batter in pan. Cut through batter with knife to create marble effect. (Cover and refrigerate additional raspberries and puree until ready to use.) Bake 1 hour or until top is firm to the touch. Cool completely in pan. Cover and refrigerate several hours or overnight. Garnish with remaining raspberry puree and additional fresh raspberries just before serving.

SERVES   10 - 12

fabulous fruity cheesecake pie

1/2 cup all-purpose flour
1/2 cup quick-cooking oats
1/3 cup packed brown sugar
1/2 teaspoon baking powder
1/4 cup butter, softened
3/4 cup any flavor fruit preserves
2 packages (8 ounces each) cream cheese
1 cup confectioners' sugar
1 teaspoon vanilla extract
1 cup heavy or whipping cream

Preheat oven to 350 degrees. In medium bowl combine flour, oats, brown sugar and baking powder. Blend in butter or margarine until crumbly. Firmly press half of mixture in 9-inch springform pan. Spread preserves on crust. Sprinkle and gently press remaining half of crumb mixture on top. Bake 20 to 25 minutes or until golden brown. Cool completely on wire rack.

In small bowl beat cream cheese until softened. Blend in confectioners' sugar and vanilla extract. In separate bowl beat heavy or whipping cream until soft peaks form. Fold into cream cheese mixture. Spoon into cooled crust. Cover and refrigerate 4 to 6 hours or until set.

SERVES   8

triple chocolate cheesecake

1/4 cup sliced almonds,
  coarsely crushed
4 packages (8 ounces each)
  cream cheese
1-3/4 cups sugar
4 eggs
3/4 cup heavy or whipping
  cream
4 ounces Swiss milk
  chocolate, finely chopped
4 ounces white chocolate,
  finely chopped
4 ounces bittersweet or
  semi-sweet chocolate,
  finely chopped
Boiling water
Chocolate Glaze
  (recipe follows)
Additional sliced almonds
Chocolate curls

Position rack in center of oven. Preheat to 325 degrees. Release side of springform pan. Trim a 10-inch cardboard circle and fit snugly within lip of pan bottom. Re-assemble bottom and side of pan. Line bottom and halfway up side of pan with foil. Generously butter bottom and side of foil-lined pan. Press crushed almonds onto bottom of prepared pan. Cover and refrigerate while preparing batter.

In large bowl beat cream cheese until softened. Beat in sugar. Add eggs, one at a time, beating well after each addition. Blend in cream. Measure out and transfer scant 2-1/3 cups of batter to medium bowl. Set aside.

Melt milk chocolate in top of double boiler over hot, not boiling, water, stirring constantly. (Or, place milk chocolate in medium microwave-proof bowl. Microwave on high [full power] 1 minute or just until softened. Stir. If necessary, microwave on high an additional 30 seconds or just until melted.) Stir into 2-1/3 cups batter. Pour into prepared pan. Set aside.

Divide remaining batter in half. Melt white chocolate according to procedure for milk chocolate. Stir into half of the divided batter. Spoon and carefully spread over batter in pan. Melt bittersweet chocolate according to procedure for milk and white chocolates. Stir into remaining batter. Spoon and carefully spread over batter in pan. Place in large baking pan. Fill with boiling water halfway up side of springform pan. Bake 1 hour and 45 minutes to 2 hours or until set. Turn off oven. Let cheesecake stand in oven additional 1 hour. Cool completely in pan. Cover and refrigerate several hours or overnight. Top with Chocolate Glaze. Refrigerate 10 minutes or until set. Run knife around edges to loosen. Release side of pan. Transfer to large serving plate. Garnish with sliced almonds and chocolate curls.

chocolate glaze:

In medium bowl place 4 ounces finely chopped bittersweet or semi-sweet chocolate. In small saucepan bring 1/2 cup heavy or whipping cream to soft boil. Pour over chocolate in bowl. Let stand 20 seconds to melt chocolate. Whisk until blended and smooth. Drizzle and spread evenly over cheesecake.

SERVES   12

chocolate cherry drops

1/2 cup butter or margarine
1 cup sugar
1-1/2 teaspoons vanilla
  extract
1 egg
1-1/2 cups all-purpose flour
1/3 cup unsweetened cocoa
  powder
1/4 teaspoon baking
  powder
1/4 teaspoon baking soda
1/4 teaspoon salt
1 jar (10 ounces)
  maraschino cherries,
  well-drained
Frosting (recipe follows)

Preheat oven to 350 degrees. In large bowl beat butter or margarine until softened. Add sugar and vanilla extract. Cream until light and fluffy. Add egg, beating well.

In separate bowl combine flour, cocoa powder, baking powder, baking soda and salt. Gradually blend into creamed mixture. Shape into 1-inch balls. Place about 2 inches apart on ungreased cookie sheet. Gently press thumb into center of each to form indentation. Pat cherries dry with paper towel. Place one in each indentation. Bake 10 minutes or just until edges begin to set. Cool slightly on cookie sheets. Transfer to wire racks. Spoon scant teaspoonful of cooled Frosting over each warm cookie. Cool completely.

frosting:

In small saucepan combine 2/3 cup sweetened condensed milk and 1/2 cup semi-sweet chocolate chips. Cook over low heat, stirring constantly, until chocolate chips are melted and blended with condensed milk. Remove from heat. Cool completely.

MAKES   3 DOZEN

italian chocolate chip cookies

1 cup butter or margarine
2 cups sugar
1 pound ricotta cheese
2 eggs
1 teaspoon vanilla extract
4 cups all-purpose flour
1 teaspoon baking soda
1 teaspoon salt
2 cups semi-sweet chocolate
  or peanut butter chips

Preheat oven to 350 degrees. In large bowl cream butter or margarine until softened. Add sugar. Cream until light and fluffy. Add ricotta cheese, eggs and vanilla extract, beating well.

In separate bowl combine flour, baking soda and salt. Blend into creamed mixture. Stir in chocolate or peanut butter chips. Drop by generous spoonfuls about 2 inches apart onto lightly-greased baking sheets. Bake 8 to 10 minutes or until very lightly browned. Cool slightly on baking sheets. Transfer to wire racks and cool completely.

MAKES   5 DOZEN

cajun cowboy cookies

1 cup butter or margarine
1 cup sugar
1 cup packed brown sugar
1-1/2 teaspoons vanilla extract
2 eggs
2 cups all-purpose flour
1 teaspoon baking powder
1 teaspoon baking soda
1/2 teaspoon salt
2 cups quick-cooking oats
1 cup semi-sweet chocolate chips
1/2 cup butterscotch chips
2 cups finely-chopped pecans

Preheat oven to 350 degrees. In large bowl beat butter or margarine until softened. Add sugar, brown sugar and vanilla extract. Cream until light and fluffy. Add eggs, beating well.

In separate bowl combine flour, baking powder, baking soda and salt. Blend into creamed mixture. Stir in oats, chocolate chips and butterscotch chips. Shape into 1-inch balls. Roll in chopped pecans. Place about 2 inches apart on ungreased baking sheets. Bake 14 to 16 minutes or until very lightly browned. Cool slightly on baking sheets. Transfer to wire racks and cool completely.

MAKES 6 DOZEN

pure fruit cookies

1-1/2 cups mashed ripe bananas (about 3 medium)
1/2 cup peanut oil
1 teaspoon vanilla extract
1/8 teaspoon salt
1-1/2 cups quick-cooking oats
1/2 cup uncooked oat bran
1/2 cup sugar
1/2 cup golden raisins
1/2 cup chopped dried apricots
1/2 cup chopped dates
1/2 cup chopped walnuts or almonds

Preheat oven to 350 degrees. In large bowl combine mashed bananas, oil, vanilla extract and salt. Blend in oats, oat bran and sugar, mixing well. Stir in raisins, apricots, dates and nuts. Drop by generous spoonfuls about 2 inches apart onto lightly greased baking sheets. Flatten slightly with back of spoon. Bake 20 to 25 minutes or until edges are very lightly browned. Cool slightly on baking sheets. Transfer to wire racks and cool completely. Store in refrigerator.

MAKES 2 DOZEN

white chocolate-macadamia nut cookies

1 cup sweet (unsalted) butter
3/4 cup sugar
3/4 cup packed light brown
  sugar
1 teaspoon vanilla extract
3 eggs
2-1/2 cups all-purpose flour
1 teaspoon baking soda
1 teaspoon salt
12 ounces white chocolate,
  coarsely chopped
1-1/2 cups golden raisins
1 cup salted macadamia
  nuts, chopped

Preheat oven to 350 degrees. In large bowl beat butter until softened. Add sugar, brown sugar and vanilla extract. Cream until light and fluffy. Add eggs, one at a time, beating well after each addition.

In separate bowl combine flour, baking soda and salt. Gradually blend into creamed mixture. Stir in chopped white chocolate, raisins and nuts. Drop by generous spoonfuls about 2 inches apart onto ungreased baking sheets. Bake 8 to 10 minutes or until very lightly browned. Cool slightly on baking sheets. Transfer to wire racks and cool completely.

MAKES   6 DOZEN

kanelkakor (swedish cinnamon cookies)

2-1/2 cups all-purpose flour
1 cup sweet (unsalted)
  butter, sliced
1/2 cup sugar
1 egg yolk
1 egg white, slightly beaten
3 tablespoons sugar
1 tablespoon cinnamon

Preheat oven to 375 degrees. In large bowl place flour. Blend in butter, 1/2 cup sugar and egg yolk with pastry blender or two forks until smooth dough forms. On lightly floured surface shape into two rolls, each 10 inches long and 1-1/2 inches in diameter. Brush with egg white. Combine 3 tablespoons sugar and the cinnamon. Dip rolls into sugar mixture. Wrap and refrigerate 1 to 2 hours or until firm. Cut into 1/4-inch thick slices. Place about 2 inches apart on lightly greased baking sheets. Bake 10 to 12 minutes or until very lightly browned. Cool slightly on baking sheets. Transfer to wire racks and cool completely.

MAKES   4 DOZEN

lemon-macadamia bars

crust:
2 lemons
1/3 cup sugar
1 cup macadamia nuts
3/4 cup all-purpose flour
1/2 cup butter, chopped

filling:
3/4 cup sugar
6 tablespoons fresh lemon juice
1/4 cup melted butter
4 eggs
1-1/2 teaspoons all-purpose flour

crust:

preheat oven to 350 degrees. Line an 8- or 9-inch square pan with heavy-duty aluminum foil. Remove yellow outer portion of peel from the lemons. (Reserve lemons for juice used in filling.) Place peel in food processor. Process until coarsely chopped. Add sugar and macadamia nuts. Process until peel is very fine. Measure out and set aside 1/2 cup mixture for topping. Add flour and butter to remaining mixture in food processor. Process just until mixture holds together. Press into prepared pan. Bake 20 to 25 minutes or until golden brown. Set aside.

filling:

In medium bowl combine sugar, lemon juice, melted butter, eggs and flour. Process just until blended. Pour over crust in pan. Bake at 350 degrees for 10 to 12 minutes or until filling is almost set. Sprinkle with 1/2 cup sugar-macadamia nut mixture reserved from crust. Bake an additional 8 to 10 minutes or until filling is completely set. Cool completely on wire rack. Using corners of foil, lift cooled bars from pan. Peel off foil before cutting. Refrigerate leftovers.

MAKES   3 DOZEN

renee's cashew bars

2 cups all-purpose flour
1-1/2 cups brown sugar
1 teaspoon salt
1 cup butter
2 cups chopped cashews or mixed nuts
1 cup butterscotch chips
1/2 cup light corn syrup
2 tablespoons butter
1 tablespoon water

preheat oven to 350 degrees. Lightly grease a 13 x 9-inch oblong pan. In large bowl combine flour, brown sugar and salt. Cut in 1 cup butter with pastry cutter or two forks until crumbly. Press into prepared pan. Bake 14 minutes. Sprinkle with nuts. Set aside.

In small saucepan combine butterscotch chips, corn syrup, 2 tablespoons butter and water. Bring to boil over medium-low heat, stirring constantly. Boil and stir 2 minutes. Pour over crust and cashews in pan. Bake 14 minutes or until golden brown. Cool completely on wire rack.

MAKES   3 DOZEN

tuxedo bars

crust:
1 package (9 ounces) chocolate wafers
1/2 cup sweet (unsalted) butter, divided
1 tablespoon sugar

filling:
10 ounces white chocolate, finely chopped
1/2 cup heavy or whipping cream
2 packages (8 ounces each) cream cheese
4 egg yolks
4 teaspoons vanilla extract
1/8 teaspoon salt
4 egg whites

topping:
6 ounces white chocolate
1/4 cup heavy or whipping cream
2 tablespoons white creme de cacao

crust:

Line bottom and sides of 13 x 9-inch oblong pan with heavy-duty aluminum foil. Brush with 2 tablespoons of the butter. Crush chocolate wafers to make crumbs. Melt remaining 6 tablespoons butter. Mix with chocolate wafer crumbs and sugar. Press onto bottom of prepared pan. Set aside.

filling:

Position rack in center of oven. Preheat to 300 degrees. Melt white chocolate in top of double boiler over hot, not boiling, water, stirring constantly. Remove from heat. (Or, place chocolate in medium microwave-proof bowl. Microwave on high [full power] 1 minute or just until softened. Stir. If necessary, microwave on high an additional 30 seconds or just until melted.) Gradually add cream. Set aside to cool slightly.

In large bowl beat cream cheese until softened. Add egg yolks, one at a time, beating well after each addition. Blend in melted chocolate mixture, vanilla extract and salt, beating 2 minutes. In small mixer bowl, using clean beaters beat egg whites until stiff but not dry. Fold into cream cheese mixture. Pour over crust in pan. Bake 30 minutes or until almost set. Turn off oven. Let stand in oven additional 30 minutes. Set aside to cool completely in pan. Drizzle Topping over cooled bars. Cool until Topping is set. Cover and freeze at least one hour. Refrigerate leftovers.

topping:

Melt white chocolate in top of double boiler over hot, not boiling, water, stirring constantly. Remove from heat. (Or, place chocolate in medium microwave-proof bowl. Microwave on high [full power] 1 minute or just until softened. Stir. If necessary, microwave on high an additional 30 seconds or just until melted.) Stir in cream and creme de cacao. Drizzle over bars while warm.

MAKES 4 DOZEN

cappuccino brownies

3/4 cup sweet (unsalted) butter
4 squares (4 ounces) unsweetened baking chocolate, chopped
1-3/4 cups sugar
1 tablespoon instant espresso powder
1-1/2 teaspoons vanilla extract
1 cup all-purpose flour
1 teaspoon cinnamon
1/4 teaspoon nutmeg
1/4 teaspoon salt
3 eggs, slightly beaten
1-1/2 cups semi-sweet chocolate chips
Confectioners' sugar

Preheat oven to 350 degrees. Lightly butter a 13 x 9-inch oblong pan. In medium saucepan melt butter and chocolate over low heat, stirring constantly. Stir in sugar and espresso powder. Remove from heat. Add vanilla extract. In separate bowl combine flour, cinnamon, nutmeg and salt. Add chocolate mixture and eggs, stirring just until blended. Stir in chocolate chips. Spoon and spread evenly in prepared pan. Bake 30 minutes. Cool completely on wire rack. Sprinkle with confectioners' sugar.

MAKES   2 DOZEN

chocolate pecan pie bars

1 cup butter or margarine
3 cups all-purpose flour
2 cups sugar, divided
1/2 teaspoon salt
1-1/2 cups light or dark corn syrup
1 cup semi-sweet chocolate chips
4 eggs, slightly beaten
1-1/2 teaspoons vanilla extract
2-1/2 cups coarsely chopped pecans

Preheat oven to 350 degrees. Lightly grease bottom and sides of a 15 x 10-inch jelly roll pan. In large bowl beat butter or margarine until softened. Blend in flour, 1/2 cup of the sugar and salt. Press firmly into prepared pan. Bake 20 minutes.

Meanwhile, in large saucepan combine corn syrup and chocolate chips. Stir constantly over low heat just until chocolate is melted. Remove from heat. Add remaining 1-1/2 cups sugar, eggs and vanilla extract, mixing well. Stir in pecans. Pour and spread evenly over hot crust. Bake 30 minutes or until filling is almost set. Cool completely on wire rack.

MAKES   4 DOZEN

bread pudding with rum sauce

6 cups coarse bread crumbs
4 cups evaporated milk
2 cups sugar
1/2 cup melted butter
3 eggs, slightly beaten
2 tablespoons vanilla extract
1 tablespoon cinnamon
1 tablespoon nutmeg
1 cup raisins
1 cup flaked coconut
1 cup chopped pecans
Rum Sauce (recipe follows)

butter a 13 x 9-inch oblong pan. In large bowl combine bread crumbs, evaporated milk, sugar, melted butter, eggs, vanilla extract, cinnamon and nutmeg. Stir in raisins, coconut and pecans. Pour into prepared pan. Without preheating oven, bake at 350 degrees for 1 hour or until golden brown. Serve warm with Rum Sauce.

rum sauce:

In small bowl beat 1/2 cup butter until softened. Blend in 1-1/2 cups confectioners' sugar. Blend in 2 egg yolks. Transfer mixture to top of double boiler. Whisk over hot, not boiling, water until thickened. Remove from heat. Gradually add 1/2 cup rum. Serve warm.

SERVES 16

white chocolate bread pudding

3 cups heavy or whipping
    cream
1 cup whole milk (Do not
    use low-fat or skim milk.)
1/2 cup sugar
10 ounces white chocolate,
    finely chopped
8 egg yolks
2 eggs
1 loaf (1 pound) day-old
    French bread, cut into
    1-inch pieces
White Chocolate Sauce
    (recipe follows)
Fresh raspberries

preheat oven to 350 degrees. Butter a 13 x 9-inch oblong pan. In medium saucepan combine cream, milk and sugar. Bring to simmer over medium heat, stirring constantly. Continue cooking and stirring until sugar dissolves. Remove from heat. Add white chocolate, whisking until melted and smooth.

In large bowl whisk together egg yolks and eggs. Gradually whisk in warm chocolate mixture. Add bread, stirring until coated well. Let stand 5 minutes or until bread is softened. Spoon into prepared pan. Cover with foil. Bake 45 minutes. Remove foil and bake additional 15 minutes or until golden brown. Cool slightly. Serve warm with White Chocolate Sauce and fresh raspberries.

white chocolate sauce:

In small saucepan bring 1 cup heavy or whipping cream to boil. Remove from heat. Add 8 ounces finely-chopped white chocolate, whisking until melted and smooth. Serve warm.

SERVES 12

nantucket cranberry dessert

2 cups chopped fresh
   cranberries
1/2 cup chopped walnuts
1-1/2 cups sugar, divided
1 cup all-purpose flour
3/4 cup melted butter,
   cooled
2 eggs
1/2 teaspoon vanilla extract
1/4 teaspoon salt
Vanilla ice cream, creme
   fraiche or custard sauce,
   optional

Preheat oven to 350 degrees. Butter a 9-inch springform pan. In medium bowl combine cranberries, walnuts and 1/2 cup of the sugar. Spoon onto bottom of prepared pan. In large bowl combine remaining 1 cup sugar, flour, melted and cooled butter, eggs, vanilla extract and salt. Stir until blended and smooth. Pour over cranberry mixture in pan. Bake 40 minutes or until toothpick inserted comes out clean. Cool 15 minutes in pan. Invert onto serving plate. Serve slightly warm with vanilla ice cream, creme fraiche or custard sauce, if desired.

SERVES   10 - 12

baked pears frangelico

10 Bosc pears, peeled,
   cored and halved
1-1/4 cups Frangelico
   liqueur
1/2 cup plus 2 tablespoons
   sweet (unsalted) butter,
   chopped
1/2 cup plus 2 tablespoons
   sugar
1-1/4 cups heavy or
   whipping cream
Juice of 2 fresh lemons
5 squares (5 ounces)
   semi-sweet baking
   chocolate, melted and
   cooled slightly

Preheat oven to 425 degrees. Butter a large, shallow baking pan. Place pear halves, cut sides down, in prepared pan. Pour liqueur over top. Dot with butter. Sprinkle with sugar. Bake 45 minutes, basting occasionally with liquid from pan. Drizzle cream over pears. Bake additional 5 minutes.

Using slotted spoon, transfer pear halves to large plate. Whisk mixture remaining in baking dish until smooth. Whisk in lemon juice. Divide among individual serving plates. Cut lengthwise slits partially through pear halves. Carefully separate slit pears to make fan shapes and transfer to cream mixture on serving plates. Spoon cooled chocolate into pastry bag with small tip. (Chocolate should be thick enough to pipe from bag.) Pipe over pear halves in decorative fashion. Serve immediately.

SERVES   10

index

recipe contributors

testing committee

recipe index

recipe contributors

Sherri Akens
Miriam Albert
Patty Armbrust
Kara Arnold
Helen Ashenfelter
Peggy Babcock
Traci Bands
Joan Banzhoff
Angie Barber
Christina Barber
Susan Batista
Lynn Bertram
Jane Best
Karen Best
Ann Biery
Marla Bigeleisen
Jenny Black
Alicia Bluis
Corinne Bodeman
Peggy Bravacos
Susan Breidenstine
Jennifer Bretherick
Ricki Briggs
Liz Burns
Ellen Caldwell
Lisabeth Capozzi
Suzanne Carbone
Stephanie Carl
Nina Castillo
Beulah Chabal
Sally Chamberlain
Renee Cichy
Baiba Clemens
Karen Close
Andrea Cohen
Michelle Cohen
Cynthia Cohn
Kathy Holtzinger Conner
Dennis Corgill
Carrie Curtis
Jean Cutright
Beth DeHaven
Johnna Deily
Lisa Delciotto

Maria De Maggio
Donna Denby
Sharon DePamphilis
Annette DeSantis
Susan Detweiler
Ann Diercxsens
Sarah Dietrich
Elaine Dilliard
Linda Doup
Victoria Eastus
Delia Egan
Lisa Egan
Clara Ely
Dot Engle
Heidi Eshback
Karen Neely Faryniak
Trish Faulkrod
Pat Ferris
Kathleen Fracasso
Jackie Francis
Diane Funston
Jacqueline Galko
Patrice Ridgway Gallagher
Marcia Gobrecht
Kathy Graham
Susan Graham
Sue Grammes
Jane Gregory
Jean Griffith
Amy Groneman
Nan Gunnett
Barbara Gunnison
Karen Gunnison
Diane Hall
Amy Hammerschmidt
Rochelle Harbick
Sue Harden
Denise Harris
Mil Hatch
Sharon Hauschildt
Ellen Hench
Barbara Hendrick
Tracy Herth
Linda Hicks
Shelly Hummer

Cindy Hund
Toquaiah Jackson
Joan Jenney
Suzanne Johnson
Karen Johnston
Tom Johnston
Carol Jones
Kathy Joyce
Lori Kashishian
Christine Mumma Kasian
LuAnn Kauffman
Joanne Keim
Phyllis Kerstetter
Sally Killian
Julia Knight
Betty Kosco
Ann Kroh
Robin Kushubar
Rita Latsha
Joan Line
Lois Loy
Judy Ludkey
Terri Maclay
June Martin
Cynthia Massie
Jennifer Masters
Margaret Masters
Sue Maxwell
Sarah McAskill
Julie McConahy
Cheryl McCune
Richard McCune
Chris Medici
Debbie Mihalik
Christine Miller
Valerie Miller
Bob Mitman
Ann Moffitt
Thelma Monroe
Juliet Moringiello
George Neely
Stacey Nelson
Kathy Noaker
Donna Nooney
Sarah O'Brien

Susan O'Gorman
Trish Olshefski
Mary Beth Osborne
Louise Parker
Janey Patton
Maria Pavone
Mary Lou Pepe
Elaine Phillips
Sheri Phillips
Barbara Pinto
Libby Pirnik
Dorothy Pittenger
Lauren Plesic
Linda Plesic
Sarah Plesic
Carla Plouse
Penny Poerksen
Peggy Purdy
Carol Quigley
Mary Alice Rebman
Sue Redmond
Stephen Reed
Anne Rempe
Kelly Renaud
Michelle Ridge
Gayle Rietmulder
Mary Rock
Susanne Roderick
Sue Romaniello
Sue Rothman
Kirsten Rucker
Lorie Ruland
Toby Ruland
Anna Russo
Kathy Saltus
Laurie Saltzgiver
Ashie Santangelo
Jill Schadle
Debbie Scheifflee
Jill Crews Schiebel
Inge Schill
Marie Schleicher
Helen Schulz
Margaret Scott
Maribeth Wilt Seibert

Michele Mumma Sen
Andrea Sheya
Lori Shields
Collette Silvestri
Julie Simpson
Jennifer Slaby
Pam Smeltzer
Pam Snyder
Angela Sontheimer
Melissa Spangler
Charlotte Stafford
Chris Stellefson
Liz Stone
Ann Storms
Doris Stossel
Cindy Stought
Connor Strauss
Robin Stuart
Pam Suan
Julie Sullivan
Lisa Thomas
Alice Tomlinson
Candi Trogner
Erna Tunno
Sue Garcia Tunon
Penny Turner
Karen Vance
Kathy Vander Woude
Melissa Vera
Edie Walsh
Louise Waters
Sharon Webb
Winnie Wetzler
Amy Wherley
Marlene Whitaker
Carolyn Williams
Valeria Williams
Katherine Wilson
Maribeth Wilt Seibert
Beth Witmer
Theresa Shade Wix
Kathy Vander Woude
Jo Wright
Pat Yanchuleff
Susy Zwally

The Junior League Of Harrisburg, Inc.

testing committee

Marion Alexander	Sue Grammes	Becky Piper
Patty Armbrust	Jean Griffith	Libby Pirnik
Christina Barber	Karen Gunnison	Linda Plesic
Susan Batista	Ellen Hench	Peggy Purdy
Lynn Bertram	Mindy Holland	Mary Rock
Susan Breidenstine	Karen Johnston	Sue Rothman
Jennifer Brubaker	Tom Johnston	Lorie Ruland
Liz Burns	Sally Killian	Marie Schleicher
Stephanie Carl	Judy Knupp	Pam Smeltzer
Mary Kevin Cawley	Rita Latsha	Melissa Spangler
Andrea Cohen	Cathy Leeds	Liz Stone
Johnna Deily	Juliet Moringiello	Candy Trogner
Susan Delaney	Karen Neely Faryniak	Ronnie Trogner
Sharon Depamphilis	Kathy Noaker	Judy Underwood
Tita Eberly	Donna Nooney	Edie Walsh
Pat Ferris	Faith Perkins	Katherine Wilson
Trish Foulkrod	Barb Pinto	Jo Wright

* We regret the omission or misspelling of any name.

recipe index

appetizers

dips and spreads:
Avocado Dip with Sesame Seeds, 24
Cajun Tuna Dip, 23
Caponata, 26
Chutney Cheese Ball, 27
Herb and Olive Dip, 24
Low-Fat Roasted Pepper Dip, 25
Roasted Garlic Pate', 20
Susquehanna Shrimp Dip, 21

cheese:
Almond-Raspberry Brie, 14
Baked Chevre with Tomatoes and
    French Garlic Toasts, 47
Cheese Quesadillas with Black
    Bean Salsa, 14
City Island Crostini, 45
Glazed Brie, 15
Goat Cheese Log with Cranberry
    Pecan Crust, 23
Harris Mansion Cheese Pate', 19
Herbed Cheese Tarts, 19
Italian Cheese Terrine, 46
Mini Feta Cheesecakes, 43
Southwest Empanadas, 13
Stuffed Camembert, 44

pizzas:
Almond and Prosciutto Pizza, 15
California Pizza, 16
Chicken Pizza with Barbeque Sauce, 17
French Onion Pizza, 18
Greek Appetizer Pizza, 17
Spinach Phyllo Pizza, 16

chicken:
Caribbean Curried Chicken Bites, 29
Chicken Pate', 20
Chinese Roasted Chicken Wings, 28
Italian Lake Bruschetta, 40

seafood:
Artichoke Bottoms with Feta Cheese
    and Shrimp, 27
Bruschetta with Shrimp and Gruyere
    Cheese, 39
Clams Napoli, 34
Crab Deviled Eggs, 36
Crab Quesadillas, 12
Crab Rangoon, 34
Deviled Shrimp, 36
Jalapeno Pesto-Topped Oysters on the
    Half Shell, 35
Mushrooms Stuffed with Crab, 31
Piroshki, 30
Sesame Shrimp, 44
Smoked Salmon Tortillas, 12
Smoked Trout Pate', 21
Thai Style Seared Scallops with
    Cucumber Pepper Relish, 33

meat:
Beef Roulades with Watercress and
    Blue Cheese, 38
Italian Sausage and Sun-Dried
    Tomato Tarts, 31
Mini Beef Wellingtons, 38
Pepper-Crusted Beef Crostini
    with Arugula, 40
Piroshki, 30

vegetable:
Asparagus Cheese Fritters, 25
Beggars' Purses with Mushroom
    Filling, 42
Caramelized Onion Quesadillas, 11
Hummus with Roasted Garlic, 45
New Potatoes with Bacon-Horseradish
    Filling, 43
Sizzling Mushrooms, 32
Stuffed Pea Pods, 28
Tri-Color Vegetable Pate', 22

others:
Antipasto Roll-Ups, 29
Crostini with Grilled Vegetables
    and Smoked Mozzarella, 41
Gingered Cream Cheese Grapes, 26
Marinated Olives, 42
Mexicali Roll-Ups, 11
Pesto Toasts, 39
Rosemary Focaccia with Goat Cheese
    and Tomato Stuffing, 37

soups
Cajun Crab Soup, 53
Chicken Corn Soup, 51
Cool Cucumber and Sweet Yellow
    Pepper Soup, 57
Garden Vegetable Chowder, 55
Gazpacho with Crab and Pesto, 60
Kareen's Tortellini and Spinach, 55
Muffuleta's Mushroom Bisque, 54
Northern Woods Wild Rice Soup, 52
Roasted Garlic and Onion Cream
    Soup, 51
Roasted Red Pepper Soup, 59
Sensational Shrimp Bisque, 56
Sherried Brie Soup, 52
Vegetarian Tortilla Soup, 58

salads
Beef Salad with Caper Vinaigrette, 77
Caesar Margarita Salad, 69
Chicken Salad with Orange-Ginger
    Dressing, 71
Chicken and Tortellini Salad with
    Honey-Mustard Vinaigrette, 71
Crab Meat and Pasta Salad, 72
Cucumber and Feta Salad, 63
First Prize Potato Salad, 69
Fruited Spinach Salad, 77
Fusilli and Shrimp Salad with
    Cucumber and Orange, 73
Greek Salad, 62
Green Salad with Pears and Walnuts, 61
Greens with Fried Tortellini
    and Prosciutto, 66
Grilled Seafood Salad Nicoise, 75
Grilled Shrimp in Chile Marinade
    with Three Melons, 74
Ham and Orzo Salad, 76
Impromptu Salad with Balsamic
    Vinaigrette, 64
Orange-Walnut Salad, 65
Orzo and Feta Cheese Salad
    with Dill Dressing, 63
Portobello and Prosciutto Salad, 68
Radicchio and Avocado Salad with
    Warm Monterey Jack Cheese, 76
Ravioli and Broccoli Salad, 67
Roast Pork Tenderloin Salad with
    Creamy Cilantro Dressing, 79
Smoked Chicken Salad with Pecans
    and Sweet Grilled Pears, 70
Spicy Broccoli Salad, 66
Summer Veggie Slaw, 68
Taco Salad with Shrimp and Black
    Beans, 73

Warm Steak Salad with Papaya
and Red Onion, 78
Warm Wild Rice and Roasted
Vegetable Salad, 72
Watercress Salad with Lemon
Dressing, 61
Winter Salad, 65
Winter Spinach Salad, 64
Vermicelli and Chicken Primavera
Salad, 67

breads and brunches and lunches

breads and muffins:

Apple Almond Coffee Cake, 93
Apricot Almond Bread, 83
Apricot Cream Scones, 95
Apricot Nut Roll, 94
Bacon Braid, 87
Beer Bread, 86
Carrot Bread, 85
Chocolate Lovers Bread, 83
Coconut Sour Cream Coffee Cake, 93
Delicious Dill Bread, 87
Dried Cherry and Cream Scones, 91
Glorious Morning Muffins, 89
Homemade Crescents, 91
Low-Fat Banana Bread, 84
Peach Muffins, 88
Pecan Bread, 84
Pennsylvania Herb Potato Bread, 86
Southwestern Corn Bread, 85
Susie's Orange Muffins, 88
Sweet Potato Muffins, 89

brunches:

Artichoke and Sun-Dried Tomato
Fritata, 102
Blintz Souffle, 104
Brie Quiche, 97
Broccoli and Cheese Pie, 100
Caramel Strata, 104
Crab Meat Brunch Casserole, 103
Greek Spinach Quiche, 98
Ham and Cheese Torte, 102
Italian Sausage Quiche, 97
Mushroom Crust Quiche, 95
Oat Bran Banana Pancakes, 92
Oatmeal Pancakes, 92
Savory Souffle Roll, 105
Sensational Sunday Strata, 103
Spinach and Ricotta Pie, 99

Stuffed French Toast, 90
Sweet Noodle Kugel, 106
Vegetable Quiche with Whole Wheat
Dill Crust, 96
Watercress Roulade with Smoked
Salmon, 101

sandwiches:

Barbeque Turkey Burgers, 107
Broccoli Reuben Sandwich, 106
Calabrian Smoked Turkey Sandwich, 109
Grilled Gruyere, Black Forest Ham
and Onion Sandwiches, 107
Indian Beef Patties in Pitas, 108
Jim's Big Sandwich, 111
Portobello Mushroom Burger with
Basil Mustard Sauce, 110
Sesame Beef Pitas, 109

entrees

seafood:

Angel Hair Pasta with Shrimp and Herb
Sauce, 127
Baked Flounder with Mustard
and Herbs, 127
Baked Salmon with Lemon Grass, 122
Cajun Pasta, 129
French-Style Grilled Shrimp, Scallops
and Swordfish, 120
Garlicky Swordfish en Papillote, 119
Grilled Scallops Provencal, 125
Grilled Swordfish with
Tomatillo-Avocado Salsa, 118
Lacquered Salmon, 123
Less-Fat Caesar Swordfish, 118
Mariner's Walk Tuna, 117
Mexican Red Snapper, 121
Orange Roughy with Basil Sauce, 130
Orzo with Spinach, Shrimp
and Scallops, 124
Penne in Tomato Sauce with
Crab Meat, 127
Red Snapper with Leeks
and Chives, 121
Salmon with Avocado Butter, 122
Sauteed Sole Fillets with Ginger
and Cilantro, 117
Scallop and Bacon Jambalaya, 124
Seafood Pastries with Dill Sauce, 115
Shrimp and Sea Scallop Stir-Fry with
Julienned Vegetables and
Soba Noodles, 126
Spinach-Stuffed Trout, 116
Swordfish alla Fiorentina, 119

Tuna Steaks with Wasabi Butter, 130
Walnut-Crusted Sole, 116

poultry:

Chicken and Leeks over Linguine, 133
Chicken and Shrimp Stir-Fry, 136
Chicken Cerubi, 135
Chicken Marabella, 131
Chicken Scallopini with
Hazelnut-Parsley Pesto, 139
Chicken with Pasta and Sun-Dried
Tomatoes, 131
French Country Chicken, 138
Garlic Lime Chicken, 137
Golden Chicken Chili, 140
Green Chilied Chicken Breasts with Sauteed
Corn and Red Pepper Salsa, 133
Hawaiian Chicken with Tropical
Fruit Salsa, 137
Island Drumsticks with Grilled
Pineapple, 135
Mayor Reed's Cranberry Glazed
Chicken, 134
Moroccan Chicken Stew, 134
Roast Pesto Chicken, 132
Roast Turkey Breast with Herb
Stuffing, 141
Turkey Chili, 142

beef:

Beef Tenderloin Au Poivre, 145
Cold Pepper Steak, 147
Festive Chili, 148
Filet Mignon with Peppercorn Sauce, 147
Flaming Filet Mignon, 146
Grilled Peppered Steaks, 147
Roast Tenderloin Stuffed with Lobster, 145
Sesame Sirloin, 144
Spicy Beef Pot Roast, 143

pork:

Fettuccine with Sausage and Sage, 150
Penne with Eggplant, Roasted Peppers
and Sausage, 151
Pork Chops with Apple and Onion, 149
Pork Tenderloin with Sesame Sauce, 150
Raspberry Pork Roast, 151
Sally's Pork Roast, 149

veal:

Breaded Veal with Lemon and Capers, 154
Veal Blanquette with Dill, 152
Veal Chops with Fennel Butter, 153
Veal in Caper Sauce, 154
Veal Princess, 153

lamb:
Parsleyed Rack of Lamb, 155
Roast Stuffed Leg of Lamb, 155

venison:
Tom's Venison Chili, 157
Venison Chateaubriand, 156

vegetarian:
Vegetable Tortilla Lasagna, 158

barbeque:
Back-Slappin' Bohemian Barbeque
    Sauce, 159
Boogie-Woogie Barbeque Sauce, 158
The Very Best Barbeque Rub, 159

vegetables and sides

pasta:
Bacon, Tomato and Ricotta Rigatoni, 172
Bow Ties with Arugula, Bacon
    and Parmesan, 170
Fettuccine with Fennel, Prosciutto
    and Goat Cheese, 168
Four-Cheese Pasta with Fresh
    Tomato Sauce, 169
Greek Spaghetti, 166
Linguini with Sun-Dried Tomatoes,
    Broccoli and Romano, 170
Mediterranean Pasta, 165
Pasta and Broccoli with
    Gorgonzola Sauce, 166
Penne with Asparagus and Brie, 171
Portofino Primavera, 167
Spinach Pasta with Vodka Sauce, 168
Wilted Spinach Penne, 172

rice and grains:
Avocado Rice, 177
Barley Shitake and Spinach Pilaf, 174
Brown Rice Pilaf with Raisins, 173
Pecan Rice Pilaf, 173
Rice with Fennel and Fontina, 178
Risotto with Roasted Asparagus
    and Walnuts, 171
Risotto with Spinach, Fontina
    and Proscuitto, 167
Saffron Rice with Sun-Dried Tomatoes, 176
The Wildest Wild Rice, 177

vegetables:
Artichoke Stuffed Tomatoes, 186
Baked Cabbage with Cheddar and Dill, 188
Baked Eggplant Extraordinaire, 175
Brussel Sprouts with Walnut Cream
    Sauce, 164
Carrots in Cognac, 174
Curried Tomatoes, 186
Eggplant, Zucchini and Bell Pepper
    Saute, 175
Front Street Zucchini, 191
Garden Medley, 185
Glazed Acorn Squash, 185
Green Beans in Yellow Pepper Butter, 163
Green Beans with Almonds and Basil, 163
Grilled Sweet Potatoes with Garlic
    and Thyme, 182
Lemon Broccoli with Pecans, 164
Mashed Potatoes with Pesto, 183
Mashed Potatoes with Roasted Shallots
    Hollandaise, 180
Paxtang Potatoes, 179
Perfect Potatoes with Dill, 181
Roasted Cauliflower with Rosemary, 184
Santa Fe Summer Vegetables, 189
Sesame Snow Peas, 189
Spanish Potatoes, 182
Spicy Roast Potatoes, 181
Spinach and White Beans with Garlic, 187
Steamed Asparagus with Almond
    Butter, 187
Stir-Fried Broccoli and Carrots, 184
Sun-Dried Tomato Potatoes, 183
Sweet Potatoes in Orange Cups, 179
Vegetable Kabobs with Herbed
    Yogurt Sauce, 190
Zucchini with Sun-Dried Tomatoes, 191

desserts

cakes:
Banana Cream Cake, 200
Chocolate Velvet Cake, 196
Gingerbread Cupcakes with
    Lemon-Cheese Frosting, 201
Hungarian Chocolate Cake, 202
Italian Cream Cake, 203
Italian Love Cake, 195
Lemon Lush Cake, 197
Nectarine Shortcake, 195
Very Berry Lemon Pound Cake, 199

Shoofly Cupcakes, 201
White Chocolate Frangelico Cake, 198

pies, tarts and flans:
Bavarian Apple Torte, 208
Frozen Mocha Pie, 202
Irish Cream Brownie Pie, 203
Jamaican Blue Mountain Coffee Flan, 207
Mrs. Ridge's Warm Apple Tarts, 205
Peach Flan, 207
Strawberry-Chocolate Tart, 204
Sweet Potato Pie, 204
White Chocolate-Raspberry Torte, 206

cheesecakes:
Fabulous Fruity Cheesecake Pie, 209
Low-Fat Chocolate Amaretto
    Cheesecake, 208
Raspberry Cheesecake, 209
Triple Chocolate Cheesecake, 210

cookies, bars and brownies:
Cajun Cowboy Cookies, 212
Cappuccino Brownies, 216
Chocolate Cherry Drops, 211
Chocolate Pecan Pie Bars, 216
Italian Chocolate Chip Cookies, 211
Kanelkakor
    (Swedish Cinnamon Cookies), 213
Lemon-Macadamia Bars, 214
Pure Fruit Cookies, 212
Renee's Cashew Bars, 214
Tuxedo Bars, 215
White Chocolate-Macadamia Nut
    Cookies, 213

others desserts:
Apricot-Pear Dessert, 205
Baked Pears Frangelico, 218
Bread Pudding with Rum Sauce, 217
Dessert Cheese Ball, 199
Fresh Fruit Cobbler, 206
Nantucket Cranberry Dessert, 218
Spumoni Dessert, 200
White Chocolate Bread Pudding, 217